Temps and Pressures

The life of a pilot who practises medicine

Includes articles written by David Cooke over his lifetime

ELIZABETH COOKE

Dedication

This book is dedicated to Rolla Maxwell Cooke 1917-1941

© Elizabeth Cooke 2023 asserts the moral right to be identified as the author of *Temps and Pressures, the Life of a Pilot who Practises Medicine.*

Sydney, the Early Years 1941-1968

To lose one parent is unfortunate, to lose two looks like carelessness. In the words of Oscar Wilde, David certainly fits this quotation. By the age of four he had lost his own father and a stepfather.

Born into a comfortable middle-class family on the lower North Shore in Sydney, David was raised in a sheltered and conservative household. Like many war babies in 1941, David was fatherless. One month before his arrival in the world at the Mater Hospital in North Sydney, his father, Rolla Cooke, was killed in faraway Yorkshire.

At the outbreak of war, Rolla had joined the Royal Australian Air Force and then applied to join the Empire Air Training scheme as a pilot. After six weeks of married life with Betty Harrison, he sailed one day on the Queen Mary to serve with the RAF as a Spitfire pilot. He never returned. His active service was tragically cut short when he was killed in a test flight at Catterick in Yorkshire. Four weeks later his son David Rolla was born.

It is easy to understand why his mother and grandparents protected him and surrounded him with love. This fatherless baby had his own brush with death. At the age of six weeks, he underwent emergency surgery for pyloric stenosis, a condition that prevents food leaving the stomach and proceeding to the small intestine. It can lead to dehydration, malnutrition and even be fatal if left untreated. This frightening emergency in a newborn would have been a terrifying experience for the young mother. After losing her husband, she so nearly lost her little son.

David lived in a basically female dominated home, but not for long. In 1945 his mother married another pilot, Ken Hanson, a longed-for stepdad for the young boy. But these were dangerous times and Ken too was a war casualty, shot down in the Celebes Islands in late July, just two weeks before the end of the Pacific War.

It was not until 1949 that Betty married for the third time and yes, Bruce Daymond was a pilot too! Fortune prevailed and Bruce, Betty and David plus two new arrivals, Ian and Debbie, settled down to a peaceful and happy home life. Life in postwar Cremorne was good. David grew and flourished in a settled family.

David knew little about his biological father. He took great pride in regaling all who crossed his path that, "… my father was killed in a Spitfire." But one thing he knew for certain was his determination to fly, just like his father and two stepfathers. How could he not?

Apart from his father Rolla, David's grandfather Lionel, had learned to fly a Bristol Boxkite in 1915 in Point Cook in Victoria. Lionel had the 11th Flying Licence issued in Australia. He was in good company having flown with Dicky Williams who became the "Father of the RAAF". Other aviation pioneers on the same course were Frank McNamara, the only Australian pilot to be awarded the Victoria Cross in World War I and Lawrence Wackett who founded the Commonwealth Aircraft Factory. Even further back before man flew, David's great grandfather William Ernest Cooke looked skywards too, as a professor of astronomy. William standardised time in Western Australia and the Perth Astronomical Observatory was named in his honour. Yes, the sky and particularly flying were in David's blood.

At fourteen years of age, he joined the Air Training Corps. For four years he soaked up the life and times of aviation. Holiday camps and weekly parades only increased his passion for flight. As his school days at Shore concluded, he won a scholarship funded by the Air Force to learn to fly. He was sixteen years old. But on hearing this joyous news, his mother burst into tears. After losing two husbands to flight, now here was her precious first born preparing to climb into a cockpit and take to the sky.

On the 4th of December 1958, two days after his seventeenth birthday, David's love affair with the wonder of flight really began.

Not many students on leaving school spend their holiday time learning to fly. David was one of ten cadets, including his best mate, Stephen, who presented themselves that damp humid morning to begin their course. This took the form of an intensive three-week camp at Bankstown Airport. Released from the confines of school, away from home and learning to fly, excitement filled their eager young hearts.

On that first day the ten cadets were lined up under the stern gaze of the instructors in charge. How old and experienced the instructors looked to these young boys barely old enough to shave. Each cadet was allocated an instructor and an aircraft. At this time most training was done on Tiger Moths, the famous workhorse biplane that had trained every RAAF airman during the course of World War II. The Tiger now had a rival – the smart monoplane, closed cockpit De Havilland Chipmunk. It looked sleek and modern next to the antiquated lines of the Tiger Moth. Yes, thought David, that's the one I want to fly. It was not to be. Of the ten students, eight were allocated the Chipmunk, while the other two, including David, were relegated to the old Tiger Moth. A shattering disappointment. It was not until years later that he appreciated being trained on the Tiger.

Under the gruff but kindly instruction of Bill Ryan, the tuition started. The Tiger Moth is a touchy aircraft which does not tolerate strong wind. At that time Bankstown Airport had no sealed runways, just a vast green area which allowed pilots to use the prevailing wind conditions to take off and land appropriately anywhere on the field. There was, however, a certain strength of wind above which the aircraft could not be flown.

Our nervous, underconfident officer cadet Cooke would watch, with trepidation, the "magic wind test". A leaf would be dropped from waist height to the ground. If it landed between your feet, the flight was on. Despite his determination to learn to fly, David was a nervous student. He was quite happy on the days when flying was called off.

The cadets as a group had a real fear of airsickness. The consumption of Kwells became a matter of habit for the cadets. Half an hour before they were due to fly, they popped a little tablet to ease a potentially queasy tummy. David was no different. Some years before while on a cadet camp he was lucky enough to score a flight on a Beaufighter from Richmond to Wagga and back. A huge thrill. Unfortunately, he was perched on the wing spar just behind the pilot and the flight experienced some uncomfortable turbulence. An undercarriage problem also meant some violent manoeuvres to shake the landing gear into position. (It worked.) No wonder that David had battled nausea there and back. Then came the day when David was hurried out to the Tiger Moth before he had the chance to take his reassuring little pill. Hey presto, no nausea! From then on, no more Kwells.

Under pain of being removed from the course, the cadets were expected to go solo by twelve hours of instruction in the air. At ten hours it was looking likely that David would not make it. Landings persisted in being difficult as he bounced and swerved the aircraft to a halt. He despaired of ever getting the hang of it. Then somehow, fate stepped in.

David's stepfather, Bruce, was an acquaintance of PG Taylor, a famous Australian pioneer of flight who had flown with Charles Kingsford-Smith. Bruce was going to interview him about a possible book. David was invited along to meet this great man. He too, he told the young boy, had experienced trouble in landing but encouraged David to keep at it. It would all fall into place. The next day at home David creatively rigged up a simulated cockpit with some dining chairs going through the motions of landing over and over again.

The following day was Monday. Back to training. After a couple of decent landings Bill Ryan clambered out of the cockpit, tapped David on the shoulder and said, "Take it round this time on your own, lad."

On 15th December 1958 David wrote the magic word "self" in the column headed "Pilot in Command" in his logbook. He was the first on his course to do so.

Solo

Written the day after David's first solo, December 1958, at 17 years of age.

> *"For once you have tasted flight, you will walk the earth with your eyes turned skywards, for there you have been and there you will long to return."*
>
> Possibly attributed to Leonardo da Vinci

"Righto m'boy, I'm getting out this time. Just do what we've been doing. One circuit."

My heart gave the proverbial thump, and I sensed the lump in my throat. Half-heartedly I reached for the speaking tube and tried to confirm that I had understood but I doubt if Bill heard me.

"Any questions?"

On the previous circuit I had got tangled up between two aeroplanes, and Bill had taken over and dived us out of the way.

"Ah, yes sir. What happens if I get tangled up again?"

"Just fly on straight ahead until they get clear."

By this stage we were facing crosswind and Bill was getting out with his three cushions and stick. As I sat there with the motor idling and Bill reaching back to close the front hatch, I recall that even though I was not singing with delight, I was nevertheless glad this moment had come for two reasons. Firstly, the previous time I had gone up, I had mucked it up so much (including turning 45 degrees when landing) that Bill had doubted whether I would go solo within the required twelve hours. Secondly, I was going to be the first on my course to do so.

Bill smacked the side of my cockpit with his stick and walked over to a white marker near the perimeter road without looking back.

My gaze came back inside the cockpit.

"Harry the mug..." (I started the pre take-off mnemonic)

As Bill was not there, I recalled the mnemonic out loud for the first time.

"Trim set for take-off, fuel on and locked, (I doubt whether I gave the fuel gauge more than a quick unrecognising glance)... mixture fully rich... temps and pressures normal."

I unlocked the slats quickly and flicked each magneto switch.

"All clear upwind. Bill's not even looking this way ... perhaps he isn't game.

... all clear downwind ... turning into wind."

With a sharp burst of motor, the Tiger bounced around to face the fence just to the left of the De Havilland Hangar. Too quickly came the green light and instinctively I pulled back the stick and pushed forward the throttle as far as I could. No sooner had I started moving than I pushed the stick forward.

The fence rose above the nose ... "Too far, back a bit ... come on Cooke you're over correcting that swing ... loosen up a bit. It just bounced. What speed?... don't dare look ... there it is again ... back stick ... gently ... climbing attitude ... say I can see straight ahead because Bill's head isn't there ... climbing speed – 58 knots ... trim back ... 58 knots! Not 50! Forward stick ... adjust trim ... 200 feet, back throttle, I'm over the boundary ... am I off course? Not much ... blow that, I'm bloody flying myself! 500 feet all clear left and right, turning left gently ... 58 knots ... sit the top wing on the horizon ... ha! Bloody awful turn ... skidding all over the place ... hell the thing seems lighter without Bill ... 58 knots ... 1000 feet ... quick, power back and nose down ... trim forward ... all clear left and right, turning left."

Now for the first time I looked out of the cockpit and focussed on something. It was the "T" (wind indicator) down to my left, and I adjusted my heading so that it was parallel. Then, for the first time, I waggled the wings.

"Hell, that's quite hard... I had no idea there was so much pressure on the stick. Is it time to turn yet ... no ... gees I'm up to 1100 feet ... nose down ... what's the speed 85 knots ... back power 1050 feet ... 1000 ... turn left ... off power ... trim

> right back ... 58 knots ... nose up slightly ... how's the field ... two aircraft landing ... that's the first time I've seen them! OK, look round ... now turn ... nose right down ... no, too far ... I'm doing 62 knots ... back stick ... round we come ... that's it, wings level ... beauty, I don't think I'll overshoot ... keep to the right of those two aircraft. Hell, my right leg is shuddering ... stop it ... I can't stop it ... move the pedals to relieve the tension ... look out you're swinging in on those two aeroplanes, over the fence, keep the wings level ... 100 feet ... 58 knots ... nose down slightly."

I violently and vainly tried to wriggle under my harness to get comfortable.

> "Look out to the left ... there's a Piper taxying back ... keep the wings straight ... 58 knots ... look out you're swinging to the left, correct! ... that's better ... getting closer ... strain under the harness to lean out to the left."

The green blur suddenly became grass. "Round out ... slowly ... wings level ... hold it ... we're dropping ... back stick ... back ... back ... back ... right back ... still not down! ... hold it and wait ... wait ... slight bounce ... we're on and sticking ... look out, you're swinging ... that's better ... lock the slats ... How the hell did you do such a good landing Cooke? We've stopped rolling! I've done it ... I've done it!"

A sudden burst of power and I was facing the way I had come.

> "A sailor told me as he died", (I sing out loud to no one in particular one of the Air Force Mess songs) ... watch that yawing ... "I know not whether the bastard lied." I better not rev the engine so fast ... we're supposed to taxi at walking speed ... round we come ... here's Bill walking over."

Without even glancing in my direction, he hopped in with his stick and cushions.

> "Righto, m'boy, take me back to the club ... how'd you go?"

Wasn't he watching?

> "Oh, er, good sir!"

A pilot's first solo flight is a monumental experience. Every pilot, no matter how many hours they have clocked up, will remember with crystal clarity that first tentative circuit when they were in sole charge of an aircraft. But what about the second?

When David taxied out two days after his first solo flight, he felt fearless. With the confidence and enthusiasm of youth he rose into the air and set off around the circuit. Forgetting to unlock the slats, David stalled the Tiger prematurely. He had to go round twice before the aircraft finally settled in a very hard landing. It was so bad that the aeroplane had to be checked by the engineers. Luckily there was no significant damage done to the aircraft but certainly a huge dent in David's pride. A humiliating experience for this young pilot, but a valuable lesson was learnt.

The words of Geoffrey de Havilland have stayed with David all his flying years. "Flying should be entered into with a healthy degree of apprehension." It can never be taken for granted. And David never has.

In February 1959, David started studying medicine at the University of Sydney. His flying scholarship from the RAAF was valid for a year. However, with the pressure of undergoing an arduous university course, opportunities for flying were limited. Weather permitting, David continued travelling to Bankstown each weekend as he slowly progressed towards achieving his pilot's licence.

Cross country flying is another ordeal that the student pilot faces. At the end of July 1959, David undertook a solo cross country from Bankstown to Bankstown via Penrith and Camden. In the dead of winter an open cockpit is a cold place to be, especially at altitude. Despite his gloves, David's hands were numb and his fingers froze. His pencil for jotting waypoints and headings snapped. David's map flew out of his hands, disappearing into the wind. His fear of getting lost escalated as he wandered around the skies looking for a familiar feature to guide him back to Bankstown. Miraculously, he found his way back, but it was certainly a flight to remember, and learn from.

Circuits, stalls, spins and cross country flying, not to mention hours of theory, became a heavy load for a first year university student. Monday to Friday was filled with a demanding program of lectures and tutorials as

Physics, Chemistry, Psychology and Zoology were studied. The load was huge, especially for someone who had cruised through school with minimal effort. Studying did not come naturally to David. And there has to be some fun too! The year crept on and by September 3 he found himself doing his pre-licence test with his regular instructor, Bill Ryan. Understandably anxious about the actual test, which was looming ever closer, he felt quite at ease with Bill as they set off on this trial run. After they had returned to the circuit and landed, Bill turned to the young man with a wry grin. "Well m'boy, I'm afraid I tricked you. That was your actual flight test. Congratulations, you've passed."

David was a pilot at last.

With three months left of his RAAF scholarship, plus a brand new licence, he moved on to the de Havilland Chipmunk, bidding farewell to the trusty Tiger Moth. He would renew his acquaintance with the Tiger some years hence. The Chipmunk was a different kettle of fish altogether. Its main advantage was a closed cockpit and therefore much warmer. A closed cockpit meant no rushing wind in the face so no more uncomfortable goggles restricting vision, no more frozen fingers, snapping pencils and disappearing maps! It also had the luxury of radio to communicate with the tower and other aircraft and it was a whole lot easier to fly than the twitchy Tiger.

Yes, flying was certainly more comfortable now with the more modern Chipmunk. Meanwhile what was going on back at the halls of academe? It may come as no surprise that first year medicine, not receiving the attention it should have, ended in a fail. A dark time in David's life began.

It became even darker when he flew with Jim Brough from the Department of Civil Aviation one day. Up until now all his instructors had been air force staff. On this flight David was told by the tower to expedite lining up on the runway. This he did but failed to realise that the tail wheel was not straight causing the aircraft to spear to one side off the runway. Brough immediately pulled David's licence. This, of course, was only temporary, but on top of failing his university year it was humiliating blow. Where would he go from here?

A glimmer of hope came in early December when he attended a camp at Williamtown and gained some dual experience in a Vampire jet. What a thrill it was to be instructed in the sleek little fighter trainer compared to the slow old Tiger and Chipmunk. Fortunately, David's licence was restored later in December by the Chief Flying Instructor Pat Gallagher. However, as the scholarship year was now over, there was to be no more flying for David until November 1965 – six years hence!

After World War II, returned servicemen had the opportunity to undertake tertiary education. As David's father had been killed in active service, this educational scholarship was handed to any surviving children under a program called Soldiers Children's Education Bursary. This covered university fees, books, a living allowance and any other incidental expenses such as a skeleton and microscope. At the beginning of 1960 David had to swallow his pride and ask for a second chance to continue his studies. At this time Qantas was offering cadetships to fast track a career in aviation – a tempting offer and one that the hopeful young student considered. However, after much family consultation and parental persuasion, he decided to continue his medical studies. Kindly Mr Duckett, the chairman of the Soldiers Children's Education Bursary understood the young man's situation of facing the shock of university study and the thrill of flying and agreed to give him another opportunity to complete his medical degree. David settled down to the rigours of university life – minus the flying. He completed his degree without any further problems.

In order to maintain contact with the world of aviation David joined the University RAAF Squadron – a two-year commitment. During this time, as well as attending regular musters each week, the squadron went on vacation camps at different RAAF bases. With luck the officer cadets usually managed to arrange the odd ride in some RAAF aircraft. David scored flights in Hercules and Neptune aircraft. Although not in command of course, it was enough to be up in the air again and only served to make him even more determined to return to flying as soon as possible.

On graduating from the University Squadron two years later as a Pilot Officer, he became a lecturer to the young school students who belonged to the Air Training Corps. Only a few years earlier he had been one of those boys. He lectured in Navigation and Aviation Medicine and threw himself into this new challenge. One day he was amused to overhear one of the boys saying that he hoped "Cookie" would be lecturing tonight. "We don't do much in his class." David felt that the best of learning is done under the guise of fun.

As a qualified private pilot and University Squadron member David was considered valuable to Queen and country. The RAAF were not simply being kind to young aviation enthusiasts by offering cadetships to school leavers. These young men were considered "insurance" should Australia be faced with a military situation that required more pilots than were readily available. The young men in the Air Force Reserve could be quickly brought up to service standard if the need arose. David was classified as Aircrew.

About four years into his medical studies, he received a letter from the RAAF reclassifying him as Medical because of his university studies. He was far from happy at this news and sent a return letter stating he would prefer to remain as General Duties Aircrew. To his surprise this was not well received and the message was clear, "You'll do as you're told." You can't argue with the armed services.

In 1960 during his First Year Medicine mark II, David went on a blind date organised by a friend. Here he met and began dating a young Arts student Elizabeth or Lizzie. It is probably wise to make clear that this Lizzie or Elizabeth I, is not the author of this book. Elizabeth II, the author, appears many years later.

Up till now David's experience of the female sex had been limited. Being smaller in stature and young looking for his age does not engender confidence. His dalliances had been brief and harmless. Flying and university commitments the previous year had left little time for a social life. Lizzie seemed to measure up. She was, and this was important to the family, from a suitable background, had attended a private school and had been gently raised. Approval from David's family! The young couple began "courting". Lizzie, however, was not quite as she seemed. Despite her WASP upbringing, she voiced distinctly left-wing views and wanted to have not only an education but also a career! Fine by David but not quite what Betty and Bruce wanted for him. According to Betty, such women did not make good wives.

In the early sixties it was hard to escape the clutches of family. To leave home was seen as a slight on the family and unless there was a suitable excuse such as working or studying away from home, it rarely occurred. As a result, early marriage was the only approved option for young people to leave home and begin independent adult life with all the joys that entailed. After five years of dating, David and Elizabeth took the plunge into wedlock in January 1965, his final year of medicine. Upon marriage, David's Soldiers Children's Education Bursary was now paid directly to him. Together with Lizzie's small wage they had enough to set up the usual humble flat that newlyweds in those days seemed to frequent.

Meanwhile, how was the medical degree progressing? After his sheltered life at school, university, as it does to all students, opened up David's world. He started to find himself, making new friends including some from European backgrounds. One of his best friends came from a family that had escaped the holocaust. How different his friend's upbringing had been compared to David's. They were Jewish, spoke Czech at home and had experienced the horrors of Hitler's onslaught. University life was another world, and David relished the experiences it gave him.

He discovered a dress style including a smart tweed jacket paired with a yellow pair of desert boots, known by their wearers as "brothel creepers". David's genteel upbringing should have meant that this young man did not know what a brothel was, let alone the location of one. This was not the case. After one faculty dinner and egged on by others, a group of the students decided to be daring and visit a well-known brothel in inner-city Newtown. Courteously welcomed by the Madame, they were ushered into the lounge area, looking around goggle eyed and faintly apprehensive. Of course no one had any intention of using the facilities, this was more of a dare and a story to tell the mates. They did stay long enough to be entertained by the sight of a woman appearing at the top of the stairs. "Next," she shouted to the clients below. Not quite what the students had expected, as this worker had a full plaster cast encasing one leg. Convulsed with laughter they fled from the scene. Not so sophisticated after all.

Dressed in his boots and jacket, he topped off his outfit with a smart little hat worn at a jaunty angle. To complete the picture, like many young people of those times, he took up smoking, but not for David the common or garden cigarette. A pipe was more dashing, adding to the sophisticated yet studious air that a university student should have. And there he was, nattily turned out in the fashion of the day, off to lectures looking smart and debonair with all the confidence of youth. No wonder he caught Lizzie's eye!

Smoking even had a beneficial effect on his studies. In second year, medical students moved on to study anatomy. At last, something that had some real connection to the end result of being a doctor. Part of anatomy involves the dissection of cadavers or a bit of a cadaver like a leg or hand. These pieces of once living men and women were preserved in formalin and exuded a pungent, unpleasant odour. Erinmore tobacco to the rescue, and looking like some caricature from a Sherlock Holmes movie, David would bend over his piece of cadaver and gently puff away the smell. Perfect! What did the female students do to protect their delicate sensibilities? Probably liberal doses of Estee Lauder Youth Dew or something similar.

The dissections were a lengthy business and were summed up at the end of the session with a report – oral and written. It all took an age and it was not unusual for our hero to decamp with a couple of mates to the local watering hole, the Lalla Rookh, for some refreshments, leaving the swots to get on with the work. Upon returning they would ask their studious colleagues to fill them in on what was needed to know, and there - no harm done!

The Lalla Rookh provided another diversion in second year during physiology pracs. The task was for the students to run around the medical school building twice. On returning to the lab they breathed into a large plastic sac called a Douglas bag which then measured the amount of oxygen and carbon dioxide in their breath. This task was to indicate the changes in levels of oxygen and carbon dioxide after exertion. This proved too dull for some students and they decided to spice up the activity a little. In approximately the same amount of time taken to run twice around the medical school building, it was possible to dash into the Lalla Rookh and down a quick beer or two and head back to the lab to huff and puff their alcoholic breath into the bag. The results, it is fair to say, were somewhat skewed and caused much head scratching among the tutors. How could these fit young men have such poor results? What would David's patients today think of this mischievous student who subverted the system?

Doing a degree in medicine is an arduous affair. The number of years to complete the degree seems to stretch into the interminable distance. Would he ever be able to put MB BS after his name? But, just to ensure there would be some letters after his name, David and a friend decided to apply to become Justices of the Peace. If not MB BS then at least he would be David Cooke JP! This qualification has stood him in good stead for over fifty years. Many patients and friends have gratefully used his services. Eventually, JP was preceded by many other letters as David's qualifications progressed from MB BS, to FRACGP, FACRRM and more recently, OAM.

On various fronts, life was moving along quite well for David. He was coping with his studies, he had a girlfriend and although the relationship was far from perfect, to have a regular girl was desirable. There was a social life, although this was limited due to financial constraints.

There was however a huge gap where an airfield and an aeroplane should have been. We can only imagine how difficult it must have been for him. To have attained his licence in 1959 and then a few months later have it all grind to a halt with his looming years of study must have been exceedingly challenging. It says much about his strength of character that he did in fact sacrifice his great love of flying for those years of study. As a young man it would have been an easy option to forget about uni, get a job and fly whenever it was possible. Six years is an eternity to a young person. Six years with no flying must have been indescribably frustrating.

Something can always be found to fill a void. David made sure he found his something. At the beginning of Fourth Year, he was appointed to the Royal North Shore Hospital for the clinical component of his studies. Medical studies now began to have some relevance as the reality of being a doctor began to take shape. He was now entitled to wear a white coat and have a stethoscope as a badge of office! New friends were made as the group from his year was together for the next three years of study. Among them was a mature age student – at least thirty and practically middle-aged as far as the other lads were concerned. This fellow had an interest that opened up a new leisure pursuit that, in some small way, helped fill the huge void that aviation had left.

On a warm Saturday morning David drove to Long Reef on the Northern Beaches, climbed into a black, uncomfortable wetsuit, strapped a tank on his back and weights round his waist and dived into the clear waters of the Pacific. It was another world. Let us not for the moment worry about the safety of this expedition, the non-existent PADI course, the lead weights, the dangers so evident. He survived and that is enough. What he did find was a world where once again he was in a three-dimensional environment, travelling up, down, around, viewing the mysteries of the ocean. This world was as close as he could be to the world of flying, another medium but strangely similar. It was accessible, close to home and cheap, a perfect substitute for the longed-for but impossibility of flight at this time. Scuba diving soon became a regular activity. The experience of being up close to a groper or wobbegong was a special privilege. There were hair-raising stories of rocks, dangerous currents and surging waves but, apart from grazes and a ripped wetsuit, no major damage was done.

As well as diving, David found he had a natural talent for penning song lyrics. Many an afternoon was spent at the various pubs frequented by students, composing ditties with another friend, usually scrawling them on odd scraps of paper, table napkins or even, if they were desperate, scratchy toilet tissue. As was to be expected these lyrics were often parodies of well-known songs and more appropriate to a pub or air force mess than genteel company. Their repertoire at the end of their studies was around thirty to forty songs. As well as writing it was usually David who led the singing at the Medical Faculty Annual Dinners. No doubt they sang some of their own compositions.

Although not quite as exciting as flying, David, like all young men, was eager to obtain his independence by acquiring his own car. University studies and limited funds of course made this impossible. His luck changed in December 1962 when he reached the grand old age of twenty-one. His grandfather Cooke gave him the eye wateringly huge gift of one hundred pounds – Australia was still in pre-decimal days. Now what would a young man do with this sum of money? Why, buy a car of course. He wasted no time and hotfooted it to McIntosh Car Sales and Service Parts Pty Ltd in Mosman, a business which is still there today. Here he exchanged his one hundred pound gift plus five of his own for Geoffrey, a smart Austin A30 sedan of a rather unattractive pale green colour.

Geoffrey liberated David, who was now free to travel wherever and whenever he liked. Such a change from begging to borrow the family car for an important function or outing. It was freedom and he seized it with both hands.

David's university life continued smoothly. He did enough work to pass each year, much to the relief of his parents. A steady girlfriend took care of his social life apart from the obligatory pub life that demanded his attention. There was also the scuba diving, an escape to the world of silence and the freedom of the ocean. The University of Sydney had its own Jacques Cousteau!

But, and it was a big but, there was no flying. After his flying ceased in December 1959 there was no more significant flying till the end of 1965 – six years, a lifetime for our aviation obsessed pilot. Apart from two brief training flights, his final hurrah for those six flightless years was some flying in a Vampire jet while attending a camp at Williamtown. Four other flights at the end of 1961, also while attending a camp at Richmond, were the sole aviation experiences during those years of study. These flights to Laverton and Townsville were a welcome contact with his dreams of flight.

It is not surprising, therefore, to hear that on 15 November 1965, the day of his final university exam, David took to the skies again at Bankstown. Things had changed somewhat. No more Chipmunks were used for training. He found himself in an Australian made aircraft, a Victa, designed by the man who revolutionised lawn maintenance for Australians. Instead of a vast field of green where pilots took off into the wind now there were sleek black runways and ordered take-offs via radio communication with the control tower. Changes had been made indeed but in only two hours forty minutes of tuition, he was once again allowed to go solo. On 8 December 1965 after less than a month, he regained his Restricted Private licence. This licence permitted pilots to fly in the local training area only. Regulations now required student pilots to complete twenty hours of cross country flying to complete their licence. After a further fifteen hours navigation his full licence was granted on 22nd June 1966.

After graduating in Medicine in January 1966, David was appointed a Junior Resident at Fairfield District Hospital, a world away from genteel Mosman and the hallowed halls of The University of Sydney. Here he encountered the rough and tumble of the real Sydney with its bustling multi-cultural population. It also meant a much shorter commute to Bankstown Airport. Weather permitting, he would head out to the airport after finishing a shift to do some much-missed flying. The western suburbs weren't so bad after all!

Being a doctor and working for a wage meant the opportunity to save some money but unlike other young marrieds, David's desire was not a three-bedroom house with garden and garage, but an aircraft of his own. In November 1966 he took the plunge. With two mates, Stephen Lovell and Ric Macready, he bought an Auster, VH-KBP, for the princely sum of $3600 split three ways. This much prized Auster was the first in a long line of aircraft that David has owned over the years.

Now what do you do when you become the proud part-owner of a new aircraft. Do you familiarise yourself with it over the next few months doing small local flights? Well, only a few, and certainly not for long. No, much better to bite the bullet and fly to Tasmania. And so they did! On Boxing Day 1966, David in the Auster with Ric and a very nervous Elizabeth, plus two other aircraft, set off for Tasmania via Albury. A flight over the water to the island state would be considered a little daunting by most pilots and is even more so in a small single engine aircraft piloted by someone with a scant 115 hours flying experience. It was not unexpected therefore to experience what is known in aviation jargon as "interesting" events.

December 27 was Day 2 of this adventure. With David at the controls, they departed Latrobe Valley for Flinders Island in the middle of Bass Strait. Alas, they had to abort the flight after fifteen minutes discovering that the oil cap had fallen off. A lack of oil in an aircraft engine, especially over water, is not a good thing. Back to Latrobe Valley they flew where a replacement oil cap was located at a car wrecker. Saved by an old Austin car! The rest of the Tasmanian adventure passed relatively smoothly despite some low cloud over Bass Strait which meant flying at a mere 300 feet above the waves. Ric accidentally turned the fuel off at one stage, but it was quickly discovered before the engine stopped.

Leaving Devonport one day the cross wind was so strong that a normal take-off was impossible for such a light aircraft and they were forced to use the taxiway as a runway. They arrived home safely after a huge week of learning and gaining invaluable experience in cross country flying and navigation. This was David's first major flying trip and gave him a taste for outback flying which he has loved to this day.

This flight led quickly to more and in March 1967 he headed inland to Alice Springs and Ayers Rock as it was known then. What a change in landscape for this city boy who had grown up in a busy city and rarely felt the dirt beneath his feet. This flight covered huge distances over vast endless plains and sand dunes. No well-maintained tarmac airstrips on hand, just the odd scratch of dirt that depicted a property which had an airstrip in case of an emergency. Remember too that in 1967 navigation was by eyeball, map and compass, a far cry from the ease of GPS and radar today. Good visibility was vital and on the leg from Marree up the Birdsville track a rapidly building dust storm made them descend to an altitude of about 50 feet. It also forced them off track. Spotting Pandie Pandie Station they landed on the racecourse, dodging beer bottles and cans as they touched down and asked directions of the amused owners. Back on track they eventually battled through the dust to Birdsville where a strong crosswind was tearing across the airstrip. Being a high-wing aircraft, the Auster is less tolerant of wind than the low wing type. It was necessary to leap out of the aircraft and hold the wing strut to prevent the aircraft from lifting.

An overnight at Birdsville means two possible types of accommodation – sleeping under the wing in a swag or staying at the Birdsville pub. The three aviators opted for the pub of course. Not quite luxury as the rich, red desert sand had found its way into the room covering the bed, floor and other furniture in its fine but gritty film. What a long way from Mosman! It is fair to say that not a lot at Birdsville has changed over the years since then, but it remains a favourite outback spot with pub hospitality second to none.

The next day took them to Alice Springs. Fortunately, the dust and visibility improved a bit making for a more comfortable flight. On landing at this city in the centre of Australia there was much relief and congratulations all round. They were enormously glad and proud to have done this flight, but swore they would never do it again! David, for one, didn't keep his word and has flown the Simpson Desert many times since, but not one of those subsequent trips was as challenging as this first.

***

Dust

1967

"Truly superior pilots are those who use their superior judgement to avoid those situations where they might have to use their superior skills."

We take off in the Auster from Marree for the flight up the Birdsville track. The forecast is for dust haze from prevailing strong westerly winds, but we are not worried. There is no cloud forecast and that means CAVOK (no significant weather) to the hotshot young pilots with 150 hours apiece.

We decide to follow the Birdsville Track as depicted on the map, obviously as a well-marked road. In the bumpy afternoon we climb to 5000 feet leaving the Afghans and the camels on the north side of the railway track behind. In the back seat is a carton of Easter eggs that the mailman had left behind, for the store at Birdsville.

Stephen is flying and I navigate with a WAC chart spread on my lap. The Auster rises and falls in the turbulence and we fly with the side windows pulled back because of the heat.

Ahead, the haze appears to thicken, and we proceed at 80 knots. The famous track stretches northwards bending here and there to avoid a gully created by some long-gone downpour. Occasionally there is a dry creek bed made visible only by a line of trees or a slight greenness in the otherwise red/brown plains. Some buildings appear a few miles from the road indicating civilisation. Someone is living down there, scratching a living out of grazing cattle. We do not envy them as we fly over. We are glad to be up in the Auster, the engine going well and the anticipation of reaching Birdsville in our optimistic minds.

The track becomes less distinct as we travel north, and in an effort to keep it in sight Stephen descends. We are an hour and a half into the flight and continue to descend. The afternoon is hot and bumpy, and we become a little insecure as to how distinct the track is. Sometimes it appears a well-marked and graded dirt road but sometimes no more than a couple of wheel tracks. If it crosses a hard plain of rocks it is barely visible at all. The parallel sand ridges of the Simpson Desert are vaguely seen to our left and the sun is just a dim redness in the brown sky.

Two hours out. I gaze up from my map which is becoming hard to justify with what I see outside, and I notice that we are down to a few hundred feet. No problems, the country is flat and there are no powerlines around. It is so foreign to our experience, this country. We are used to green paddocks and cities and beaches and we are surprised that the forecast dust is so thick. I look to the west again, past the captain and notice that the tops of the dunes are level with the cockpit. Ahead the visibility is down to a quarter of a mile if that, and the road beneath only just visible. By calculation we have half an hour to go and we come to a branch in the road. One track goes west into the Simpson Desert and one to the right. We circle at 50 feet above the gloomy landscape, bumping around and thirsty, but not daring to take our eyes off the ground beneath. No signpost! We opt for the easterly track – stay out of the desert at all cost.

The aircraft is crabbing sideways in the strong westerly and we find a few buildings and a cleared area that is obviously the airstrip. Stephen banks steeply looking down as a man looks up at us from the ground.

> "Birdsville!" I say triumphantly as Stephen pulls on flap and bounces to a halt. The watcher drives up to us in his Land Rover.

> "Birdsville?" I ask.

> "Hell, no mate, this is Pandie Pandie homestead. Birdsville is twenty miles further up the Diamantina River."

I climb out to start the engine again, wishing I could remain on the ground and not return to the sky. How my mindset has changed in two hours. I remark on the fact that there are a lot of beer bottles and cans on the strip only to be informed that we have landed on his racecourse!

> "Just follow the Diamantina and you will hit Birdsville," is his parting call and we wobble into the air, trying to see any water beside the tree line.

> Ten minutes later we do see the town, grey red in the late afternoon haze and with the windsock streaming out across both runways in a huge crosswind.
>
> "As soon as I slow down to taxi you will need to jump out and hold the wing down, Cookie," says the pilot and I do just that.
>
> We taxi up to the pub with me hanging on to the wing struts with the gusting wind doing its best to turn us over. The engine stops but the howling wind takes over and there is no peace in reaching our destination. No peace, too, because tomorrow we are to fly across the Simpson Desert to Alice Springs, and we begin to doubt that we are the clever pilots that 150 hours flying time has made us after all.

A visit to Alice Springs means a visit to Ayers Rock or Uluru as we now call it. In 1967 it was possible to land right beside the Rock and experience its awe-inspiring, powerful presence as you come in to land. David and Stephen also flew to Yuendumu Aboriginal Settlement, a privilege not available to many as it is a closed community. When they were in Alice Springs, they met up with a schoolteacher who kindly invited them to visit this Aboriginal community. David in particular found this experience a fascinating eye-opener and was possibly part responsible in his subsequent work with the Indigenous communities some time later.

The flight home to Sydney took them over the huge salt pan that is Lake Eyre. The brilliance of the sun shining on the white salt flat created a rather frightening "whiteout" effect in which pilots can easily become disoriented and lose the idea of which way is up. It can be a very disturbing experience especially for the first time.

David and his longtime school and flying mate had lots of aviation exploits together. As well as the first hair-raising flight to Tasmania, David and Stephen revisited this experience when Stephen bought a smart little Tiger Moth, christened the Red Baron. The two of them plucked up courage and set off one weekend in 1980 to fly to Tasmania and back. This was no mean feat in the slow old Tiger Moth with its minimal instruments and open cockpit. The Bass Strait is known for its fickle weather and icy winds. It would be much more comfortable to be in an enclosed cockpit with autopilot on. The Red Baron triumphed, and two very happy pilots returned safely. Some years later, making good use of the Easter holidays, they attempted a four day fly around the coast of Australia. This was not in the airy Tiger Moth but a much more civilised Grumman Traveler.

Sadly, this was the last safari that Stephen and David did together. In December 1987 Stephen died suddenly on the dance floor at his company's Christmas party. He was only 46 years old and a great loss to David. At the time, David commented that his old mate would do anything to get out of paying the restaurant bill! He has never been forgotten.

Meanwhile when he wasn't haring around the outback in the Auster, David was slogging away at Prince Henry Hospital at Little Bay. This premier site was commandeered for expensive housing and the hospital closed some years ago. David developed an interest in surgery, particularly neurosurgery. A decision was made to travel to England and undertake the training necessary to become a neurosurgeon. With the British academic year commencing in September there was a gap of some months to fill before leaving Australia. David had a brainwave. and on seeing an article in a medical journal he applied to a hospital in Port Vila in the New Hebrides, now Vanuatu. His idea was to conduct a flying doctor service visiting outlying areas and providing medical services for communities that did not have ready access to medical care. At this time the New Hebrides was conjointly governed by France and the UK. In true political fashion no decision could be agreed on the funding of the project. For various reasons this project did not come to pass. Instead, David applied for and obtained a job with the Northern Territory Aerial Medical Services as a flying doctor. This was the NT equivalent of the Royal Flying Doctor Service.

And so it was that in January 1968 he and Elizabeth, barely clinging on to a rocky marriage, packed their bags and travelled to Darwin to begin a new life far from suburban Sydney.

He found himself in a totally different, exciting environment and blossomed under the hot, territory sun. He never returned to Sydney to live.

Darwin 1968

Arriving in Darwin in January is probably not the most sensible thing to do. The wet season certainly lives up to its name with the constant monsoonal deluge being enervating and inconvenient from a flying point of view.

Just imagine, this Sydney born, middle class North Shore boy was thrust into the frontier life of Darwin. All his life David had been expected to think, act and speak in the appropriate way of someone from this environment. He was friends with, and generally mixed with people of a similar background. They had all gone to "good" schools, were of the same ethnicity and believed in the same religion.

In Darwin, this mattered not one bit.

For the first time in his life David was free. No one was interested in where he was from, what school he went to or how he voted. Darwin in those days was often a refuge for those wishing to "escape" from personal, legal or financial problems. It was populated by "characters". Everyone was accepted for who they were with no questions asked.

Medically, life in the Northern Territory was a real eye-opener. Up until now David's medical experience had consisted of working in hospitals with all the assistance that modern city hospitals could provide. Now, in the Northern Territory, he was on his own, flying around this vast outback area treating mainly Indigenous patients and having to improvise in remote areas that lacked any sophisticated equipment. He loved the stimulation of this new and challenging form of medicine. No doubt it added greatly to his overall skills in diagnosis by relying on little more than his eyeballs and stethoscope.

Geographically, he flew long distances to places such as Elcho Island, Millingimbi, Maningrida, Gove, Oenpelli, Borroloola and the beautifully named Snake Bay. These places were not on the tourist trail and hence little visited by anyone at that time.

Prior to leaving Sydney, David had begun his studies to attain his Commercial Pilot Licence. Despite his busy working life in Darwin, he managed to complete this in September 1968. The test, however, was not without incident. David found himself slightly uncertain of his position somewhere in the middle of Arnhem Land. This was still unfamiliar territory to the young pilot. Fortunately for David, the Department of Civil Aviation testing officer began to suffer some uncomfortable bowel urgency and was keen to complete this test in record time! It only took the offer of some anti-diarrhoea medication in return for a location fix and both men were happy. David continued to complete the flight test, the testing officer's rumbling innards calmed down allowing him to reach the ground with dignity. A win-win situation. Nothing more was said about the temporary navigational hitch up there in the sky and David gained his commercial licence.

With his brand new commercial licence, David set out to fly just as much as he possibly could by obtaining a weekend job flying a large Cessna for a buffalo meat company. Instead of payment he was offered unlimited hours in the company aeroplane. This was an opportunity to log many hours honing his skills. He was often fortunate to have a retired RAF test pilot willing to share his knowledge with David. He completed a course in aerobatics, which, apart from being enormously exciting if you like being turned upside down, also improves a pilot's handling of unusual attitudes in an aircraft.

David's daily work with the Northern Territory Aerial Medical Service, (NTAMS), involved flying with Trans Australia Airlines pilots. This was invaluable experience observing these pilots and how they operated an efficient, safe air service for the local people.

The NTAMS had never had a doctor who was so keen to fly. It didn't matter to David – day, night, fair weather or foul it was all a wonderful opportunity to grow as a pilot. His skills increased exponentially. He became good friends with pilots, sometimes persuading them to fly low over the East Alligator River flats chasing buffalo. All this safely out of sight of air traffic control!

Medically the Northern Territory was so very different from doctoring down south. One significant medical challenge was an outbreak of typhoid fever in two Aboriginal settlements in Arnhem Land. David was directed to go with four nurses and fix it. Now our city doctor, of course, had never seen a case of typhoid let alone an epidemic, so where does he start to diagnose and treat such numbers of infected people? He decided that treating individuals might not do the job. Reinfection could occur, with those who were not actively ill spreading the disease. Instead, he chose to treat the whole community with antibiotics for two weeks in order to break the cycle of infection. It worked a treat. As a side benefit it also cleared up other common infections such as middle ear infections, impetigo and even gonorrhea!

He had also decided to remove the canine population as they too could have transmitted the disease. However, word had got around. When it came time to remove the dogs they were nowhere to be seen! They had mysteriously vanished and were hidden from view. What a learning experience this was. David realised that removing dogs was tantamount to removing children from the community, they were just as important. As a token of thanks for eradicating typhoid in the community, the Yirrkala people gave him a tribal name, a great honour for a white person. They named him, "Bungali".

Treating the Indigenous people of the outback was a new and different form of medicine for David. He soon picked up their sense of humour. Once their trust was gained, they would joke and make fun of him. One day as he was walking down the dusty road in a small community, he could hear giggling and scuffling behind him. He was being followed by a gaggle of local kids all imitating David's slightly rolling gait and laughing their heads off!

Christmas 1968 saw David being asked, at age twenty-seven, to don the Santa suit and be the jolly round man at the Christmas celebrations at a local mission. Dressed in the red suit, complete with flowing white wig and beard, off he went in a Connellans Airlines Piper Comanche; a flying sleigh laden with gifts for these children who had so little. This was a tremendous opportunity for David to display his not inconsiderable acting ability. He practised his cheery wave and "ho, ho hos" with relish. He was going to be a Santa the kids would never forget! In 40 degree heat the aircraft landed. David hitched the padding around his middle, adjusted his beard and stepped forward for his big moment. How thrilling for the kids to have their very own Santa in this remote area. With only his eyes visible and sweat running down his face, he jumped down from the aircraft to greet the mob of excited kids. Ho, ho hoing for all he was worth, he strode towards them, hands outstretched in greeting.

"Hello Doctor Cooke," shouted some bright young faces as they ran towards him. So much for the great disguise and getting into character. It was

Doctor Cooke who stepped off the aircraft and nothing could disguise that from these astute youngsters.

David came to appreciate a different philosophy towards medicine. The people had a fatalistic view of their health. They would just shrug their shoulders and simply say, "Bidi' – if I die, I die. The doctor and nurse were never blamed if things went wrong. Then again, profuse thanks were rarely offered when things went well. Life was what it would be, and this was accepted uncomplainingly. They were eager to please the doctor and questions had to be carefully asked to avoid eliciting the wrong response in their desire to satisfy the doctor with what they perceived was the expected answer. David soon got into the swing of it and was greatly flattered once when a woman had to have a toe removed in hospital. She requested a visit from the traditional medicine practitioner. On hearing none was available she replied, "Oh well, get David Cooke, he's just as good."

Contraception was a difficult medical issue for Indigenous women. The convenient IUD was popular at this time but was not permitted in the Indigenous communities. The insertion of a foreign body was an alien idea, not acceptable to the women. The contraceptive pill which was relatively new at this time also proved problematic. The Indigenous idea of community and sharing of everything, plus the necessity of regular dosage, made this a difficult choice.

David found himself in the position of giving sex education lectures to the school children - a challenging job for our somewhat naïve young doctor. These kids could probably have taught him a thing or two!

There was a leprosarium located just outside Darwin. David's only knowledge of leprosy, or as it's more correctly known, Hansen's Disease, was limited to gruesome Biblical references. Who knew it still existed in some form in Australia in the 20th Century? He quickly learnt about the disease when he was seconded to the leprosarium to relieve the Superintendent for a few weeks. The existence of this curable disease in the Indigenous population of Northern Australia was a huge shock to this city born and bred doctor. It showed without doubt the shocking divide that occurred between black and white, let alone rich and poor in modern Australia. Diseases rarely, if ever, seen in the south still thrived among those who were living in third world conditions in this country. More and more David felt driven to do whatever he could to improve in some small way this appalling situation.

Aboriginal women generally birthed easily but certainly not always. One case involved performing an operation on a woman in labour. This occurred beside the airstrip at the Rose River Mission in the Gulf of Carpentaria, certainly nothing like a sterile operating theatre. The patient was experiencing difficulties with postpartum haemorrhage but refused to be transported the 300 miles to Darwin Hospital. To be moved away from the family and the security this provided was greatly feared by the Indigenous community and this woman would rather risk her own life and that of her baby than be sent away to a strange hospital. Of course this occurred in the rainy season and the pilot found himself assisting with the operation by holding an umbrella over the doctor and patient. Uncrossmatched blood (O negative) was used to transfuse the patient as this blood can be given to all blood types in the case of emergency.

David also diagnosed a case of yaws; a bacterial infection present in some tropical countries but unknown to a first world city doctor. In one dramatic incident David was the target of a spear thrower (it missed!) but what had he done to provoke such anger? Apparently he was telling jokes and laughing with the pilot and nurses much to the displeasure of the spear carrying patient!

Another obstetric emergency occurred late one thundery afternoon with an Aboriginal woman dying of blood loss from a retained placenta. The community of Umbakumba was on Groote Eylandt, two hours flight time from Darwin. Then followed a four-hour drive in a Land Rover up a dry riverbed before reaching the Umbakumba Anglican Mission on the far side of the island. Because of its remoteness, no doctor had attended this mission in thirty years. Luckily the woman survived. The missionary praised the lord. "Alleluia," he exclaimed, "the Lord has sent David Cooke". On the medical team's departure, the community members bowed as if to royalty or a saint. A long day's travel for the life of one patient, but typical of what was done in the outback to provide care to the isolated people who lived there.

By this time, it had become apparent to David that his desire to travel to the UK to become a neurosurgeon was fast fading. September came and went. The academic year commenced in the UK without him. Understandably, this decision was not such a happy one for Lizzie, causing a deal of friction between them. This proved the final straw. Lizzie left the Northern Territory to return home before subsequently moving to the UK by herself.

During the last three months of 1968 David was appointed to the hospital at Alice Springs as the resident obstetrician. In his hospital years in Sydney, he had delivered a total of ten babies under supervision, but here he was, in charge of obstetrics.

On his first day in charge the midwife on duty showed David how to use the Ventouse vacuum extractor. This involves attaching a suction cup to the baby's head, which allows the mother to deliver the baby naturally with the doctor helping to manipulate the head and shoulders from the birth canal. It is an alternative to a forceps delivery. That very night at 2.00am David was called to attend a woman in protracted labour. The midwife suggested using the Ventouse and proceeded to fetch it. All went well and with the baby safely delivered David said to the midwife, "That's my eleventh!"

"Oh, you've done eleven Ventouse?"

"No, it was my eleventh delivery!"

Not long after arriving in Alice Springs, he had the thrill of delivering a young woman of fraternal twins. This was his first multiple birth, which fortunately was a straightforward delivery. The mother decided to name these two babies after the attending doctor and midwife. It was common within the Aboriginal community to name a male child after the father, but in this case that was obviously not David!

Let's hope that David Cooke Lynch and Jean Gricks Lynch, now fifty-three years old, are still happily living in the Northern Territory, constantly reminded of who helped them into the world.

His experiences in Alice Springs resulted in a love of obstetric work which he continued to practise until 1990. He never tired of the thrill of easing a new life into the world.

Alice Springs offered new experiences in aviation. Although the Auster had been left in Sydney with the other two part-owners, David still managed to fly. At the weekend, he would hire a Cessna 172 and fill it with three nurses and fly to Ayers Rock, as it was known at the time. He quickly fell in love with the beautiful McDonnell Ranges surrounding Alice Springs and was never happier than when flying around the spectacular landscape of central Australia.

In December 1968 he noticed an advertisement for a Medical Officer with the Royal Flying Doctor Service in Mount Isa in Queensland. The incumbent doctor had fallen ill, and a replacement was urgently needed. During these last few months his marriage had come to grief. Although he would have liked to continue working in Alice Springs, he felt that a change would be appropriate.

In late January 1969 he moved by himself to Mount Isa. Another adventure had begun.

Mount Isa

1969 - 1972

The city of Mount Isa was a different kettle of fish from Darwin and Alice Springs. This was a mining town and a service centre for the vast grazing areas around it. The RFDS serviced an area the size of Texas. In the Northern Territory there had been several doctors, three aeroplanes, three pilots and four nurses. At Mount Isa there was one doctor, two pilots and a nurse. They flew in a Beechcraft Queenair and David was on call 24 hours a day, seven days a week. Despite this heavy work load he soon loved working and living in this hostile environment where temperatures commonly rose to 35 or even 45 degrees during the day.

After two months it was mutually decided that David would be permanently appointed as the Medical Officer at the Mount Isa base. It was now time to once again have his own aircraft to enjoy during his leisure time. The other two part-owners in the Auster were more than happy for David to buy them out. Flying this old aeroplane all the way from Camden near Sydney to Mount Isa was a huge undertaking, not one to be done alone. David's stepfather, Bruce, a retired flying boat captain, jumped at the chance to be the co-pilot. Over three long, hot days they slowly made their way north. They flew at a low altitude with Bruce insisting on navigating with the Shell road maps, declaring them more accurate than David's flying maps!

One of the stops was at Winton in central Queensland. In good outback style there was a man at the airport who happily gave them a lift into town for a lunch break. No such luck on the way back to the airport. Despite David's year of living and working in these hostile conditions they recklessly set off on foot to walk to the airport. On the point of collapsing from the heat they were once again rescued by a passing driver who conveyed them safely to the aeroplane. It was a learning experience that made David aware of the dangers of the outback. Respect the country or it will kill you.

As in the Northern Territory, the medical work was challenging, relying on a great degree of improvisation and commonsense. Flying out to isolated communities or properties often meant setting fractures by eyeball only, no such thing as x-rays being available. It was impossible to do blood tests. Cardiographs were not available either, as most properties had only 32 volt direct current generators. With the flying, of course, there was no GPS. Maps and compass were how you found these remote airstrips scratched in the dirt of the outback. Medically, too, it was isolating with no one to discuss the cases with apart from the nurse and pilot. It was real flying by the seat of your pants medicine.

Although David had graduated with MB BS from the University of Sydney, he soon discovered that some patients were decidedly harder to treat. An absence of vets and dentists in the outback meant that he quickly learnt how to pull teeth and treat cats and dogs, including spaying them. After completing his regular clinic at Normanton one day a few people wandered in with the odd dog which needed spaying. Without thinking too much about it, David set to, fixed up the animals and sent owners and pets on their way. Unfortunately, one day as he was busily at work a hospital board member wandered in, no doubt to have a cheery chat with the flying doctor on his monthly visit. Imagine this man's horror on seeing a red kelpie bitch on the examination table! Some words were exchanged, and this practice was never done again on hospital property. But private arrangements were another thing!

David thinks he only had one fatality in the feline population! A much-loved young female cat required spaying. With the beautiful animal laid out on the kitchen table and anaesthetised, he picked up the scalpel and set to. Carefully he removed the ovaries and stitched up the incision, thinking as he did so that the ovaries seemed quite big. Days later and many miles distant from the property he heard that the cat had unexpectedly died a few days after the surgery. It was then that David realised he had inadvertently removed the poor cat's kidneys.

With horses it was mostly guesswork based on size to calculate the appropriate dosage of antibiotics. One frightening consultation involved a horse with a stake in its foreleg. This required the "vet" to crawl under the distressed and very twitchy horse to access the wounded area. Remember that this "vet" is a city boy with little experience but plenty of apprehension when it comes to horses. Of course the horse used one of his perfectly good rear legs to deliver a "hands off" kick to David. All in all, he definitely preferred treating the human animal!

The RFDS doctor was not simply an emergency doctor dashing to patients in the middle of the night by aeroplane. Each morning at 8.00am there was a radio session where people could ring in for a radio consultation about the kind of health problems that would take town residents to their local GP. Unlike a GP consultation, this one was not exactly private as the radio was open to all to listen in each day and find out who had tummy trouble or the flu. It was popular entertainment, and despite having to listen to the progress of the colour of a bronchial patient's sputum or the frequency of little Susie's diarrhoea, most people wouldn't miss it for the world.

One morning, at 4.00am a woman called up on the radio as her husband had woken up with swollen testicles. Not the sort of thing you want the whole of North Queensland to know! Advice was given and of course follow up calls were made each day with discreet general enquiries as to size and progress of the swelling. No mention of the location of the swelling was ever made in what was most likely a pointless attempt to protect the owner of the swollen bits!

Each property in the area was provided with a chest which was kept under lock and key in the homestead. The chest contained a veritable chemist shop of basic drugs, painkillers, antibiotics, ointments, dressings; everything to assist the family with everyday medical complaints, preventing the need for a visit or evacuation to town. The chest was scrupulously organised. If medication was required, the doctor would direct the patient to, for example, "take two of Number 34 twice a day for five days," with follow up radio calls each day to check on progress. It was a wonderful system providing quick medical relief without long distance travel. This system continues to provide reassurance to remote homesteads today.

The system of morning radio calls, the medicine chest and of course the regular clinics and emergency aeroplane flights enabled these isolated property owners and their workers to live safely in this huge area, secure in the knowledge that the flying doctor service would be there if needed. These hardy people who had chosen to live and work in such a hostile environment were deeply grateful for the security this system provided, doing everything they could to support and show appreciation to the flying doctor. This was done often by feeding the visiting doctor, pilot and nurse enormous quantities of food. Home baking of cakes, scones and sponges would be provided at one property only to be repeated a few hours later at the next place to be visited. No wonder the weight crept up. Refusing such generosity seemed ungrateful.

Weight gain, as most people know, can gradually just happen and be conveniently ignored. In David's situation this is exactly what occurred. Living on his own, he was only too happy to avail himself of the bounty provided by these country women as the meals provided by his own efforts were far from healthy. It was not a good diet for a young man. Crunch time came over two events, both of which severely dented his ego. One day he overheard his current young lady referring to him as, "my little round friend." Who could that be, he thought briefly before realising the horrible truth! The other "crunch" occurred just before boarding a flight in Hong Kong after a visit to the UK. Bending over to pick up his bag there was a horrible rrrip as his trousers split from stem to stern! To cover his modesty there was only one solution. Despite the tropical Hong Kong heat David donned the heavy overcoat that had been essential in chilly London. Once on board the aircraft and safely aloft he was supplied with a rudimentary sewing kit and managed to cobble together the ripped seam in the privacy of the cramped toilet.

Back in Mount Isa he started the regime, severely reducing his calorie intake. Just to make things even harder, he decided to combine weight loss with ceasing smoking. These two things do not normally go together, but David, being an extremely disciplined person, managed to accomplish it. He emerged a few months later fifteen kilos lighter and no longer smoking 60 cigarettes a day.

Another practice was the giving of gifts, often just appearing in the back of the aeroplane in the form of kilos of prawns in an Esky or a piece of butchered beef or pork. Yes, the locals appreciated the RFDS and were determined to keep it. David has frequently remarked that during his time in North Queensland there was rarely any need to buy meat because of this generosity.

When a radio call was received to attend an emergency or a regular visit was being made for a clinic, it was customary for the doctor or pilot to ask if the property or community needed anything brought out. This could turn out to be something as simple as fresh fruit or vegetables or perhaps a tractor part or a drum of cattle drench. This was another way that the community worked together to help those who lived and worked there.

During his time in Mount Isa, David was responsible for setting up regular clinics in small communities that had not been serviced by the RFDS before. This meant that isolated settlements and stations like Urandangi, Mt Oxide and Canobie, had the benefit of regular visits by the doctor and nurse to undertake work such as vaccinations and children's health issues. Ear and skin infections were common. Regular visits kept these in check more successfully.

Late one night a radio call was received from Brunette Downs station in the Northern Territory. This was outside David's area and under the control of the NT Aerial Medical Service where he had previously worked. There was a sick child who required evacuating to hospital, but the NT service would not attend until the following morning - a cause of great concern to the child's family. It was decided that the Mt Isa RFDS would attend. Off they went in the dark and safely evacuated the sick little girl to Mt Isa hospital.

The following day a letter arrived from Dr Tim O'Leary, the roguish Irishman who was David's boss as the head of RFDS Queensland. It was a letter of reprimand as this event had breached protocol, causing a "diplomatic incident" between the RFDS and the NT Aerial Medical Service. Basically, David had pinched their patient and shown them up as well. After dutifully reading the reprimand from his boss David turned over the letter. Written on the back in Tim's scrawly hand was, "Good onya Davey!" Nothing more was said about the incident.

The outback was full of "characters". One such character became a patient when he sustained an injury competing in a rodeo. The RFDS received a call to attend an unconscious man after he had fallen from his horse. Off they went to the rescue, lodging the flight plan as they flew across the deserted landscape to the aid of this man. As they landed on the dirt strip a Land Rover raced to meet them with an update on the status of the patient.

"He'll be with you in a minute, Doc, he's just competing in this event!" So much for the emergency, but it does say something about the stoicism and sheer guts of these outback men.

The characters were not always patients. Every month David attended a clinic at Middleton pub, a community of two buildings until the store burnt down. The pub, however, provided a social hub for the station hands and others who lived in this empty land. It was run by a wiry older couple who of course showered the visiting RFDS staff with typical outback hospitality. David got to know them well and learnt all about their numerous children and their goings on. He was amused to hear the wife admit they had never married. Coming to the area thirty years ago it was always something they were going to do when a visiting member of the clergy called through on a mission visit. By the time they had one grandchild they decided there was really little point. The ceremony was never performed.

Another incident involved a man who had broken a leg whilst working on an outstation. He required evacuation to a hospital. His mate radioed the base and was asked if they had any painkillers which could be given to the man to ease his pain before the flying doctor arrived. It would take a good hour or two for the aircraft to reach him. The only analgesia available was Bex powders, which was a blend of aspirin, phenacetin and caffeine, and a popular drug at the time. It was used not just as pain relief but more commonly as a pick-me-up. Subsequently it was found to cause kidney damage and was removed from the market. They also had a flagon of claret, good old Red Ned. The medical advice was to administer Bex and some claret. By the time the help arrived the patient had consumed six Bex powders and half a flagon of claret. He felt no pain and grinned and babbled as the leg was manipulated into position prior to his evacuation to hospital. Improvisation is a wonderful thing.

Now that he had his beloved Auster with him in Mt Isa, David, of course, made sure he flew at every opportunity. Because he had the same flying licence as the pilots, he was often unofficially allowed to do some of the flying. No doubt the pilots were glad of the break and were still in the left hand seat to satisfy regulations. It was a wonderful experience for the young doctor to rack up some hours on these twin engine Queenairs and all at no cost. The Auster was his first love, however. His leisure hours (such as they were), involved hanging around the airport, having fun with his own aircraft. At all times he was in contact with the Mt Isa control tower who could relay to him any emergency that might come up.

Unfortunately he managed to create a slight emergency of his own. On a routine scenic flight one day, the Auster developed a rough running engine, and a forced landing was made in a paddock. He was about fifteen nautical miles west of Mt Isa. A local charter company was galvanised into action. The pilot, Graham Lingard, prepared to head off on a search and rescue.

"I'd better take the flying doctor," he said to the control tower.

"It is the flying doctor!" was the reply.

The aircraft and the flying doctor/pilot were safely located and with the engine repaired they flew back to the airport.

The Auster began to make a habit of rough running engines but on one occasion decided that a total engine failure would provide more of a challenge for the pilot! Just after take-off, a loud bang followed by a stationary propeller indicated something was seriously wrong. David called the Mt Isa tower requesting an immediate land and fortunately managed to glide the aircraft back to the safety of the runway where of course it came to a halt. Passenger and pilot leapt out. The first the tower knew of a problem was the sight of the two men pushing the aeroplane off the runway!

Apart from the lack of X-ray equipment, cardiographs and other facilities that are taken for granted in most small rural hospitals today, the RFDS on an emergency call could never guarantee that electricity would be available. Electrical storms and faulty generators meant that a reliable supply of electricity was not always possible. One emergency at Julia Creek hospital involved a young girl with abdominal pain. It soon became clear that an appendicectomy needed to be performed, and urgently. But the town power supply had failed. In the fast-fading light the surgery was performed with the aid of torchlight. All was well and the patient recovered from the operation in hospital. More improvisation.

It is common knowledge that emergencies often occur after hours. The outback is no different. Flying to a remote station at night is a little different to flying to Katherine or Tennant Creek where a runway is equipped with an efficient lighting system to guide the pilot to the landing strip. There is no such luxury at a station airstrip but once again, improvisation will find a way. Empty cans of powdered milk make excellent flares when half filled with sand for stability then filled with cotton waste which is doused in fuel. These are then set alight when the aircraft is approaching. Cars can also be used, with flashing headlights locating the airstrip from a distance before the flares are lit. Where there's a will and a need, a solution can be found.

Sometimes, however, this solution can run into problems. Late one night David was called to attend a sick child, and by chance a local reporter came along to report on the situation. They landed on the strip marked out with flares and the child was stabilised with an intravenous drip. As this was being done Adele, the attendant nurse, glanced up to see one of the flares had toppled over. The long dry grass quickly ignited spreading fire down the strip. A mad scramble ensued to load the patient and expedite a take-off. Adele was still pulling up the door as the pilot, John, was taxiing down the as yet fire-free part of the runway. Fortunately, it was an uneventful flight back to Mount Isa, the only notable thing was a casual remark by the reporter passenger.

"Are all emergencies like this one?"

The media took a great interest in the RFDS. This provided much needed publicity for the service as it relied on a one-for-one system for its operating costs. Every dollar raised was matched by a government dollar. Fundraising was active and all publicity was good publicity. Consequently, rarely a day went by without the local or state press calling to find out what had been happening. As can happen with all keen journalists, a casual remark about an evacuation of a man with a broken leg would morph on page 3 of the *North West Star* to,

"Daring RFDS rescue saves injured man!"

As a result of this the papers were frequently full of stories and photos of the doctor, nurse, pilot and of course the patients. This culminated with a huge double page spread in the *Courier Mail* weekend Colour Supplement headlined "Angels of Mercy in Modern Dress".

David, an angel?

Beside the Auster, David's other prize possession was a golden cocker spaniel pup. The little creature grew up being accustomed to travelling as co-pilot. Over the years he accrued about 400 flying hours, a notable achievement. Sammy had an affectation that marked him out from other dogs. Sammy wore a tie. When David visited the lounge area in the local pub where ties were mandatory for men, Sammy was refused entry. David quickly slung a tie around his neck to allow him to comply with pub regulations. The publican relented and Sammy's tie became his trademark. The dog liked nothing better than playing with it and flipping it in the air.

It soon became evident that due to the wet season weather, it was often difficult to fly into the normal airstrips. The occasion could arise when it would be more appropriate to parachute a doctor plus medical kit into an emergency possibly with the aid of a helicopter. Never one to shirk from a challenge, David decided he would bite the bullet and learn the art of parachuting. Not for him the common practice of tandem skydives that are the generally accepted method today. No, he undertook some hours of instruction in packing the parachute and learning the technique of landing and rolling safely. Wearing the full flying suit plus parachute on the back was uncomfortable in the tropical heat but he spent a great deal of time leaping from the verandah to practise the landing technique. Not quite the real thing but better than nothing.

After the requisite training he finally accomplished two solo jumps but never put this new skill to medical use. All this derring-do attracted a deal of attention from the media. Photos and articles were splattered across the pages of the *North West Star*, *The Australian* and some medical journals showing the young flying doctor prepared to parachute to save a patient. The powers that be in Brisbane were slightly apprehensive at this latest exploit of the doctor, firstly from the safety point of view and secondly, they feared they may have difficulty recruiting doctors if it became common practice to expect them to skydive as well as heal the sick!

David's personal life also underwent a change during his time in Mount Isa. Arriving as a newly single man and no doubt wary of making another serious commitment, he enjoyed being a carefree young man in the outback. At one stage he had a girlfriend who would accompany him in the Auster for a scenic flight. Now normally when a young lady has a new boyfriend it is her father who makes the enquiry, "And what does his father do?" This time it was David who should have asked that question. After going out together for some time the young lady's father came to Mount Isa to visit his beloved daughter. Imagine David's horror when he found out that Daddy was the senior airworthiness inspector for the Department of Civil Aviation (now called CASA). What would he think of the old Auster and its unreliable engine? He didn't have long to find out. Daddy took one look at the Auster and sternly said to his daughter, "You are not to go up in that aeroplane with David. It is a liability to my good statistics." Being a dutiful girl, she didn't.

Daddy may well have been right. David also started doing aerobatics in the Auster although it was not strictly rated for it. It was only equipped with a car battery. Unbeknown to David when the aircraft rolled upside down acid leaked out of the battery and rotted the fabric covering of the fuselage. One day as David leaned slightly on the fabric it gave way beneath his hand. After doing a quick repair he never again turned it upside down in the air.

A year or so later his eye was caught by Pamela, a young blonde lady who had recently arrived to work at the Barkly Hotel. This was the place to be seen and to entertain any visiting dignitaries. The RFDS had some doctors from Mexico inspecting the Queensland branch with the prospect of starting up a similar service. Pamela was the meet and greet staff member on duty that night and this resulted in David using his winning chat-up line, "Would you like to come for a fly?" A time was made for this first date.

Of course, at this stage in the relationship, Pamela was not to know, but would quickly learn, that David was, above all things, obsessed with time and in particular, punctuality. Safe to say it did not go down well with the pilot when his pretty young passenger failed to show up! Oh well, that's that, he thought. She must have got cold feet. Later in the day, remember this is pre mobile phone, he received an embarrassed and hugely apologetic phone call. Generously he gave her another chance and a second time was set. Huge relief, she turned up, on time and more importantly, loved the flying including the added test of some aerobatics. The relationship flourished and after a suitable courtship they married at the Gold Coast in 1971. David's family were happy with his choice. A nice normal, wholesome girl, even if she wasn't from Mosman!

Part of the job description for the doctors was a four week vacation and four weeks doing a refresher course somewhere in the world. In early 1970 David decided to spend his time in the UK working in a hospital. He planned also to use this time away to travel to Yorkshire where his father had been killed in a Spitfire crash during the war.

As David had grown up and matured, the loss of his father had weighed heavily on him. His childish pride in a heroic Spitfire pilot gave way to a deep sense of loss. His only mementos of his father were a gold watch, poignantly stopped at 11.13am on the day he died and his logbook showing 228 flying hours and the graphic "Killed on this flight," beneath the final entry. He also had a few photos.

The RAF Station Catterick was located on the outskirts of the township of Catterick, an unprepossessing town in Yorkshire close to the historic and much prettier Richmond. It is not a place sought after by tourists. The Commonwealth War Graves were located in the Parish Cemetery. The entry to the cemetery was down a narrow laneway between tidy suburban dwellings. It was hard to see and poorly signed. But there it was. Among the general rows of graves were three rows of clean, white war graves standing proudly in carefully manicured garden beds. Rolla Maxwell Cooke was flanked by a Canadian on one side and a British pilot on the other. The sight of the grave with the remains of this young Australian, so far from home, was a deeply moving experience for David. For the first time in his life his father seemed real to him – not just a concept from the past. Aged 23 years, said the gravestone. David was 28, already older than his father by five years. What a tragedy this young pilot's life had been.

Before leaving Australia for this first trip overseas, David had been contacted by the Iranian Oil Company, an associate of BP. He was asked to visit to advise on how an aviation medical service was organised. Imagine, in 1970 leaving Australia for the first time and visiting the mysterious country of Iran. After arriving in the early hours of the morning he went to his hotel where the rooms were decorated with gold leaf. Waking up some hours later, he threw open the curtains to be met with a vision of snow-capped mountains close to the town. David was escorted in a company Fokker Friendship to visit a possible centre where a Flying Doctor Base could be set up. One of the suggested places was the ancient city of Isfahan. It was an interesting and eye-opening few days and a stimulating and worthwhile experience for David. He even asked permission to take to dinner the daughter of one of the executives and was given a firm "No"! That was definitely inappropriate! Bad luck David.

Perhaps the most dramatic and life-threatening evacuation flights took place in 1971, a year of the biggest wet season witnessed. An emergency arose when a young woman on an isolated property miscarried and subsequently haemorrhaged severely and would not stop bleeding. The homestead was beside a flooded river which had spread over the plains, under the raised houses and through the other buildings. The airstrip was out of action because of the continuous rain. It was thought that perhaps David could parachute in, but the low cloud prevented this too.

After two days, with the weather and the patient no better, a helicopter was obtained and the pilot, with David on board, headed off through the deluge to the stranded homestead where the young girl lay in desperate need of help. The journey was slow. Because of the driving rain, frequent stops were required until the visibility improved sufficiently to continue. By late afternoon they had run low on fuel and could not continue as far as the property. They had no choice but to land on a slightly elevated section of gravel road and wait out the night until a plane could drop some fuel to them next morning. What an uncomfortable night it would have been, with no food and big aggressive mosquitoes keeping them company. As well as dropping fuel, the delivery aircraft was asked to bring along some much needed cigarettes! The pilot was a non-smoker, but David had a strong attachment to cigarettes at this time and a lack of them was not to be tolerated. It is interesting to learn that the clean-living pilot, by the end of this adventure was hooked on nicotine as well.

The next day the mercy aircraft duly arrived and dropped enough fuel to get them to the nearest property where they were able to fill the tanks and continue the journey to their destination. Meanwhile the workmen on the property had been desperately clearing a ditch around a patch of ground to keep it clear of the incessant rain. The helicopter landed safely, and David went to the aid of the girl to prepare her for the return trip to hospital.

The patient was loaded on to the helicopter and it prepared to depart.

The drama was not quite over. Because of the condition of the ground and the extra weight on board, the helicopter could not lift off the ground. David was left behind wading through the murky knee-deep floodwater. The helicopter took off and landed half a mile away on a slightly more elevated and firmer road where they picked up David then set off for the long flight to Mt Isa and safety. The patient was hospitalised and recovered.

This heroic rescue mission in the direst of weather conditions gives real meaning to the motto of the Royal Flying Doctor Service, created by the Reverend John Flynn, "A Mantle of Safety".

The locals who were on the receiving end of this level of care could not have been more grateful. A keen fundraiser for the RFDS said of David, "…he is wonderful. Even in the floods we knew he was close by, and we knew he would get to us if we needed him. There is something in the Bible that says, 'I will not leave you comfortless' – that is David."

Life in the outback for the RFDS employees was a solitary affair with family and old friends left behind in cities. This meant that friendships were formed quickly, and a new social network was created. Some of these friendships can last a lifetime while others are for a short time only and yet others can be reformed many years later in a different location.

Understandably many of David's acquaintances came from the aviation side of life. One was Graham Lingard, the pilot who came to David's rescue when his Auster came to grief and landed in a paddock. Graham was a charter pilot working for a local company. He soon became keen on David's RFDS nurse, Adele. They quickly became an item and eventually married. They moved out of David's life when Graham advanced his flying career into airlines. Now, forty years later, they have reappeared, retired and settled in Port Macquarie where friendships have been renewed via the flying club. It's a small world.

Another friendship was formed with a military man, Captain Russell Smith. He was in charge of the Citizens Military Force in Mt Isa after serving in Vietnam during the war. Russell, too, was interested in aviation and would eagerly jump at any excuse to fly with David. Much fun was had exploring the local area, testing each other's flying skills. Russell however, being a military man, proved useful. On one occasion, during the wet season of course, an elderly man on a property near Normanton fell ill with pneumonia. The property was isolated by floodwater and the aircraft could not land. Russell, with his contacts, located a helicopter in Townsville which met the RFDS aircraft at Normanton airstrip to ferry the doctor to the property to evacuate the patient. The old man was appalled at the sight of this rescue machine, an army chopper, with no side doors. The man was understandably afraid of falling to his death. He quickly realised he was securely strapped in, and after take-off, began issuing requests. "Fly over there to check me cattle!" No doubt the stranded beasts were terrified of the strange monster overhead. This was in the days when cattle were checked by man and horse, not helicopters.

Russell's friendship with David has continued until this day, a friendship forged in a harsh environment where people need and rely on others for support.

In 1970 a brave young single mother of three arrived in Mount Isa to take up an appointment in the tiny township of Dajarra. Annie was nudging thirty and, with three preschool children in tow, had accepted a job as Bush Nurse in this dusty little town. This would have been a monumental move for any young mother, but for Annie it was more so. Annie came from Bridge of Allan in Scotland, a genteel and cultured town near Stirling, the gateway to the highlands. It is hard to imagine what she thought of her new surroundings. Annie settled in and became a much-loved addition to the community. She established an instant rapport with the Indigenous community and treated all her patients with dignity and care. David visited Dajarra each month with his clinic and liaised with Annie at other times should she need advice. Annie had never seen a child with dead flies impacting their ear in Scotland. This was a whole new way of nursing for her. Annie and David have remained firm friends ever since. Friends made under such harsh working conditions are very special and much valued.

Not all the exciting flying was for work. One night David decided to do some night circuits in his Auster. Now an important thing to know about the Auster is that it did not have any lights. No problem, thought David, this will add to the challenge. Equipped with a torch gripped between his teeth, he decided to call the control tower and advise his intentions.

"Sure David, go ahead," came the cheery voice from the tower.

Away he went and on doing the obligatory radio call when turning in to make his approach to the strip, the tower controller replied in a puzzled voice,

> "I can't locate you, could you make this a 'full stop' and call me after landing."

Oops!

> "I couldn't see your landing or navigation lights," said the controller.

> "No, I don't have any," replied David.

> "But you were doing night circuits!"

> "But I asked permission and you gave the go ahead, I thought you knew I didn't have lights."

A weary voice replied, "David, don't do it again, you're giving me grey hairs."

This poor air traffic control officer put up with a lot. On another occasion David was enjoying himself in the Auster one afternoon when he caught sight of the Inlander train heading for Mt Isa. In that part of the world there were no power lines and no trees of any size. The land was covered in low scrubby spinifex and hence an aircraft could easily fly at a very low altitude. Not legally of course, that is 500 feet, but who would see this young aviator having a bit of fun? Lowering the nose of the Auster he descended until flying almost level with the locomotive and waved cheerily to the engine driver. Strangely he did not return the greeting. Later that afternoon, on returning to the airport, he received a call from the long-suffering air traffic controller.

> "David, I've had a call from the driver of the Inlander reporting a low-flying aircraft flying beside the train."

> "What did you say?" said David.

> "I reported that we had no known aircraft in the vicinity," he replied, "but for pity's sake don't do that again!"

In the 1970s, Outback Tourism was virtually non-existent. Only the hardy few ventured into the desert and the popular four-wheel drive safaris that are so prevalent today did not exist. There were no endless streams of mobile homes and enormous caravans driven by fit and energetic grey nomads happily spending their well-earned superannuation. However, an aeroplane does give one a certain advantage in accessing remote areas. David used the trusty Auster (in spite of some engine wobbles!) to explore the surrounding landmarks. He had been told of some Aboriginal engravings located at Carbine Creek near the small township of Dajarra. He determined to see them for himself.

One day he hopped in the Auster to do a recce to see if a visit was feasible. Approaching the area, he performed some low-level flypasts to check the surrounding terrain for a suitable landing spot. He located a tract of land that would be long enough to plonk the Auster safely down. He soon realised that it would not be long enough to enable a take-off. Ever able to improvise, David decided that with the help of an axe and a mattock the "airstrip" could be extended to enable take-off.

The following weekend he set off with June, the flight nurse and another friend. An axe and mattock were carefully stashed in the stowage area. After a safe but bumpy touchdown they proceeded to root out some scrubby growth, hot and tiring work under the outback sun. It wasn't quite like Mt Isa's smooth tarmac but at a pinch it would do. And it did! Elated with creating this magnificent airstrip, they almost forgot why they were there in the first place so keen were they to test it out. After following the vague directions given, they did come upon the ancient Aboriginal rock etchings that very few Europeans would ever have seen. It was a rare privilege and coupled with the Boys Own Adventure take-off made for a great day – one of many adventures that made living in North Queensland so special.

Despite David's rapidly improving obstetric skills thanks to his experience at Alice Springs, there was one time when he was surplus to requirements. A call was received from Wollogorang, a dot on the map near the Northern Territory border and one and three quarter hours flight time from Mt Isa. A young woman had arrived at the local police station in labour. It was clear that she needed to be evacuated to hospital. The cavalry set off on the rescue mission and the policeman was able to keep in touch with David via the radio. It soon became evident that this baby was in a bit of a hurry to arrive in the world and was not prepared to wait for any aeroplane, doctor and nurse.

With the doctor in an aeroplane hurtling at speed through the sky, a young woman struggling with contractions in a room at the police station and a frantic officer manning the radio while checking the labour's progress, the outcome could have been a disaster. In a pantomime that would have been comical to see but a huge drama for those involved, the police officer proved himself the hero of the hour. Dashing from the labouring woman lying on the station floor to the radio in the other room, he relayed the progress of the patient to David in the air. In turn, David questioned and offered instructions in what to do as the labour progressed. Toing and froing, the frantic officer, to his amazement, successfully delivered the baby, carefully following the advice given by the doctor. When the doctor did arrive, he was greeted by a serene and happy new mother with a beautiful infant in her arms. Slumped in a chair in the corner was the stocky, outback defender of the people, white of face and shaking from head to foot. Mother and baby declared fit and well; policeman required sedation!

Although David was a careful and dedicated doctor there was also the young man with a devilish streak who got up to mischief when the opportunity arose. One day on the way to a regular clinic at Kynuna things didn't go according to plan. Normally, on hearing the approaching aircraft a vehicle was sent out to bring them to the clinic. Not on this day. After a short wait and growing increasingly impatient, they decided to take off and wake them up. Flying low down the main street they opened the cargo door and threw out an enamel chamber pot that was kept in the aircraft for emergency use. It bounced and clattered down the street narrowly missing a car. The pick-up vehicle arrived at the strip shortly thereafter! It is said that this chamber pot is still displayed in the pub, but the truth has probably been lost in the mists of time.

Another outback experience, which was in fairness not of David's doing, involved a drinking session at the Burketown pub. At 10.00pm as the licensing laws of the day demanded, the local policeman arrived and announced that it was closing time. He proceeded to shut and lock the pub doors, enclosing the drinkers and himself within. The revelry inside continued, and continued in fact until 2.00am when the police officer, now in the role of genial barman, decided it was time for all to go home. Outback law in action.

Sometimes what might look like a prank or vandalism actually was, in fact, the right and only thing to do. One day a bad car accident occurred on the Barkly Highway miles from any airstrip. Fortunately it was near a roadhouse which serviced a tourist area called Barry Caves. In order for the aircraft to land safely on the road the sign, "Slow Down, Barry Caves" had to be removed by those on the ground. This was done, the aircraft landed safely, and the patient was quickly stabilised and retrieved. A couple of the locals stood guard to warn any approaching B doubles or trucks. What a shock they would get to come across a Queenair blocking their access north!

Accidents were part and parcel of outback life. Most of the retrieval work was to attend either an accident on a station or a road trauma. One man who was involved in a truck accident deteriorated rapidly, and by the time the aircraft and medical staff arrived, he was in a bad way with dangerously low blood pressure. It was imperative that he be evacuated to Mt Isa hospital. He was a large man. In the rush to get off the ground there was no time to secure the belt around him on the stretcher. Consequently he kept rolling about. Adele, the attending nurse, had the difficult job of hanging on to the IV drip and holding him steady on the stretcher. Luckily it was a short trip, but the poor girl was left with bruised legs as a memento of the occasion.

Not all accidents involved adults. A young boy in Dajarra had a nasty accident climbing a chain attached to a large hook. His normal boyish fun soon turned dangerous as he slipped, embedding the rusty hook in his scrotum. After its removal, the hook, still attached to the chain, was carefully presented to the very relieved parents. A very frightening experience for this young boy.

The case that probably best sums up David's dual role as doctor and pilot involved a patient who needed urgent evacuation to hospital. The property had a dirt airstrip which was not long enough to accommodate the Queenair. Luckily, the station owner next door (about twenty miles away) at Lorraine station had a small Cessna. A quick radio call was made to arrange for David to borrow it. The RFDS Queenair landed at the large Lorraine airstrip and David hopped into the owner's Cessna to fly to the property where the patient waited. With the patient safely aboard the Cessna he then returned to the waiting Queenair and the patient was soon on his way to Mount Isa hospital.

On hearing of this tale, the superintendent of the Queensland RFDS Dr Tim O'Leary remarked from Brisbane, "Davey, you're not a doctor who flies, you're a pilot who practises medicine."

In 2016 David returned to Mt Isa. He had been invited to attend the celebrations commemorating the 50th anniversary of the RFDS in Mount Isa. Sadly, he was unable to attend the official event but submitted a speech to be read on the night. By chance, a few weeks later he was on his way to Darwin. Of course he stopped en route to visit the base and catch up with the RFDS in the 21st century.

It was a wonderful experience with the current staff welcoming him and treating him like royalty with a splendid dinner. The changes since the early seventies were amazing with five doctors rostered on a two week on-off roster. The doctors worked on a fly-in fly-out basis and did not live in the town. There were three shining new aircraft that were fitted out like an intensive care unit. This was a far cry from the Queenair which only had a stretcher for the patient, oxygen if needed and the facilities for installing an intravenous line. The personnel could not believe that David was the sole doctor for the region, working on call as needed. He was declared a "legend" and many tales were shared around the table. The visit was inspiring. It showed that the RFDS is thriving and providing a first class health service today for the people of the outback.

In the early seventies the RDFS was undergoing some changes. As well as the base at Mt Isa there was also one at Charleville and Charters Towers. The state was covered by these three sites. Charters Towers was a small base, and the aircraft were not kept on site but located in Townsville on the coast. When an aeroplane was needed it had to be brought from Townsville to Charters Towers and thence to its destination further afield. A decision was made to close the Charters Towers base and open up a new one in Cairns to service this area of the state. Thus it was that David was appointed the senior medical officer at Cairns, charged with setting up and bringing into being RFDS Cairns, and taking over the Cairns Aerial Ambulance.

In July 1972 David, Pamela, the Auster and Sammy the cocker spaniel, moved to Cairns to start a new chapter in life.

Goodbye dusty Mount Isa, hello tropical Cairns.

Cairns

1972-1974

The move to Cairns was a culture shock.

Mt Isa was a rough and ready mining town plus a service centre for the vast rural community surrounding it. It was dusty, searingly hot and full of goodhearted people.

Over on the tropical coast, Cairns sulked beside the ocean and was overlooked by a mountainous ridge. It was not the slick, tourist city it is today. Certainly, the Great Barrier Reef was a drawcard and tourists enjoyed the warm and sunny winters. There was an endless expanse of mangrove swamps where the impressive esplanade dominates the city front today. No free public swimming pool, fitness stations and bustling café scene; just a sullen milky sea which probably concealed large reptiles. It was a town about to take off and become the drawcard it is today.

The new RFDS Base changed the focus of David's work. Instead of being the happy-go-lucky young doctor ready to tackle any emergency with gusto, he found himself in a slightly more administrative and even political role as head of this new set-up. There was some animosity in sectors of the community to the taking over of the Air Ambulance by the RFDS. Patients were accustomed to calling the air ambulance which would pick them up and transport them to the city for medical attention. The RFDS changed this by sending a doctor onboard the aeroplane. This did not always result in a trip to Cairns. Often the situation could be dealt with on site by the doctor and nurse much to the irritation of some patients. A free trip to Cairns was greatly desirable.

David was lucky to have the services of an experienced older doctor, George Ellis, as his second in-charge. George had wide experience in all areas of medicine having served for years as the doctor in Charters Towers. He was a much-loved doctor. The inhabitants of Charters Towers were devastated when he encountered some health issues and decided to retire. But retirement did not sit well with George. After recovering his health, he realised that he still had a lot to offer. He was appointed as David's offsider at the Base, a job which would not be too onerous but would allow him to share his vast experience with the younger man. David adored him, and George became an almost father-like figure to him. George called David "son", and David in cheeky fashion called him "Grandpa". It was an extremely happy working relationship and one which, considering the boss was thirty-one and the second in charge sixty-five, could have been a whole lot different.

One day, as George and David were ambling down a hospital corridor, David turned to look back at a pretty nurse who had just passed them.

"I know what you're looking at son, but I can't remember why!"

That was George.

As well as being the boss of a man old enough to be his father, David also had another challenge to face. For the first time in his life, he was faced with a female pilot! Beth Garrett is something of a legend among female pilots in Australia and particularly with the RFDS where she was their first female pilot. She started learning to fly at the age of twenty-one. She paid for all her own training, no mean feat considering her meagre secretarial salary. Beth obtained her private pilot's licence in 1947. She continued her training, gaining her commercial licence and instructor's rating by 1952.

The following year she married the love of her life, Martin Garrett. A young TAA pilot, Martin was seconded to the RFDS soon after their wedding and Beth joined him in Townsville shortly after. A few months later on a hot Queensland day the wood and fabric Dragon biplane failed to gain altitude on take-off from Cheviot Hills cattle station. Martin attempted to circle trying to gain height but the aircraft went into a spin and hit the ground. Of the six people aboard the aircraft, two were killed, including Martin, Beth's young husband. The other fatality was Catherine O'Leary, the young Irish bride of Dr Tim O'Leary. Tim later became the superintendent of the Queensland RFDS. David came to know Tim very well during his time in Queensland. Two young people killed and two young people widowed. It was a terrible tragedy and the only fatality with an RFDS aircraft.

Beth was devastated. She faced the difficult task of providing not just for herself, but for the child she was carrying at the time of Martin's death. In 1954, eight -months after the accident she gave birth to a daughter, Catherine

Martyn. When Martyn, as she was known, was twelve months old Beth decided to forge a career in aviation, a difficult task for any woman, let alone one with a child to care for. After working for a small regional airline and instructing, she was lucky enough to obtain a job with the RFDS. She was thrilled to have a steady job and one which she loved.

Apart from the shock of flying with a female pilot, the most obvious difference between Mt Isa and Cairns was the weather. David was lucky to arrive in the tropical winter with sunny days and little rain. Winter however, soon passed. The wet season arrived with its heat, humidity, rain and of course storms. In the early seventies, reverse cycle or refrigerated air-conditioning was not commonly installed in houses. Relief from the heat was gained with ceiling fans. Humidity caused shoes, curtains, even walls to be covered in an attractive film of greenish mould which required constant vigilance to keep in check.

The stormy tropical weather was not merely an inconvenience - for flying it was a major issue. If there's one thing pilots wish to avoid up in the air, it's thunderstorms. A Cairns wet season had plenty of these. The old aviation motto, "Take-offs are optional, landings are mandatory" does not sit well when an accident or emergency has to be attended. Bad weather flying became the norm.

One of many hair-raising flights that David did with Beth was to a mining community at Greenvale about 200 miles southwest of Cairns. They had been called to pick up a man who had a severe crush injury to his foot. The flight down was bad enough through constant rain and thunderstorm activity, but the return flight was one for the record books. After loading the patient, they were faced by a line of thunderstorms blocking the route back to Cairns. It was decided to fly to Townsville instead – a shorter flight with marginally better weather. Ten minutes into the flight the electricity failed, due most probably to a lightning strike. Beth was faced with flying the Queenair in the dark through cloud, driving rain and thunderstorm activity using a medical torch which she shone on the compass. The compass itself may have been damaged by the strike and was perhaps not totally reliable. The aircraft was without any navigational aids, the undercarriage and flaps were out of action and they had no radio. It was a nasty situation. Beth took it in her stride, sitting quietly at the controls and doggedly flying the aircraft. David helped with the intermittent use of a small pocket torch. She headed east to the coast, finally flying into clear skies and then on to the Townsville control zone. All was not yet over as the aircraft landing gear had to be lowered manually This job fell to the doctor/co-pilot. The landing also had to be done without the aid of flaps which are normally used to help slow the aircraft down.

The patient was safely tucked up in Townsville hospital and after being checked, the aircraft and crew returned to Cairns the following day.

This flight and David's recommendation led to Beth being awarded the Brabazon Award which was given for the most outstanding piece of flying in the Commonwealth. Some years later in 1978 Beth was featured on Roger Climpson's television series *This is Your Life*. David was invited to be a guest on the program to narrate the story of the stormy flight. Not shy of a chance to perform, David seized the opportunity in front of the cameras and enthusiastically held the audience enthralled. Afterwards at the production party it was suggested by the director that David might like to consider a career in comedy!

David managed to adjust to this unique phenomenon of having a female pilot. The two soon developed a humorous tolerant relationship with plenty of good-natured banter. Beth kept the young doctor in his place and David wasted no opportunity to remind Beth of her gender, age and abilities. It was a situation born of its time, and one which would not have arisen today when the sky is full of strong, capable female pilots.

Years later, in 2000, Beth called to visit David and family in Port Macquarie. David's youngest child Michael was living and working there at the time. Michael was forging his career in aviation, working as an instructor with the local flying school. Like all young people he was absorbed in his own achievements and escapades. At this point in time he had successfully flown a De Havilland Dove from Australia to New Zealand. A huge task for this young man barely twenty years old. During dinner that night Michael was regaling this little grey-haired old lady with the details of this latest flight. She listened with indulgent attention to the young man. Then, quietly, she murmured,

"I've got a few hours in Doves."

"Oh?" said Michael.

"Yes, I clocked up 6000 hours in Doves. Lovely aircraft to fly."

The look on Michael's face was priceless. That this quiet old lady had accomplished what to him had been a momentous feat was almost unthinkable. Never judge a book by its cover gained new meaning. Michael was hugely impressed.

Living on the coast meant that emergencies sometimes meant a flight out to sea. David's first flight out of Cairns, his baptism of fire, was a trip to Lizard Island. A call came to attend to a man with an injury caused by a marlin spike. Lizard Island was not the exotic destination it is today. In the early seventies, the only residents were a young couple who acted as caretakers on the island. This visit involved a flight to the island's airstrip then a bumpy tractor drive to the coast followed by a speedboat out to the reef where the patient was waiting in the fishing boat. The patient had a collapsed lung and was having breathing difficulties. After being stabilised and strapped up, the return trip was made to the aircraft. A patient with breathing difficulties cannot tolerate much altitude and David requested a low altitude flight across the water to Cairns.

"What altitude would you like, Dave?" asked Nick, the pilot. Nick was an experienced, decorated ex RAAF pilot.

"About twenty feet," suggested David.

"What's wrong with ten?" replied Nick.

Off they went practically skimming over the waves dodging, as they went, the Low Isles lighthouse. Wonderful fun, totally illegal under normal circumstances but with a sick patient on board, this was the way to fly.

Lizard Island became a regular spot to visit when the caretaker's wife became pregnant. Each month they flew to the island for her monthly check up.

It was common knowledge at the time that these two young people enjoyed a relaxed and carefree life on the island. Part of that lifestyle included a reluctance to wear any clothing except when visitors were expected. The pregnancy check-up was always at approximately the same time each month apart for one notable time. Nasty weather meant that the visit should be done much earlier in the day before the storms formed but no one saw fit to inform the residents of this change in plan. Imagine the reaction of all concerned when the aircraft, swooping low as it lined up for landing, saw this delightful young couple "au naturel" on the sand. By the time the aeroplane landed both were respectably clad in their sarongs ready for the check up! A far cry from the Lizard Island of today with its luxury accommodation and day spa guests wearing designer bikinis!

One patient evacuation to Cairns Hospital involved a large and generously endowed woman from Yorke Island. Polly had many mental health issues and was showing signs of a severe psychotic episode. She required urgent evacuation to hospital. Polly was on board a trawler anchored in the lagoon, and strenuously defying all attempts to remove her. Beth and David went to the rescue. Yorke Island is part of the Torres Strait Island archipelago and is north-east of the tip of Cape York peninsula. After landing on the island David had to be rowed out to the trawler where the recalcitrant Polly was waiting. Polly, wearing only a very small pair of pants, took one look at this young man coming to her rescue, decided he looked pretty good and, yes, she would go with him. She was even willing to wear the accompanying policeman's large shirt but then felt slightly overdressed and proceeded to remove her pants. Only then did she agree to get into the rowing boat and head for land.

After much gentle cajoling and the offer of a new pair of pants she was persuaded into the aircraft where she seriously began making advances to the apprehensive doctor. She was a terrifying sight and while it makes for a good tale after the event, it was no joke at the time. This huge woman could have created a dangerous situation on the flight home. Poor Polly just wanted this cute young doctor. She produced some talcum powder which she gently rubbed over her shoulder and arm murmuring seductively, "Look, David, white". Thinking quickly David pointed to Beth in the cockpit blissfully unaware of the potential catastrophe behind her. "My mother wouldn't like it", he said. Not to be put off Polly simply reached over and pulled across the curtain that separated the cockpit from the cabin. "Now," she purred, "mother can't see".

It was the longest three hours of David's life as Polly persisted with her attempted seduction until the aircraft landed. It was tactical warfare of a very strange kind but finally Polly was admitted to the psychiatric unit at Cairns Hospital where she would receive the care she so desperately needed. Her parting effort after disembarking the Queenair was to turn to David and pick him up, clutching him to her voluptuous bosom. It was a flight to remember all right and one which David and Beth hoped never to repeat. Beth too was riled. David calling her his mother, the cheek of him!

As in Mount Isa, the press was constantly contacting the RFDS base to find out what the young doctor had been up to today. One time, instead of the media turning a routine evacuation into a full-blown emergency, things went the other way.

A call came over the airways to attend a stabbing. A man injured, lots of blood, possible violence or maybe self-harm. Here was a story that would surely make the front page! Pilot, doctor and nurse headed off to save the man's life. On arrival, the truth was plain to see. A man, yes, covered in blood with only a tiny scratch on his chest but a massive nosebleed which was the cause of the blood-soaked clothing! Was this an outback version of man flu? There are wimps everywhere, apparently even among the tough outback workers.

David was always skilled at managing some extra flying under the guise of work. The huge area north of Cairns, the Top End, was full of small unlicensed airstrips that locals knew about but which were not well known to the general public. It would be hugely beneficial for the RFDS to have access to these airstrips in case of emergency. David decided to do something about it. He took a few days off, leaving George Ellis in charge. He and a retired DCA inspector, Percy Barwise, proceeded to fly around the whole top end in a Piper Cherokee, landing on these private strips where Percy would measure their length and note their surface quality and any local hazards in the area. This served a real purpose, making more of this huge expanse accessible by air if need be. But not only that, it was also great fun.

George and David, despite their age difference, were great mates. George could even tolerate the flying, in the Auster as well as the Queenair. On one occasion when David was off duty, George received a call about a young man in Miranda about 200 miles west of Cairns who was fitting, probably the result of a brain tumour. Apart from the distinct possibility of a haemorrhage, he knew that the boy's father was a doctor from the Gold Coast. Yes, this patient needed urgent transfer to hospital.

Because of the rainy season the strip was rather wet and unable to take the weight of the Queenair. There was a dry area that would allow a smaller, lighter aircraft to land safely. Unfortunately they could not find a charter pilot with a suitable aircraft prepared to venture to Miranda in such nasty weather. It looked like the young man would be left to his fate, hopefully managing to hang on to life until the weather improved. It was this sad possibility of losing a patient that encouraged David and George to cook up their own solution to the problem. It was decided to hire a Cessna 182 from the local Aero Club. David, being technically off duty, would be the pilot and George would be the doctor.

It was essential of course to find out exactly where on the strip was the drier area that would be safe to land on. George contacted the owner of the strip and made arrangements for the dry part to be outlined in toilet paper. Not pretty but it certainly would serve the purpose. In decidedly unpleasant, stormy weather the two set off, dodging the worst of the weather and weaving and wandering until they approached the airstrip at Miranda. Sure enough, the appropriate part of the airstrip was lavishly outlined in best quality Sorbent. Thank goodness the outback folk have few shopping trips and when they do, they buy in bulk. It is safe to say that after this evacuation, a trip to the big smoke might have been in order.

Not only was the drier area of the strip outlined in the toilet paper, it also had a gentle boomerang shaped curve in it which meant after touchdown the aircraft had to be carefully turned instead of just slowing down as usual. The same applied to the take-off. It was not an easy task adding to the workload of bad weather and unfamiliar aircraft. After the obligatory country lunch, the patient, who had been stabilised and sedated, was loaded into the aircraft and they set off on the return leg. Of course the weather was even worse. A stop had to be made to obtain fuel at Wrotham Park, the nearest station which had any. The Cessna 182 does not have a huge range and by the time they had flown to Miranda and then on to Wrotham Park, they were down to the legal minimum of forty-five minutes of fuel remaining. Not a comfortable situation to be in, especially in such stormy, rainy weather, where it might be necessary to change course.

After fuelling and waiting out a heavy storm, off they went heading for Cairns, dodging towering thunderstorms while praying for a break in the weather. Fortunately, the patient was blissfully unaware of any drama having been suitably sedated for the entire journey. Yes, the weather in the tropics certainly made the workload a great deal harder, requiring those on board, both pilot and doctor, to have nerves of steel.

After landing on boomerang shaped runways, battling the tropical weather and saving the patient's life, this heroic pair were feeling pretty chuffed with themselves. Not everyone was of this opinion.

Head office in Brisbane contacted David. He and George were both given a severe admonishment. Despite saving a life, (that was good!), they were extremely foolish to undertake this flight in a single engine aircraft flying in marginal weather. With both of the Cairns base doctors on board too!

"David, you are a RFDS doctor, not a pilot."

"But I was off duty that day, therefore a pilot."

Back came the counterclaim, "No, as boss of the Base, you are never off duty."

After this event George made a private decision never to put himself in that sort of situation again.

David? Not so sure about that!

As well as battling with the weather in the course of the working day, David managed plenty of private flying in his Auster. There was nothing better than heading off over the ocean to the reef where, out of sight of land, he could soar and swoop and be like the many sea birds that used the low isles of the reef as a landing, resting and breeding spot. Once, instead of doing what any sensible person would do and hop on a jet from Cairns to Hobart, he decided to go in the Auster. Less comfortable, a whole lot slower but certainly to an avid pilot, a whole lot more fun.

The trip got off to a bad start. The track down the coast flies over the Hinchinbrook Channel, a stretch of water between Cairns and Townsville. As usual the weather was cloudy with light rain. Providing company in the cockpit was a friend, an engineer who was hitching a lift to Mackay. Pamela had sensibly decided to take the more comfortable option of airline travel and would meet up with David in Hobart.

Heading down the Hinchinbrook passage, the aircraft got lower and lower in an attempt to keep below the threatening clouds. A channel enclosed by towering mountains combined with low altitude, made it impossible to turn around without coming into contact with the water. After a nail biting thirty minutes the cloud lifted a little and it was a relief to land at Townsville for fuel. The accompanying co-pilot, however, disembarked deciding to make his own way to Mackay rather than go any further with David. Later, after David made it safely to Hobart, he asked his friend at what point in the flight should they have turned back.

"On the way to the airport," was his cryptic reply!

With great trepidation the now solo pilot made it safely across Bass Strait to Hobart. On the return journey north of Rockhampton the engine started running rough and not delivering much power. There had been flooding recently here so there was no convenient spot to make an emergency landing. David had no alternative but to return to Rocky where the problem was repaired. Finally he made it safely home successfully completing this mammoth 45 hour trip.

It was just sinking into David's head that it was probably time to do two things. One was to obtain an instrument rating to allow safe flight in cloud. This he achieved in 1978, not before a few other "interesting" flights in marginal weather. The other was to acquire a newer, better equipped aeroplane and this he did in 1974. He was beginning to realise there was some truth in the famous saying, "There are old pilots and bold pilots, but there are no old and bold pilots."

David made a decision to become an old pilot.

Regular clinics to outlying missions and stations were a normal part of the RFDS. Because of the watery areas in the gulf many settlements were not serviced by the RFDS because of a lack of a suitable airstrip. David decided that what could not be reached by the Queenair could easily be accessed by an amphibious aircraft. Bloomfield River Mission north of Cairns was able to have a regular visit thanks to this innovation. A Lake Buccaneer amphibian aircraft was hired from Cairns airport. After flying to the mission, it would land in the river on its floats. The wheels were lowered and the aircraft taxied up the bank on to the shore. It was important at this point to keep a close eye out for lurking crocodiles before leaving the aircraft. No one wanted to become lunch for a hungry reptile.

Not wishing to miss out on a new skill David somehow managed to persuade the pilot to teach him how to land on the water, a skill he further developed years later with a floatplane endorsement.

David pestered and pestered the RFDS to allow him to obtain a Queenair endorsement. It seemed good sense to have two qualified pilots on board as well as allowing David to log the odd leg that Beth would, if she was in a good mood, allow him to do. Finally, the manager weakened and said yes. It probably would have been a good idea to wait for written confirmation, but the impatient flier did not bother about that. Off he went out to the airport to line up an instructor to get the job done as soon as possible. As luck would have it the instructor had not flown a Queenair for some years and was happy for David to just "fly round for a bit and I'll sign it." As luck would not have it, on landing and receiving the endorsement David was given a message from RFDS head office that they had changed their minds. There was to be no Queenair endorsement. Too late, the deed was done and a win for David against the bureaucracy!

Leisure for David has also revolved around aviation. He could not believe his luck that the RFDS combined a regular steady job using his medical skills with his passion for flight. How lucky was he to be paid for doing what he loved. Another leisure activity which did not involve actual flying was working with CART, the Cairns Aircraft Recovery Team. A number of local pilots and engineers worked to recover a crashed Bell P-39 Airacobra from mudflats on Cape York where it had been since wartime. Once recovered, the group set about restoring the aircraft, working one night a week for years. The project was completed long after David had left Cairns but working on bringing the Bell 39 back to life had been a great experience. It was a satisfying and fulfilling project to be involved in.

Cairns provided David with the opportunity to develop organisational and managerial skills. Instead of simply enjoying the flying and medicine with the RFDS he was now in a position of authority. It did not sit well with him. He came to think that perhaps it was time to move on and develop his medical skills as a General Practitioner. Where to go? He had developed a love of country life hence a return to Sydney, despite the family connections, was out of the question. Likewise, despite Pamela's connection to Brisbane a return to city medicine was not an attractive proposition. A line was drawn about halfway between Sydney and Brisbane running through or close to a variety of towns. Did any of them require the services of an eager young doctor? Yes, one did - the inland town on the NSW north-west slopes and plains called Gunnedah.

David's time in Cairns was fulfilling and challenging both workwise and in his flying life. He had learnt much and experienced an incredible variety of medical cases and interesting flying moments. The most incredible event that happened in his time in Cairns, however, was becoming a father. Pamela gave birth to Sarah Alexandra Cooke on 10th May 1973. The young couple had become a family. Life as they knew it had changed forever. Fifty years later, Sarah made the courageous decision to begin a nursing degree and is now following in her father's footsteps with a medical career.

Thus it was that on April 1st, 1974, David arrived in Gunnedah with Pamela and baby Sarah. Their worldly goods at that time consisted of one Auster aeroplane, one bright orange sports car, one golden cocker spaniel with 400 flying hours and little else. It was now time to be a grown-up with both job and family responsibilities. What would life in Gunnedah bring to them?

Gunnedah

1974-1998

The town of Gunnedah in 1974 was a prosperous rural community nestled on the northwest slopes and plains and backed by the Liverpool Ranges. It was a wealthy farming and grazing community growing mainly premium wheat in winter and sorghum in summer. Cattle were raised and feedlots were beginning to appear in the area. The town with its surrounding area also had a couple of coalmines and an abattoir that processed the animals raised within a wide radius. Unemployment was rare; there were jobs for all who wanted them. It was a wealthy, conservative area. How would the daring young flying doctor fit in here?

After running away from the stifling suburban environment of his childhood, David had blossomed in the free and easy attitude to life that existed in the Northern Territory and North Queensland. Even Cairns had a pioneer atmosphere about it. What would Gunnedah bring?

The social structure of Gunnedah plunged him well and truly back in the conservative society of his youth. He was welcomed with open arms into the rural community of grazing and professional people. Once again, the importance of school and background were a topic of conversation. Dinners and invitations flooded in. The new family in town was accepted into this social circle.

Working with the RFDS had made David something of a local celebrity in Queensland with constant photos, interviews and newspaper articles keeping him in the public eye. How would he cope with sinking into the obscurity of life as a GP? Now life was the daily five-minute drive to his surgery, seeing his patients, then returning to the family at day's end. Where was the glamour, the excitement, the unpredictability of each day? Settling down to a less dramatic life happened gradually, as his experiences in the north provided rich fodder for the Gunnedah service clubs who were always on the lookout for interesting speakers. David attended many a dinner and meeting, informing and entertaining these rural people with the thrilling tales of life as a doctor with the RFDS. He sometimes wondered on looking around the room as he spoke if they actually believed him. The rescues, parachute jumps, terrifying flying through storms and operating with torchlight seemed a world away from the price of steers or the wheat crop destroyed by hail.

In 1974 the medical practice that David had joined consisted of four doctors. The town itself had nine doctors, a good doctor/patient ratio for a town of 10,000 people. David was the youngest and created something of a talking point among the older doctors by wearing shorts and long socks instead of the traditional white coat. This flared up one day when David was called into the senior doctor's surgery and formally asked to dress more appropriately as befitted his status. This did not go down well with the free and easy David.

> "Out in the waiting room," he said, "there are twenty people, eighteen are for me and two for you!" He turned on his heel and stormed out. Nothing more was said about appropriate dress.

Private practice soon proved a good fit for David. His patient base quickly grew as he became known and established in the town. The medicine of course was very different to the RFDS. David was used to emergency medicine or the regular clinics that provided screening services. The RFDS covered an area the size of Texas but medically it was not busy – most people nursed themselves through simple ailments, using the service for the more dramatic events that life threw at them. The good people of Gunnedah, however, liked the convenience of a doctor who was at the most a few kilometres away and would, without too much persuasion, visit you at home. It was a shock to David to have consultations and house calls for minor colds that would pass without any professional intervention. They were spoilt, using the system cheerfully and willingly.

When David arrived in Gunnedah the other three doctors breathed a collective sigh of relief at the thought of another doctor sharing the load. They helped David build up a patient base by promptly taking turns to take leave from the practice for some rest and recreation.

As the young doctor of the practice, David became the doctor of choice for obstetrics. This became an important and much enjoyed part of his working life. He never tired of the thrill of bringing new life into the world. He had come a long way from the raw obstetric "specialist" at Alice Springs Hospital. These early days were the beginning of the "cradle to the grave" medicine that family doctors love. It is true that a doctor's patients age with him and in those early days of booming obstetrics, these babies grew up, suffered the normal childhood ailments, teenage dramas until, in time, they too were delivered of their babies by the same family GP. A doctor's ability to practise medicine is related to how well they know not just the patient, but the whole family situation. Country medicine allowed a doctor to really know a family, their relationships, their financial situation, their work situation, their cultural life as well as their health. The doctor knew the whole person.

As well as obstetrics, David also enjoyed surgery. One morning a week would be set aside for operating at the hospital. He performed tonsillectomies, appendicectomies, set fractures, did skin work and of course at any time of the day or night, caesarean sections.

A medical day was lengthy. It started in the morning around 7.30am when David left home and headed to the hospital for rounds. There could be anything from one to ten patients to see, check their progress through the night and discuss with the RN about their ongoing care. Then it was off to the surgery for the morning session, to check results and do other paperwork before facing the patients. If he was lucky there might be a lunch break. If he was really lucky, he went home for a spell before the afternoon session. There was no such thing as finishing time. Patients can't be hurried. What looked like a routine checkup could quickly change into something much more complicated. Flexibility was the key here. Every third night one of the practice doctors was on-call for emergencies and the ring of the phone quickly became a thing to dread. The people of Gunnedah were used to getting instant medicine and calls and visits to the hospital at all hours of the night were common. After a disturbed night's sleep, it all started again next morning. It was definitely a job for the young and fit.

David relished the challenge of being busy and enjoyed the variety of work that general practice provided. This level of work however took its toll, and the aeroplane provided a perfect release from the stresses of work. The old Auster, complete with dodgy engine, enabled the family to weekend away in Sydney, Brisbane or the Gold Coast. The weather, however, did not always allow him to return in time for work on Monday! One day when David had baby Sarah on board, the Auster decided to cough and splutter a bit. With more than himself to worry about he decided it was probably time to upgrade the Auster to something more sophisticated. In December 1974 he bade a fond farewell to the Auster and bought a Cessna 172. He revelled in the aircraft's all-metal fuselage and reliable engine and most importantly, its more modern equipment allowed him to fly at night.

Life in Gunnedah was quiet, sedate - not nearly as dramatic as life up north. The people were nice, the patients were nice, the weather was nice. It was all very nice.

Life needed to be spiced up a bit. What better excitement than the acquisition of a new aircraft? Well, not new exactly, in fact quite an elderly aircraft – none other than a Tiger Moth. A desire to own a Tiger Moth had been lurking in David's mind for some time. David was well acquainted of course with Tiger Moths, having trained on them all those years ago. Buying a second aircraft might seem an extravagance but what if it was shared with others? Word got around the local flying community. Soon six eager buyers were keen to share the costs and buy an aircraft as a syndicate.

David located a 1940 model in Perth, just about the furthest point in Australia from Gunnedah. It was in original condition, with no radio or tail wheel or even brakes. This would be a real challenge!

Of the six syndicate members, David Macpherson put his hand up to help ferry the Tiger back to Gunnedah. David Mac was a local farmer and he and his wife Leigh were both keen pilots. He had an airstrip on his property not too far from town. It was the perfect place to while away a Sunday afternoon with flying and plenty of space for young children to enjoy themselves without the usual, "When are we going home?"

The flight home in the Tiger Moth took four and a half days, a stark contrast to the four and a half hours it took to fly to Perth with Qantas.

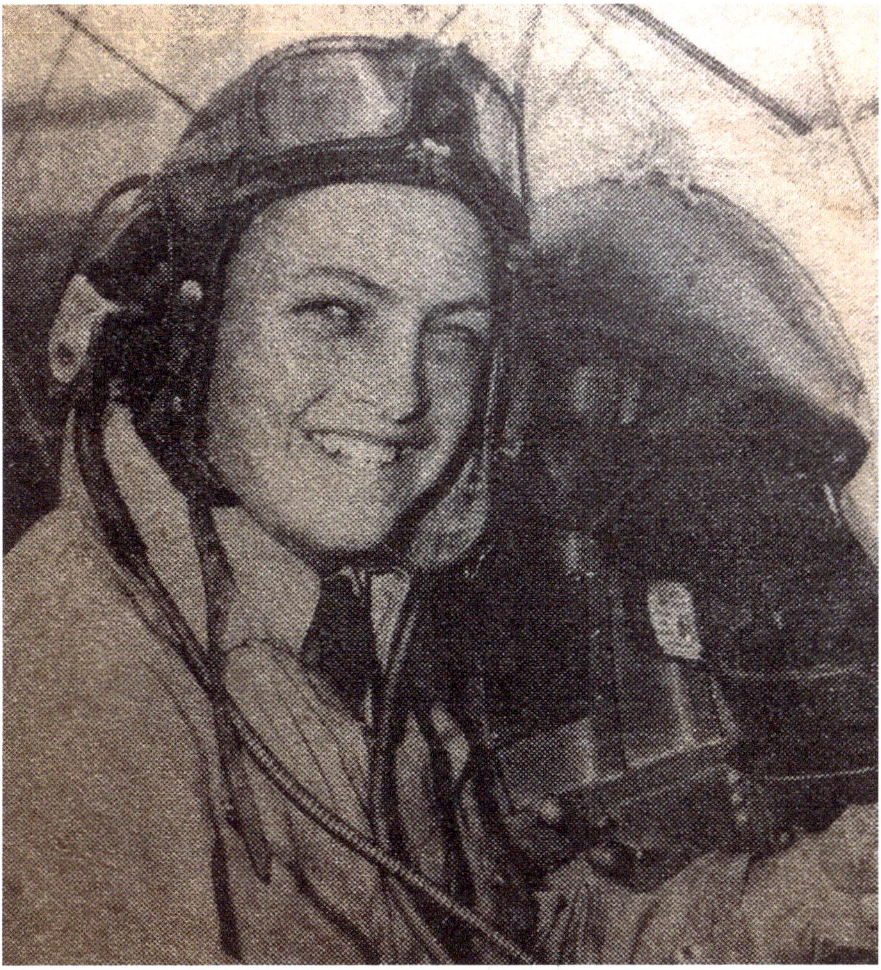

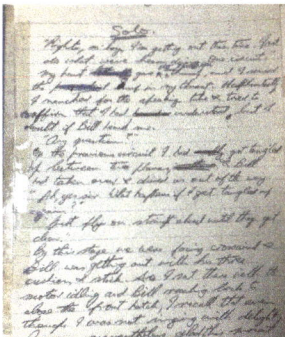

Day after first solo.

David with co-owners of Auster, Ric Macready and Stephen Lovell, Flinders Island 1966.

David's first solo, handwritten on 15th December, 1958.

David with brand new stepfather, Bruce Daymond, 1949.

Lionel Cooke and Boxkite, 1915, Point Cook.

Officer Cadet David Cooke on Pilots Course, 1958.

With Cy Cyganiewicz, parachute instructor, 1971.

"Dr. David Cooke, I presume?"

Lionel Cooke (in dark jacket) on running board, 1915

With Sister June Beatty, Normanton,

Newspaper cartoon when doing parachute training, Mt Isa, 1971.

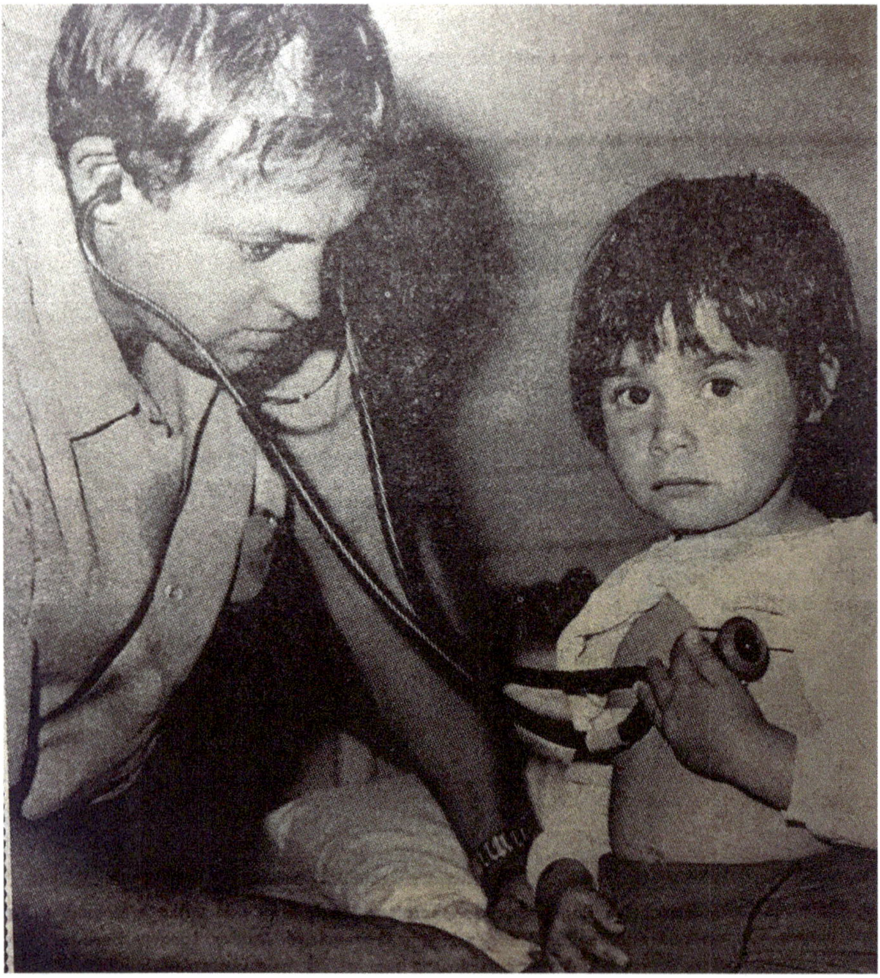

A young patient, Normanton Queensland, 1969.

Overweight flying doctor, Doomadgee, 1969

With Captain Johnny Murkin, Mt Isa, 1970

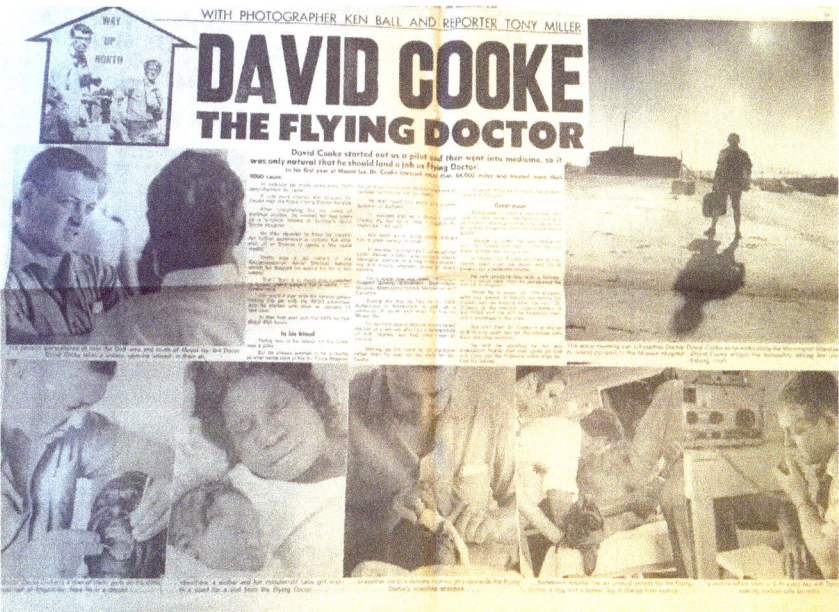

Press articles 1969

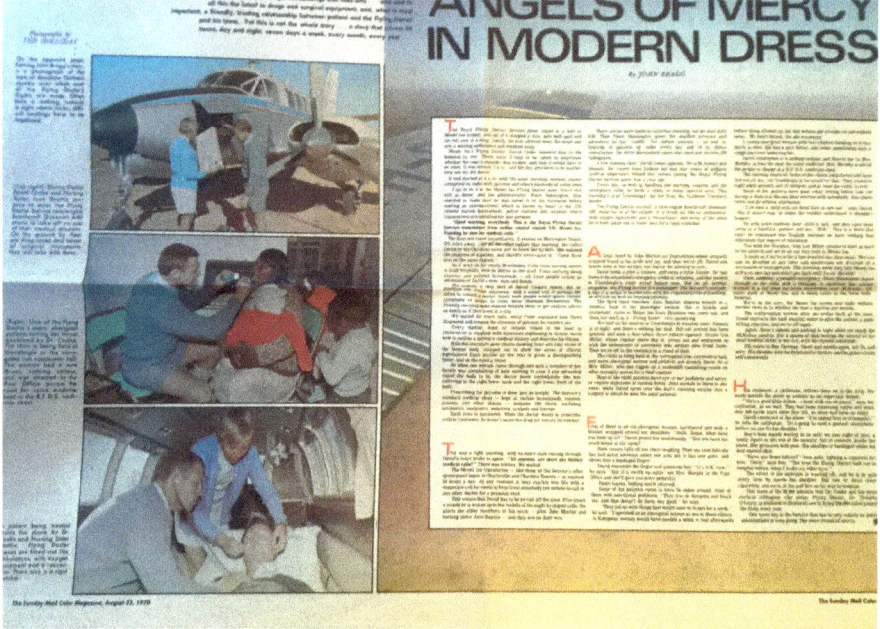

With Captain Beth Garrett on "This is Your Life", 1978.

Centrefold Brisbane Sunday Mail, August 23, 1970.

With David Macpherson, Tiger Moth from Perth to Gunnedah, 1977.

Tiger Moth, Gunnedah, 1978.

Press article, leaving Mt Isa, 1972.

With Beth Garrett, Yorke Island, Torres Strait, 1974.

Off to work, 1969.

Flying the Clancy Skybaby, Gunnedah.

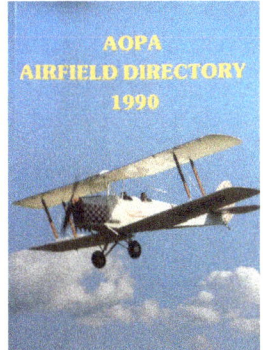

Playing "Herod" in Jesus Christ Superstar, Gunnedah, 1986.

"Ali Hakim" in Oklahoma, Gunnedah.

1st Edition Airfield Directory created by David, 1990.

Painting of Western Scotland.

First painting, 2011.

With Anthony and Michael.

In formation over Port Macquarie.

Low and Slow

1977

"I don't think you're ever the same after seeing the world framed by the wings of a biplane."

Richard Bach

There are many ways of loading oneself up with problems, but none quite so memorable perhaps as crossing the continent of Australia by Tiger Moth; and I can recommend it.

With a lot of wind in the wires, the face and a certain amount in the stomach, David Macpherson and I brought the said flying machine from Perth to Gunnedah, NSW mostly at 500 feet, over four and a half days.

It is hard to pick up a real Tiger these days. Many have been polluted with radios, tail wheels, brakes and worst of all, canopies.

It was necessary, therefore, to go to Western Australia to find such a beast.

At 500 odd knots we crossed the continent at 32000 feet sipping cool drinks and munching chicken wings and looked down at the great expanses of Australia and pondered on the next few days heading back.

The Tiger was in good condition and we, armed with a hand pump, three gallons of straight oil, a comprehensive set of tools, and many nuts and bolts – (anyone operating a Gipsy Major engine for more than twenty minutes straight must have the latter) set out.

Naturally our personal effects consisted of a toothbrush and an alarm clock plus some water, a VSB (survival beacon) and a few dried apricots.

As the dawn crept over the hills next morning, and fifteen minutes before the Jandakot tower opened, we thrust ourselves at the east. At a reckless forty knots groundspeed and a dizzy 3000 feet we soon became aware that little old ladies doing their shopping were gradually but firmly overtaking us.

From time to time, I was able to divorce myself from this disturbing fact as I applied myself to the 500 pumps of the wobble pump to convey the auxiliary fuel to the main tank, and to the placing of the Bandaids on the blisters caused by same.

After refueling at Kellerberrin we found that we could not possibly reach Kalgoorlie at forty knots groundspeed, and therefore lined up a drum of fuel to be left at Southern Cross, a small town about 300 kilometres east of Perth. Sometime later, following the road at 500 feet, we found that we had increased to fifty-five knots and a decision was reached to bypass Southern Cross.

Once past this place, of course, as can be expected, the ground speed dropped to fifty knots, and one experienced that nagging doubtful feeling in the stomach, unhelped by the turbulence until Kalgoorlie hove into sight three and a half hours later.

The next morning at a breakneck sixty-five knots we followed the railway out on to the Nullarbor Plain. Each tiny fettler settlement turned out to wave and the trains, doing very little less than us, became friendly as they took five to ten minutes to be overhauled. Waving of arms and apparel was carried out by both sides, and at one time my Notams concerning the Kalgoorlie DME were accidentally lost over the side.

We were to pump fuel ourselves out of a drum dropped at Rawlinna, but on arrival there we were informed that it had not arrived due to a derailment. We thought of spending some weeks at this "social capital of the Nullarbor" when someone suggested a property, Kanandah, twenty-five miles away where fuel was available. This got us out of trouble, and we were off again above the world's largest forced landing field to Forrest.

Fuelling with us at Forrest was a RAAF VIP Falcon. After offering to swap aeroplanes with the crew we decided to keep ours as there were more hours to run on our engine and they left us in a cloud of kerosene haze with two cans of soft drink out of their fridge.

Climbing into the 115 degree air at Forrest we headed south for Eucla where it was necessary to rug up. The coastal air was cool and we were surprised to find an empty hangar to use.

Following the Great Australian Bight the next morning, 500 feet above the sheer cliffs and with a low overcast was really something. Anyone who says you do not see the country if you fly should take a Tiger next time.

After pumping fuel at Nullarbor Homestead, and posing for two American tourists, we were up and climbing for Ceduna with the suggestion of a tail wind. Some hours, two bandaids and a couple of crosswind landings later, we collapsed into a motel at Whyalla.

The leg onwards next day saw us reach nearly 4000 feet to Waikerie. My feet were numb, my head and nose were numb and the aircraft shuddered as I shivered. My uncomplaining co-pilot reveled in the warmth of the firewall up front.

By mid-afternoon we reached Griffith where the local agent assured us that there was no chance of getting fuel (it was after all four o'clock) until he learned we were in a Tiger Moth and en route from Perth. "Anyone with the guts to do that deserves fuel", and we were away and pointing to Dubbo. There was one storm on the entire continent that day and it sat over Dubbo as we landed. With negligible ground speed we fell upon the grass and my wiry navigator leapt out on to the wing and lay bodily across it to stop the already lifting wheel as we taxied in. Nine hours and twenty-five minutes that day, rounded off with such conditions, made a great day for masochists.

A ridiculous two hours was all that was left to Gunnedah the next morning and as we knew that half the town and local press were waiting, we elected to skirt the town out of sight and appear up wind from the wrong direction.

We drew a few conclusions.

Firstly, it can be done.

Secondly, people are very interested in this type of aeroplane and tend to be more helpful than usual.

Thirdly, it is a long way, and fourthly, if anyone wants a Tiger Moth ferried from Western Australia, give us one week's notice.

Once the Tiger Moth was safely installed in its new home, it was up to David to train up the other members of the syndicate to fly this beautiful old flying machine. David's training on the Tiger had shown just how tricky it could be to fly. It is a "tail dragger", an aircraft that lands on the two forward wheels and then drops back on to the tail wheel. Visibility is poor and the pilot, who flies from the back seat, has to lean slightly to the side to look down the runway. It has an open cockpit and consequently freezing cold even in relatively warm weather. It is noisy with the wind blowing around the pilot and co-pilot. But it is enormous fun. The others took to it with great enthusiasm and of course David didn't mind one bit all the hours he needed to spend with each member to learn the wicked ways of a Tiger Moth.

The Tiger Moth enjoyed its life in Gunnedah with this crew of dedicated pilots. It had a relatively trouble-free life except for a couple of heart-stopping incidents. One lunchtime David thought it might be fun to dash out to the airport to do some aerobatics in the Tiger before returning for the afternoon surgery. Shouldn't be longer than forty-five minutes. Oh, the best laid plans… The Tiger climbed to 4000 feet. David put the aircraft into a roll. Normally the passenger control column should be removed but David had difficulties getting it out and had decided to leave it in place. At first all went well, and the township of Gunnedah circled around him. As he came out of the roll the aircraft wouldn't straighten up. The stick was jammed! The Tiger wanted to just keep rolling, a situation that would not have a happy ending if not corrected. Desperately David tried to free the controls but with no success. Thinking quickly, he worked out that by jamming on one of the rudder pedals and putting the throttle forward the wing would come up for a few seconds. Using this strange method, he descended over the airstrip like a falling leaf but held out little hope. A crash was inevitable. He wondered what would happen to the patients who would be waiting back at the surgery. This was not a good situation to be in and remembering the old pilot mantra about take-offs are optional but landings are mandatory, David had no option but to continue swooping and wallowing his way towards the very hard runway. Fortunately for all concerned the "falling leaf" manoevre coincided with the runway for just enough time to allow a safe landing. It was only then that he realised that the seat insert in the passenger cockpit had jammed the other control column.

They say he was white-faced for a week.

The other incident was equally heart stopping. David learnt very early on in his flying life that the Tiger does not like wind. Remember the dropped leaf between the feet? How could one anticipate a willy willy, that twisting violent wind that strikes unexpectedly with frightening force? On Christmas Eve 1977 one grabbed the Tiger Moth on take-off and flung the aircraft back to the ground on its nose, damaging the wings and propeller. Surprised to still be alive, he jumped out in a hurry, fearing it would flame, and jarred his back as he hit the ground. It could have been a lot worse and showed how quickly things can go wrong just when you least expect it.

Fortunately, Christmas Day 1977 was not a disaster and Daddy was still there to do his Santa duties. Yes, David had been busy on the home front since arriving in Gunnedah in 1974. Amelia was born in May the following year and Anthony in September 1976. David firmly states that Amelia was not named after his favourite flying female, Amelia Earhart, but who's to know the truth of that?? Anthony was given the middle name Rolla in memory of his unknown grandfather.

The world of aviation at that time was branching out with lighter, cheaper, easy to fly ultralight aircraft. It was the start of the popular recreational aircraft that now allow so many more people the joys of flight. One weekend David was invited out to a local farmer's property to inspect his newly purchased Thruster ultralight. Keen to experience something new, David was only too pleased to accept the invitation to take it for a test fly. Away he went up above the newly sown wheat paddocks enjoying the lightness and freedom of this little aircraft. Coming in to land he was surprised to see his way blocked by an unexpected power line. Following usual procedure David pulled back the control column expecting the aircraft to respond immediately. The Thruster dragged itself over the power line, stalled and headed for the ground in rather a hurry. David sustained a bump on the head and the Thruster $1500 of damage. The gathering crowd around the aircraft was quick to offer advice to the dazed pilot. "Why didn't you go under the power line?" was the not so helpful comment after the event. It was simply because, after flying for twenty-five years, it was second nature to climb and go over the obstacle. It was an expensive flight. He recovered after a short time and returned to Gunnedah in the Warrior albeit in the co-pilot's seat. Another adventure, another learning experience, another lucky escape.

In the seventies there were few, about three per cent, of private pilots who had gained their instrument rating. David continued to further his own flying knowledge. In 1978 he became friends with an East-West Airlines captain, Neale Crawford who lived close by in Tamworth. Neale became David's instructor and with this expert training he gained his instrument rating later that year. David wanted not just to have his instrument rating but to be trained to airline standards, to be the best he could be. This meant being within 50 feet of the required altitude, within 2.5 knots of the required airspeed and 2.5 degrees within the set heading. Neale would also challenge David by progressively covering up the instruments until only one or two were visible. This simulated instrument failure required the pilot to rely on whatever was available, plus instinct and common sense to fly safely. This training was all done at night, generally after a hard day at the surgery. Factoring in the flight to and from Tamworth and it made for a very long day. Neale's rigorous training made the final test with the DCA inspector something of an anti-climax. David had been taught so well by Neale and performed at such a high standard that the testing officer granted David a Class 1 licence instead of the expected Class 3. Since 1978 he has continued to renew his instrument rating and maintain the highest standards possible in his flying.

Having an instrument rating enables a pilot to fly in cloud. Prior to that a pilot has to ensure that his scheduled flight must not take him into cloud where of course there is no visibility. Flying on instruments involves lodging a flight plan and knowing exactly what are the lowest safe altitudes that can be flown in mountainous or hilly countryside. This enabled David to travel to and from the Gold Coast across the Northern Tablelands in weather that would have kept him at home before gaining this qualification. It does not, however, mean flying in any weather. Thunderstorms are to be avoided and ice way up there at altitude is something no pilot wants to experience. Caution and careful assessment of the weather is still the way to go.

Flying on instruments may have its advantages but can also create some awkward problems. Yes, you can fly in bad weather, but a person has still to board the aircraft often while carrying a bag or two. And yes, the raincoat or umbrella has probably been left at home. This was the situation one flight from Coolangatta after dropping the family there for the school holidays. The aircraft had to be fuelled for the return flight. This meant standing in the Queensland rain (minus any protective rain gear), steadily getting soaked. Into the aeroplane and off. David climbed up through the coastal rain until he popped out into the beautiful sunshine at 8000 feet. Alone in the aircraft, it seemed like a good idea to remove the wet garments and drape them around the cockpit to dry. What would the press have made of this had anything happened on this flight? A reputation in tatters! "Naked doctor found in light plane wreckage." People are quick to assume that flying in one's own aircraft is the height of decadent luxury but it does have its other side - negotiating fences and gates at outback airstrips, carrying one's own bags instead of watching them disappear on a conveyor belt, drinking thermos coffee and eating a muesli bar in a cramped cockpit instead of enjoying a proper meal and of course the worst thing of all, controlling the bladder on a lengthy leg.

With the arrival of another son, Michael Rolla in December 1979 the family was now six in number. David decided that a slightly bigger and more comfortable aircraft was needed to ferry them around. In 1981 the Grumman Traveler was traded in on a brand new Piper Warrior. The list of aeroplanes that had passed through David's hands was increasing and he was far from finished. The Warrior was a reliable, sleek little aircraft and trips to Brisbane and Sydney were now done in greater comfort.

Despite its reliability, the Warrior could not defend itself against the weather. On 29 December, just a year after buying this beautiful little machine, its proud owner was devastated when it was damaged as a twister tore through the airport. Ensconced in the hangar, the Warrior was picked up by the powerful wind and thrown up against the hangar wall damaging a wing, propeller and cowling – not a happy Christmas present. Having a damaged aircraft and negotiating the world of insurance and aviation engineers is no fun at all, the worst of it being unable to fly for one whole week.

Another indignity happened to the aircraft a few years later, this time in Tamworth. The family was returning to Gunnedah after attending the christening of a friend's child. It was late afternoon with the sun hanging low on the horizon making visibility a bit tricky. Nobody knew what the horrible metallic sound was. There were sparks and the aircraft slewed around. Without wasting a second, Pamela and the four children scrambled out leaving a bewildered pilot wondering what had just happened. He soon found out that the noise was caused by a very fast spinning propeller coming into contact with a large metal sign, a sign which read in bold black letters, "Tamworth City Council takes no responsibility for aircraft parked at this airport". What about taxiing aircraft? No, not responsible for them either!

What an embarrassment for our pilot, but over the years it's been a good aviation tale to tell. The damaged prop hangs proudly in the stairwell at home as a reminder to look, and look, and look again.

The Warrior experienced a couple of "interesting" flights. On both occasions the other seats were filled with anxious, questioning children.

David decided to take the children on a holiday across Bass Strait to Tasmania. This flight involves at least a one hour expanse of time when there is water beneath the aircraft, not solid ground. An hour generally passes quite quickly but, on this occasion, the acrid fumes of a battery simmering at a gentle boil tended to spoil the flight. With air vents fully open and the little storm window allowing a blast of cold air into the cockpit, the Warrior managed to reach Launceston unscathed. The battery had boiled causing it to melt. No wonder the smell was overpowering! Apparently, the battery had been overcharging. The engineer in Launceston had to change the voltage regulator as well as installing a new battery. An inconvenience during this family holiday but all was well, and the Warrior was soon as good as new and ready to continue its flying adventure around Tasmania.

Another interesting flight had David flying Sarah and Amelia to Brisbane. The flight was smooth, the weather good until they reached the jagged Great Dividing Range around Tenterfield, when a rough running engine began to spoil things somewhat. The engine coughed and spluttered, spat and hissed and two anxious girls in the back said hopefully, "Is everything all right Dad?" Between reassuring the girls, flying this uncooperative aircraft and liaising with Air Traffic Control David had his hands full as the brave little Warrior slowly limped towards Archerfield Airport.

"What happens if the engine stops, Dad?" was the second anxious question.

"Oh, no problem, we'll just land in a paddock somewhere," replied a hopeful pilot. Could the girls not see that down below was simply hostile looking tree covered mountains and gullies, not a paddock in sight! Such is the faith and trust the girls had in their father. Yes, he would know what to do and everything would be fine. David declared an emergency and the airways were cleared to facilitate their entry into the airspace around Archerfield airfield. In case the engine did decide to cease totally, David flew at 9,000 feet altitude right up to the circuit area over the field. This would give David some chance of gliding safely to the runway without the help of an engine. After landing safely he discovered that the Warrior had a shattered valve guide. According to the engineer it had about one minute left before it stopped completely. It was a lucky escape. The broken Warrior was left in Brisbane and another aircraft hired to return to Gunnedah. Work the next day will not wait while an aeroplane is fixed.

Despite these occasional excitements, David's flying career was by this time a fairly stable affair. Gone were the exciting, unpredictable flights with the RFDS. In Gunnedah flying involved mainly playing with the Tiger Moth on a calm Sunday afternoon or flying the Warrior to the Gold Coast or Sydney. Imagine the excitement when an old friend rang one morning asking if David would be interested in being co-pilot to ferry an Australian N24 Nomad to the USA! Would he what!

The Nomad was an aircraft that held great promise for Australian aviation. It was useful as a short field passenger, charter or freight delivery aircraft. The USA was hopefully going to be a big customer.

The ferry flight from Gunnedah, where David was picked up, to San Jose in California took fifty hours of flying and six days to complete. An aircraft of this size flying across vast expanses of ocean with no convenient landing spots every few hours has to make other arrangements. This means that the fuselage behind the cockpit where normally passengers would be seated is now full of large, smelly tanks containing extra fuel to take the aircraft from one airstrip to the next fuelling stop. The Nomad also had no autopilot as this needed to be fitted in the USA. Flying by hand for endless hours, weaving through weather and possible thunderstorms, is hard and exhausting work. To add to this the cockpit was cold at altitude; maybe this was intentional to keep the brain alert. It was not a flight that is normally taken across the Pacific thanks to the airlines; this was a flight for the brave and those who could suffer discomfort.

On his return home and back at work in the safety and security of his surgery, David could not understand why his gentle and genial partner, Dr Arthur Lundie, seemed to avoid his company, and engaging only the most essential of conversation. Arthur had no truck with such reckless foolishness. He took a good couple of weeks to forgive David for undertaking this dramatic journey.

It's a Long Way Between Seagulls

1980

> *"Flying is safe as long as you remember it is dangerous."*

How quickly could I get a US visa? It was not a question I hesitated much about. To fly the Pacific as co-pilot in a Nomad was not something to pass up.

En route to Brisbane I became familiar with the delightful all white N24, its cabin filled with twelve ferry tanks, biscuits and bully beef, a couple of suitcases and of course, two large-necked plastic bottles.

Early the next day found us slowly climbing into the back of a trough heading out from the Queensland coast. The absence of autopilot in such a stable aircraft was not a problem as we weaved between towering cumulus clouds. The first leg of eight hours to Honiara was filled with enthusiastic conversation about flying and philosophy interspersed with noises of munching upon almonds and dried apricots. Perhaps every two hours would come a series of jokes and laughter, or perhaps a few rugby songs, sung perhaps a little haltingly due to the lack of sea level pressure in our cabin. A crawl back over the tanks to find the plastic bottle in the fifth hour helped to increase the circulation in one's legs before the clouds of a mild tropical depression wove around us.

With one hour to go we started discourse with Honiara who informed us that the weather was down to minima and the QNH was 990! This sounded awfully like a cyclone until, following a further request, it turned out to be a much higher pressure. After an instrument approach we landed at Honiara where it was fascinating to still find relics of the Pacific war in evidence. The old control tower still stands, sundry guns lie around and under the water off one of the main beaches lie countless aircraft in generally unserviceable condition. The car which took us into the hotel appeared to be held together by rust interspersed with areas of metal and one could watch the road running by beneath one's feet quite easily through vents which I gather were not part of the original design. The second day proved better weather and we part filled the tanks for the nine hour leg to Majuro, an atoll in the Marshall Islands.

The captain arranged his washed underpants and singlet on the coaming next to his flight plan and instructions for operating the Loran and sat back to let me work. This was the area of the inter-tropic convergence zone and we therefore spent most of the day weaving away from huge tropical build-ups. Every so often, however, a great wall of cloud barred our way and we plunged into it at the most innocuous part, both hands on the wheel and teeth grinding away.

Within five minutes of the captain's ETA we circled the tiny atoll barely wider than the airstrip. Here we met a couple of Australian pilots, flying the Marshall Islands Airways Nomad and coincidentally maintained by an engineer who came from within a few miles of my hometown.

After a night of tough chicken and rice, a hard bed and the telling of countless aviation "lies", we nursed the heavy aeroplane into the humid air for a sixteen hour leg to Honolulu. The day wore into night broken up with laughter and quiet times, dried apricots and crawling back to the plastic bottle. After dark a tiny light appeared in the dark sea in front of us. This was Johnston Atoll, a US submarine refueling base. For want of someone else to talk to, my mentor called them up and was greeted with a delightful southern drawl, "Why don't you all come on down here and have some coffee and get some gas?" … and, "What's a Nomad?" and, "You all have a nice flight then."

Getting into Honolulu at 3.00am is no time for enthusiastic chatter to customs people. We were ready for bed but in response to the usual questions, we did declare the plastic bottles!

My suitcase had been sitting under a tank vent all day and as we climbed out of Majuro, expanding fuel had seeped out all over my clothes to the extent that wherever I went after this, I was followed by quizzical stares about my personal freshness!

A few hours later we surfaced to organise our entry into America and to study the local inhabitants. We could not leave until 3.00pm the following day in order to avoid fogs on the mainland and this enabled the body to start catching up on its rest. Loaded to the gunwales we waddled to altitude but it was some hours before we appeared to get on to the step. As the night progressed the cold started to seep into one's body. It was preferable not to use heaters and so the skiing pants and Tiger Moth boots had been produced to maintain circulation.

At times we would call up a Boeing tracking above us to pass a position. There would always be a pause, no doubt as the cup of tea was put down, before we would receive an answer.

As the horizon lightened, I was sitting there blinking with my fearless leader asleep beside me, when I noticed a small light up ahead just above the horizon moving in a very odd way. I looked at my wings to ensure that I was not moving the aircraft and then it struck me that this light must be a UFO coming to take me off somewhere. It was an eerie sensation and when I could bear it no longer, I woke the captain to ask what he thought we should do. "It's a ***** star!!" he said and went back to sleep; and of course, it was – moving in the refraction area.

As the fifteenth hour came up (our ETA for San Jose), we were still over the sea and in fact not even in DME or VHF range of what we hoped must be the USA up ahead.

The dreaded feeling in the pit of the stomach crept in and thoughts of scrambling the Coast Guard flooded to the surface, however eventually land loomed up and I remember thinking how sorry I would feel for someone who had to do an instrument approach after sixteen hours in the air. Needless to say, we did in fact have an ILS approach!

Breaking out of cloud we were immediately aware of being in the USA – there were three parallel runways being used and we were bracketed between a tiny Cessna 150 and a Boeing 727 all on final.

We had spent fifty hours over six days hand flying down in the weather altitudes experiencing the same Pacific that Kingsford Smith had. All that sea just sitting there every day independent of the overcrowded world surrounding it. It was not the excitement of achieving a goal that I felt when we landed, but that vague feeling of disappointment that we experience when we must come back to earth and reality again.

That night I was sipping my coffee on QF4. As I peered out of my pressurised window, it was a different Pacific Ocean that I saw, but one that will not be quite the same for me again.

This life-changing flight in the Nomad must have settled quietly in the back of David's mind for some years before popping up in a slightly different guise. In 1990 David became the part owner of VH-KEY, an A36 Bonanza. The aircraft belonged to an old friend Dr Peter Andersen. It was Peter's daughter who was christened the day David decided to run into the sign at Tamworth airport. David, and a Tamworth radiologist, Dr Trevor Stewart, each bought a share in the aircraft. This bigger, heavier aeroplane was a six-seater with a longer fuel range and enabled the family to undertake longer trips in greater comfort.

Not long after, the subject of doing an overseas safari in the Bonanza arose. David, the expert with his Nomad flight to California under his belt, was the one with the knowledge. Soon a round trip to Bali was organised. Now it is one thing to be a willing co-pilot on such an adventure. You do what you're told by the pilot in command, do your fair share of the flying and generally provide moral support and company. It's a totally different thing to be in charge. Flying overseas involves negotiating immigration and customs without the reassuring organised business of flying with an airline where you follow the signs, fill in the forms as required and maybe answer the odd question. It's all quite a different affair as a private operation.

The flight departed Australia from Darwin with a three-hour leg to the port city of Kupang on the island of Timor. With the Australian mainland fast disappearing behind them the three aviators settled into the routine of observation, flight checks and radio calls and, of course, endless chat. On board the aircraft was a dinghy in the event of a water landing and each of them wore an uncomfortable Mae West while over water. A six-seater aircraft does not have the convenience of toilet facilities and so each person has to provide their own wide-necked bottle for use if need be. Modesty is not possible in these situations! Heading across the sea with no land in sight is a strange and fearsome situation to be in. There is trust in the instruments that are guiding you ever closer to your destination and great relief when a smudge on the horizon slowly forms a stretch of land. The GPS has worked.

Kupang is a large port - not the happy holiday place that people associate with places like Bali. After an overnight stay, they headed to Mataram on the island of Lombok. Lombok, next to Bali is quieter and charming. After negotiating volcanic craters, lakes and streams of cloud this was a good spot for some R&R for a few days. It was only a half hour flight to Bali for fuel and an overnight before heading for home.

Negotiating foreign airports involves the exchange of money ($US) to enable service crew to fuel the aircraft, clear customs and immigration, transport the crew to the terminal and generally facilitate the bureaucracy involved with aviation in a different country with a different language and culture. No doubt too much money was handed over but to these local workers, three men from Australia flying their own aeroplane to their country for a few days must have seemed unbelievably wealthy. It was money well spent. Where to next? Just wait and see!

Indonesian Adventure

1990

"Flying is hypnotic and all pilots are willing victims to the spell."

Ernest K Gann.

"I'm sorry but Denpasar airport will be closed at 7.00am for two hours". The briefing officer was adamant.

"But we have to get off now to make it through to Darwin today."

"Sorry, very important person coming to Bali today," he smiled.

"Please can you ask the tower? We are ready to go now."

It was 6.55am.

"It is not possible," he said politely.

I thought of producing a few American dollars, but there were too many air force pilots in the room.

"Please try."

He picked up the phone – the dialogue was in Indonesian. I was almost speechless. We had been already held up for almost an hour because Customs had found inconsistencies in their own processing of our entry five days before. Customs in Kupang had cleared us in and out of Indonesia at the one time and as we went to leave Bali, they discovered we were not in Indonesia at all!

He looked up. *"You must be off the ground by 7.05am."* It was now 6.59.

Grabbing my fellow aviators, Dr Peter Andersen and Dr Trevor Stewart, we sprinted to the service bus, urging them to go quickly to our waiting and still *un-preflighted Bonanza. Wet behind the ears in this overseas flying this "Ground Handling" had cost us $US100 and we felt they could at least go fast for that price.*

At 7.01am the bus pulled up and the three of us unceremoniously piled out with our bags.

By 7.03am we had inspected the aeroplane, drained the fuel cocks and thrown in the luggage. As the aeroplane taxied quickly, almost swerving past a Boeing beside us, we closed the doors. It was Peter's leg and he turned to line up on the runway pulling on his belt and exercising the prop at the same time.

"Clear for take-off, please expedite."

"OK!"

We lifted off at 7.05 and 30 seconds shaking from the rush and breathless from the excitement. It was only as we climbed through a layer of stratus at 1500 feet that we were able to put on our Mae Wests and pull out the flight plan.

It was a momentous feeling five days before as we started our Bonanza outside the overseas terminal in Darwin. We were through Customs and had ceremoniously put on our Mae Wests. A minor staining of oil in the engine compartment had prompted me to ring our engineer in Tamworth, waking him from sleep at 6.00am on this Sunday morning.

Trevor, in the left seat for our first overwater leg was very slow and deliberate in his checks. Using the international system, we called ourselves by the full, "Victor Hotel Kilo Echo Yankee, ready".

Gently bumping as we climbed through the early morning stratus over Fanny Bay, it was exciting to set course on the three-hour leg to Kupang in Timor. I had been flying for thirty-four years, but this was the first time I would be flying as a pilot in command on an international flight.

The cloud dissipated and we found ourselves seemingly motionless over a shimmering calm sea. It was a beautiful day and the engine hummed reassuringly as the GPS ticked off the miles and we served ourselves morning tea.

It was good to keep our link with home through the Adelaide HF officer and how difficult it proved to jostle in the small cockpit to use the wide-necked bottle with a life jacket on!

With half an hour to go the volcanic mountains of Timor started to materialise above the misty inversion layer.

It was time to talk to Indonesia, and this proved to be anti-climactically easy – the heavy accent told us that the wind was "calem" and the altimeter was ten ten.

"Are you coming from Bali?"

"No, Darwin!" So much for thoughts of SAR (Search and Rescue) protection.

The smiling Indonesians swarmed around us and told us they would organise fuel, customs and weather for tomorrow. Little did we realise these services would cost us $US150 on the following day.

Kupang was the port where Captain Bligh made landfall after his epic journey in a long boat. It is a dusty, hot city with throngs of happy people staring at us, the only white people to be seen.

At breakfast the following morning I discovered a local airline crew and pumped them for information about en route frequencies for the day's flight to the island of Lombok.

A phone call from Darwin came through from a friend, Bernie Saroff. He was about to leave with his nine aircraft safari on a similar route. I was able to give him a Kupang "actual".

We headed north west to the large island of Flores and turned west weaving in good weather for over two hours between beautiful volcanic mountains and colourful lakes in craters. There were no large towns to be seen and thousands of islands dotted the gleaming, calm sea. Little wisps of cloud hung over the windward slopes of the hills and some anabatic condensation appeared as a stream of cloud climbing up a valley in one of the rocks. I weaved around these peaks reaching well above us at 6500 feet.

One hundred miles distant, the 12000 foot volcano on Lombok appeared towering over the surrounding islands and clouds, and we started a slow descent to keep visual as we had been unable to maintain the appropriate 13500 foot – the lowest safe altitude.

I tried the Mataram control tower and cursed them under my breath for not replying until I discovered I had turned the radio volume down in my excitement at this beautiful terrain. Lombok, next to Bali is much less known to the tourist industry and yet we found it charming and relatively unspoilt compared to its popular neighbour. We spent three days there before flying the thirty minutes to Bali for fuel and an overnight. Taxiing out for the only IFR weather for the trip we saw women with heavy loads balanced on their heads waiting at the edge of the runway for us to take off before crossing, apparently unchecked by air traffic control.

Leaving Bali, we sat over unbroken cloud for three hours barely seeing the island of Sumba on our track and saying goodbye to the Lombok volcano away to the north.

We were determined to avoid another "Ground handling charge" at Kupang and by being firmly pleasant, fuelled and were away from Timor in twenty minutes with only a small "service charge" to the cheerful tanker driver.

As we climbed out over the sea, I could not resist trying Adelaide on HF. A welcome female Australian voice came through very clearly. Of course, she would maintain our SAR from the Australian end and would I please give her the details.

We celebrated our smooth flight across this well travelled Timor Sea with lunch. I sat there with the autopilot connected to the GPS, musing on all the ghosts that had preceded us – Ross and Keith Smith, Bert Hinkler and many more.

At eighty miles we sighted Bathurst Island to the left and then the line of dark Darwin shore became more material and we started our descent.

As I lowered the wheels in the circuit at Darwin, we had already started to plan next year's flight to New Zealand and Fiji!

The "Three Musketeers" didn't have long to wait. The following year saw them once more poring over maps and performing calculations involving fuel flow, range and distance of legs in preparation for their next overseas jaunt. This time they headed north-east to the South Pacific.

By now these three were old hands. The process of getting ready for the expedition was a little more relaxed. Travelling this time to Lord Howe Island, Norfolk Island, Noumea in New Caledonia, Vila in Vanuatu and then back again, it was reasonable to assume that the organisation of fuel, immigration and customs would be less stressful than in Indonesia. They would be friendlier places altogether.

Pacific Adventure

1993

"The only thing that scares me about flying is the drive to the airport."

We were quite lost.

It was dark, as dawn had not yet crept over the eastern hills. There was a rising anger and frustration in our crew as we realised that time was passing and we had no idea which way to turn. The map was no help and my pulse was quickening as we seemed to be getting nowhere fast. If only we had the GPS!

This incredible situation occurred not over the Pacific Ocean, but as we drove from Noumea, New Caledonia to the international airport of La Tontouta, fifty-two kilometres north of the city.

The road was not signposted, the few pedestrians around at 5.00 am spoke neither French nor English and the roadworks in progress altered what should have looked like a highway into a rough back street. The situation was compounded by a left-hand drive vehicle which put me at a great disadvantage. It took half an hour to find our way and head north to the waiting Bonanza.

With eight days free, fellow doctors Peter Andersen, Trevor Stewart and I had decided to take the Beechcraft to Lord Howe Island, Norfolk Island, New Caledonia and Vanuatu.

Armed with a dinghy, Mae Wests, wide-necked bottles, a French-English dictionary and lots of noise and bravado, we set forth on a clear Saturday morning. Climbing over the dividing range from Tamworth we became aware of cloud building over the coast. A small glimpse of the beach at Port Macquarie through a hole in the undercast gave us our last look at the mainland and we changed into "insecure mode". As if to add to our anxiety, we started to pick up ice and I climbed a thousand feet to remain in the clear.

As is usual over the sea, the NDB on Lord Howe Island sang its reassuring song in our headsets almost from the mainland shore and of course, almost cheating, the GPS gave us the accurate information which we would broadcast when the engine failed!

At a computed point in the sky, we started our descent when this beautiful island was still invisible, and as we broke out of cloud at 1500 feet, the romantic mountains piercing the clouds appeared in the rainy gloom. We were fortunate that the wind was light and after a curving "Spitfire" approach and minor turbulence we were down for fuel and customs.

The imposing scenery around us was almost overpowering as we readied for our next leg to Norfolk Island, three and a half hours away.

Despite all these modern aids, it is a great act of faith to head out over featureless ocean assuming that almost 1000 kms away lies refuge in an airstrip on a piece of land five miles by two. It was indeed an almost spiritual experience when we saw that tiny dot looming out from under a cloud and suddenly we were on the runway and had become earthlings again.

The quaint Norfolk Island is soaked with history both of convict gaols and descendants of the Bounty Mutiny, and we loved the gentle rolling hills and tiny NIKI car which we hired for $12.00 a day.

After two days we headed over the sea in solid IMC, a stinging rebuke from the airport manager for jumping the fence ringing in our ears. The Norfolk wet season, missing for two years, decided to start that very day!

It is a lovely feeling to climb out the top of the clouds and sit motionless in the sunlight knowing that underneath all is dark and raining.

Eighty miles from New Caledonia we switched to the Tontouta frequency and tried our luck with the courteous but fast-talking controllers. We were informed of our clearance in English, but they spoke to everyone else in French and so we had no idea of the traffic or what was going on.

The representative of the airport authority approached us as we stopped. She was, to our surprise, young, slim, beautifully groomed with low cut neckline and split skirt. Very French! Our fuelling stop and paperwork was completed too quickly, and we headed up through the 5000 foot hills en route to Port Vila in Vanuatu.

Fifty miles out of Vanuatu I called the Vila tower to be greeted by a Kiwi accent and the information that his airport was below minima. Seeing a few small holes in the clouds we descended over the sea and finding we could track at 500 feet visually, followed what amounted to a most interesting approach into this attractive island.

Peter rang a local resort and arranged a 50% aircrew discount and immediately put on his wings and four gold bars. As I was in t-shirt and jeans, I looked for a phone booth to change. There being nothing appropriate, I surprised several cleaning ladies and security guards by leaping behind the Airport Information counter and changing my shirt, trousers and shoes. The next moment I surfaced resplendent in my captain's uniform to claim our bargain. After two great days of seafood including the famous coconut crabs, smiling Melanesians and duty free shopping, we flew back to our chic airport lady in Tontouta. The happy French controller informed us he did not fully understand our, "Australian language!"

Noumea did not disappoint us, and we were amazed at how our schoolboy French came back after so many years. We hired a little Renault and explored the island for two more days before we started our homeward legs.

After fuelling in Norfolk Island, we spent two days in perfect weather at Lord Howe Island, climbing the hills and even swimming despite it being mid-winter.

It was with regret that we climbed away from the lagoon on the eighth day and headed west and yet there was a patriotic excitement as the dim outline of Australia materialised in the haze. More appropriately, the approach to Tamworth was in rain and gloom and suddenly we were back to the reality of winter.

Thanks to modern technology, the navigation was never in doubt as we hopped from island to island across miles of empty sea. How spoilt we are, crossing the ocean that men like Kingsford Smith conquered by turn and bank indicator and sextant. I feel humbled by their achievements when all we have to do is select autopilot to GPS and open the thermos. For our crew, however, it was a great experience, tinged by both a little fear and a lot of laughter to enrich it. With the long range tanks we are installing, the way is opened up for us to fly the North Pacific to Alaska in a couple of years!

Hopefully my ground navigational skills will have improved by then.

A third overseas flight took place a year or so later. By this time the syndicate was dissolved. The Bonanza VH-KEY was now owned entirely by Trevor. This trip had a newbie on board, Grahame Deane, a long-term fellow doctor and flying enthusiast friend of David. Local Gunnedah GP and flying mate, Grahame was not without a degree of nervousness about this new adventure. The other two tell of KEY forging out to sea with David and Trevor stoically looking forward, while in the back seat there is Grahame giving himself a severe crick in the neck as he grimly watches the coast of the mainland slowly disappear from sight. Welcome to overwater flying, Grahame!

David and Grahame have spent many hours flying together. A quick couple of circuits after work in Gunnedah, outback safaris, the overseas flight to Pago Pago have continued to this day as Grahame and his wife Karen moved to Port Macquarie to work in a medical practice in Lake Cathie in 2015. Many hours have been spent doing "training" flights as well as holiday adventures to Cairns, Darwin, Alice Springs and Adelaide. They have clocked up over 600 flying hours together.

Recently they discovered a connection that goes back almost two hundred years. Grahame's great, great, great grandfather was Colonel George Barney who came to Australia with the Royal Engineers in 1835. He was responsible for the building of defence installations of Fort Denison in Sydney Harbour, Nobby's Head in Newcastle, Victoria Barracks in Paddington, Sydney and the gaols in Norfolk Island. By a strange coincidence it was discovered in a personal document that he was a close acquaintance of David's great, great, great uncle, Archibald Mosman. Archie and his twin brother, George arrived in Australia from Scotland in 1828. Archibald set up the whaling station in Mosman Bay, named after him and George headed north to Charters Towers. The town of Mossman in Far North Queensland bears his name, even with the wrong spelling!

Now although David may have liked to, it is probably impractical to fill all one's leisure hours with flying. He certainly tried, even spending time at the weekends when off duty flying the local "jump" aircraft for the parachute training school. This involved multiple take-offs, and landings ferrying groups of eager young people to altitude for the thrill of a lifetime. Having trained years ago and done some parachute jumps himself, he certainly understood the lure and excitement that each jumper experienced.

However, our energetic "doctor who flies" needed to find another diversion to enrich his life. As an eager young school student David had appeared on stage in such epic productions as *Campbell of Kilmohr* in which he appeared as the mother. He even gave Lady Macbeth a go and to this day is still word perfect in her major speeches. It is no surprise then that he decided to launch himself into the local amateur dramatic scene. At first he performed in the annual musical staged by the Gunnedah Musical and Dramatic Society. These entertainments were greatly enjoyed by the local community who relished seeing their businessmen, shopkeepers, teachers, tradesmen, doctors, dentists and farmers up on stage in quite a different role.

His first performance with the group was in *Camelot* where he played one of the knights, Sir Sagramore. Tights and swords became his latest attire and although it was a minor role in the production, he made it his own paving the way for larger roles in upcoming performances. David's fine tenor voice was an asset to these productions, but he preferred to play a character or comic role. This allowed him to play to the audience with quips that were topical or local in their appeal. One of his two favourite roles was Herod in the controversial production of *Jesus Christ Superstar* in 1986. This production caused some problems with the local churches which of course resulted in great publicity for the impoverished amateur group and hence great houses each night it was performed. David's character Herod has one appearance in a hit song made famous by the likes of Reg Livermore in the Sydney production. It is the showstopper of the night and David's rendition was no exception.

His other favourite character was playing Fagin in Gunnedah High School's production of *Oliver!* in 1984. David was the only adult in the production and had been approached by the Director to play the part. It was not a difficult decision to make and just required a bit of reorganisation of the patients in the waiting room. The school students took all other parts, from the Year 7 boys with their sweet young voices playing the workhouse boys through to the senior students playing the other adult roles. What annoyed David was the fact that these young performers became word perfect with their parts very quickly while poor old Fagin struggled up till opening night to be word perfect. He also had to master the art of singing and dancing at the same time. All in all, it was an excellent physical workout.

The most challenging role he performed was the part of Escamillo, the hero toreador in the opera *Carmen*. Now this is serious stuff; no dialogue, no comedy, no playing to the locals, just beautiful music and a tragic story. The production was an enormous challenge for the cast and crew as few had trained voices to make the most of Bizet's music. However, they rose to the task in hand. After a rigorous and difficult few months of rehearsals the production was an outstanding success. Despite the sleek black wig that really didn't suit him, David's performance was flawless. His voice filled the hall right to the back row.

Gilbert and Sullivan musicals are always popular. David performed in two of them – the lovelorn Nanki-Poo in *The Mikado* and the villain Dick Dead-Eye in *HMS Pinafore*. Dick required him to enact a tortured body with withered hand and evil voice, difficult to maintain over the whole performance. Nanki-Poo was the hero striving for love and hoping to get the girl, and yes, he did!

The expression, "the show must go on," was never truer than during the production of the musical *The Desert Song*. Amateur companies do not have the luxury of understudies for the major roles. It is not feasible to expect people who have a day job to prepare two roles in the unlikely event that someone falls ill. However, these things do happen. David unfortunately underwent surgery for kidney stones just before the production was due to hit the stage. He was playing the character of Benny, a comedy part which fortunately could be adapted to allow the show to go ahead with a full cast. It was not acting that caused David's legs to tremble in his voluminous Bombay shorts but weakness, being so recently hospitalised. He would be appalled had a patient done what he did, but the old show must go on.

The after-hours and on call roster could always be organised with the other doctors to fit around the rehearsal times and performance nights. The other doctors in the practice were accommodating in swapping nights on call to fit in with the rehearsal schedule. What is not easy to predict or schedule is the delivery date of David's many obstetric patients. Babies as we know come when they want to, usually at the most inconvenient time and generally in the middle of the night. So it was that one night as David was psyching himself up for his debut with the Gunnedah Music and Dramatic Society's performance of *Camelot*, a patient came into labour ready to deliver her first-born child. There was no time to waste changing into doctor clothes hence she had the delightful pleasure of her attendant doctor delivering her baby while nattily dressed in his lime green tights and with his rapier by his side. The hospital gown concealed a deal of this outfit, but the young mother was mightily relieved that neither the episiotomy nor the umbilical cord was the work of the Sir Sagramore's sword. It was certainly good publicity for the production.

Although he enjoyed performing in the musicals immensely, David could not help harking back to his schooldays on the stage. These productions were straight drama, no singing or dancing there, and many of David's roles had him cast as a female. Being young for his age and smooth of face meant the hero roles went to the brawnier types. Now as an adult maybe it was time to tread the boards again but in drama not musicals. He took to it like a duck to water, enjoying the break from learning dance routines and trying to sing at the same time; an exhausting experience after a full day's work. For the best part of a decade, he performed in a series of one-act plays, some Irish and some Noel Coward. The wordiness of Noel Coward was a challenge, especially so in *Blithe Spirit*, the one three-act play that he performed in. David's role, the pompous Charles Condamine, meant he was on stage for much of the play. The script was demanding and incredibly wordy with the fast moving dialogue that Coward is famous for. Although performing in a full length play was a challenge, it was certainly worth the effort.

As well as acting David undertook singing lessons to polish up his naturally fine tenor voice. For some years he would perform solo at the local Anglican Church and at times join with others to perform in a duet. This interest in music, acting and singing was a significant creative outlet for him and a huge contrast to his medical work and his other great love, flying. Medicine and aviation were science based activities whereas the stage was a different side of the brain entirely.

In the 1970s David became involved in the general aviation body AOPA, the Aircraft Owners and Pilots Association. The association's aim was to promote, encourage and foster aviation in the private sector. He was elected to the committee of twelve in 1978, rising to the position of Senior

Vice-President in 1990, a position he held for three years. The committee met bi-monthly in Sydney with the AGM being held in various locations around the country - Canberra, Adelaide, Albury and Launceston to name a few. During his time in office David assisted another doctor, Arthur Pape in his work fighting for the right of colour blind pilots to fly at night. At this time pilots were allowed to fly if they were colour blind, but not at night. This was a hark back to the days of maritime navigation when red and green marker buoys were used to indicate left and right. These were then used during the early years of aviation but with modern navigation this seemed unnecessary. Arthur fought a long battle to allow these longstanding rules to be changed. The success of this project has enabled many pilots who would otherwise have remained grounded, to gain their wings.

His other notable achievement was the production and publication of the AOPA Airport Directory. This immensely useful book provided pilots not only with the details of the airfield and runway information but also information about facilities, accommodation, transport, taxi and telephone availability, toilet amenities and anything else you could think of. In pre-Google days this was an invaluable tool for anyone finding themselves in a small outback town or a private airstrip. Even in today's tech age it is a handy little volume to keep in the pilot's nav bag. You never know when you might need it.

During his time on the committee David began to write more regularly. As has been shown, he recorded accounts of his various flying exploits, starting with his first solo. As well as that he wrote short articles on other aviation related themes. These he submitted to the editor of the AOPA monthly magazine over the years accumulating a solid body of published works. His other challenge was the writing of book reviews. Always an avid reader of aviation books, he was delighted to be forwarded a book by the magazine editor. Each month he would have the pleasure of reading and reviewing several books, and, the best bit, the book was his to keep! It always amazed the editor when David, having received the book on Monday, would have faxed the review to the editor by the Friday of that week! David is a true example of the phrase, "If you want something done, give it to a busy person." His reviews were generally humorous, personalised writings which always connected his own experiences to the book's topic. These years of steady book reviews have helped create his extensive aviation library that has been acquired over the years, causing something of a storage issue. Part with a book? Never!

Not content with book reviews and general aviation articles, David decided to turn his hand to fiction. The result was a novella called *The Circular Rainbow*. This phenomenon is seen from an aeroplane when the sun reflects on cloud to reveal a perfectly circular rainbow, not the usual arc or semi-circle seen from the ground. It is a special and beautiful sight as at the centre of the circular rainbow is an image of the aeroplane itself. It is considered a lucky omen. The novella involved a young journalist, a pretty young girl, an aeroplane which crashes in the desert and the heroic events which follow. It is still awaiting discovery.

In 1995 an upheaval on the AOPA committee took place resulting in a change of leadership. After 17 years David found himself off the committee. As a consolation prize, and to provide a distraction he purchased a small unit at Flynn's Beach, Port Macquarie. Instead of trundling off to boring committee meetings, he now could head off on Friday afternoons for two days at the beach. Much better fun! It also sowed the seed for a sea change in the future.

Meanwhile, let's not forget, David was working in the busy practice, delivering babies, operating once a week as well as his regular general consulting. To add a little excitement and variety to the week, he commenced a weekly clinic flying into the small village of Premer, about 20 minutes flying time from Gunnedah. This was held in the premises of Community Health. Each Thursday morning he landed on a strip attached to a local property and a car was supplied to take him into the village. This system worked well and enabled the people living in the area to have access to a GP instead of driving an hour into town and back again. If scripts were needed, they were taken to town on David's return, filled by the chemist and sent back to Premer via the school bus. It was a simple and efficient way of ensuring quick assistance to these isolated patients.

Premer was a tiny settlement. A pub, a petrol station, a few houses, that was about it. It serviced a rural area of farming and grazing properties just south-west of Gunnedah. One Thursday David took an American visitor along for the experience. This man was the brother-in-law of a Qantas pilot who lived in Gunnedah and farmed in his spare time. On arrival at the Premer strip they drove into the clinic and they both climbed out of the car.

"Now if you could just point me in the direction of the town, I'll look around until it's time to return," asked the visitor.

"This is the town," replied David. "There's not a lot to see!"

The trips to Premer were not without their complications and problems. The weather could be difficult. In winter David had to take a thermos of hot water with him to de-ice the windscreen of the aeroplane before take-off. Rain, when it came, could make the airstrip marginal and he had to rely on the opinions of other non-aviation people as to its condition. Of course, there were also the kangaroos. It was not unlikely to have heartstopping encounters with a marsupial but fortunately never a significant issue.

Flying to Premer each week was a happy experience. What pilot would not love to fly to work? It also provided a service to a small community and to David, well it took him back to his time in the RFDS. Not quite as dramatic, but a connection nevertheless.

Doctoring, aviation, stage work, writing and a busy family life certainly kept David busy. He was burning the candle at both ends and did not know how to slow down. Inevitably something had to give. In 1981 he contracted a respiratory infection. It was nothing serious but instead of shaking it off in a few days as he expected to, this ailment hung around and he was left with a debilitating chronic weakness, tiredness and inability to concentrate. It was of course what today is called chronic fatigue syndrome. In 1981 such a disease did not exist. Strangely enough David was not alone in his suffering as there were others in town with the same symptoms. There was no official diagnosis, no medication, no pathology to help. Specialists were puzzled, people were accused of being malingerers and little could be done to ease or control the symptoms. David, as he struggled with his own health, became the unwitting expert in the field of chronic fatigue, and with a combination of rest, nutrition and careful exercise, he gradually climbed out of it. Some people never do.

In the late eighties David's personal life too underwent a dramatic change. After seventeen years of marriage David and Pamela went their separate ways. They have remained friends ever since and share family celebrations when the occasion arises. Shortly after, David and I married setting up home in Gunnedah with a blended family of his four children and my one son, Christian on a week about basis. The town locals accepted this new setup in the fullness of time, and ten productive years were spent in the town before a move was made.

In the early nineties David decided to reassess his aircraft fleet. With the Bonanza partnership dissolved he was reduced to the little Piper Warrior for his regular flying and of course the sale of the one third share of the Bonanza was burning a hole in his pocket. There was an obvious solution; sell the Warrior and with the proceeds plus the Bonanza share money he could upgrade to a better aircraft with minimal outlay from consolidated revenue. The hunt began. Soon he decided on a French aircraft, a Trinidad. This sleek aeroplane had some definite street cred, or should that be "sky-cred". It was sporty with a cruising speed of 150 knots and a six and a half hour fuel endurance. One of its first flights was a trip to Tasmania. How strange to take off from Gunnedah and five hours later to be climbing out of the aircraft in Launceston. No fuel stop, but that means no comfort stops either! The Trinidad had five comfortable seats and two "gull-wing" doors that allowed the pilot easy access instead of clambering into the left hand seat from the right door, as is the case in most aircraft. Visibility was excellent - all in all a most comfortable aircraft to fly in and a great aircraft to fly too!

Like anything which has had a previous owner, the Trinidad had its technical problems. The first eight months of ownership were spent arranging repairs with the local aviation engineer in Tamworth. Some were minor and some not so. They were trying months with its proud owner tearing his hair out wondering what else would go wrong and beginning to regret his decision. One evening a dinner outing to Tamworth was arranged. It was winter and dark by the time the landing approach to Tamworth airport was made. Neither pilot nor co-pilot was happy to see only two green lights showing on the undercarriage switch. Thus started a dialogue with the control tower, emergency vehicles were summoned, and the engineer was called to check the wheels as a low level flypast was made. Like something out of a war movie the aircraft flew at low altitude above the runway while the engineer shone a huge searchlight at the aircraft to see if the wheels were locked or not. Good news, the wheels looked fine, but by the time the aircraft came in to make the landing, the Oxley Highway which runs parallel to the airstrip was lined with numbers of cars waiting to see the excitement to come. Ambulances, fire engines and of course the press were all awaiting the arrival as a safe touchdown was made and the aircraft taxied to a halt.

The TV reporters appeared with cameras and microphones and after a brief interview the reporter asked if the dinner was still on.

"We're not hungry," was David's reply. The engineer kindly flew us back to Gunnedah and the Trinidad was left behind to have its undercarriage checked. The Italian restaurant was never visited!

A similar incident happened again but this time in daylight at Archerfield airport in Brisbane. It was Michael's 21st birthday and he was waiting at the airport and hence watching the drama that was about to unfold. As before, there were only two greens showing but this time on a fly-by it appeared that the two wing wheels were locked, but the nose wheel was down but not at the right angle and definitely not locked. Again, the emergency vehicles were summoned and again this drew the gawkers to accumulate along the fences. Michael spoke to the TV reporter and filled him in with some details of the reason for the trip and the experience of the pilot.

There was no choice but to come in and give it a go, probably ending up with a damaged aeroplane sliding along the tarmac but hopefully no damaged people. The landing was perfect. The cool head at the controls decided to come in at a higher than usual angle and land first on the two good wheels and then on the questionable nose wheel. The force of the thump on the main wheels caused the nose wheel to jolt forward and lock in place. The Trinidad ran true and taxied normally to the hardstand. Michael was more than delighted to still have a father for his birthday bash although the father was slightly pale and certainly didn't like being described as a "sixty-year-old pilot" on the Brisbane news. David had just turned fifty-nine but had been described as "nearly sixty" by his younger son to the reporter!

Reluctant undercarriage

2000

"Flying is hours of boredom punctuated by moments of stark terror."

We are starting to relax a little as I call over the Logan Motorway inbound to Archerfield Airport, Brisbane. It has been a pleasant three-hour flight from Bankstown with only half an hour of solid instrument flying and very little turbulence.

The forecast thunderstorms are still a few hours away. The green airfield lies before us and we are thinking of a cappuccino already. In only two minutes we will be shutting down. We have our joining instructions and the Trinidad is slowing on base leg.

I select the gear. My wife, who has experienced an undercarriage problem with me seven years before is always interested in the number of green lights on the panel, and almost as quickly as I realise there's a problem, she comments, "The wheels aren't down."

After consulting the flight manual, I reselect the lever up and down. Nothing.

"Lima Quebec Charlie cleared to land 28 left."

"Ah, tower, we have a problem with the gear. I'll stay at 1500 feet and circle left if I may."

I pull the circuit breaker, slow the aeroplane and release the emergency extension. Thump, thump. My smile is shortlived as I see both mains are locked but no nose green. I pitch the aeroplane a couple of times but there is no change. My wife is not impressed.

"May I do a fly-by at 500 feet?"

The aeroplane circles past the tower. The controller tells me that the nose leg is down but does not look forward in the over centre position.

I climb back up so that a light twin in the circuit can formate on us. He agrees with the tower. My son, waiting for us to land has been watching the proceedings from below. As a commercial pilot he is used to the position of the undercarriage and the tower allows him to talk to me as we circle endlessly over the now closed aerodrome. He concurs with the others. The nose wheel will collapse on landing.

The tower asks us to hold while the emergency services are summoned. Meanwhile I feel sorry for the various aeroplanes held outside the zone. I offer to land on the grass to avoid blocking the runway, but the recent rain has closed all but the sealed areas. The two remaining minutes of the flight have now turned into seventy-five. Below us, two ambulances, a fire engine and three police cars take up position beside the runway and I am aware of people lining the fence and standing on the apron ready for the show.

How quickly the flight has changed from routine to a looming disaster. I dare not think of the cost to come or the downtime for my beautiful French aeroplane. Needless to say, the possibility of injury to ourselves is not to be ignored either. Thoughts of a coffee are long forgotten.

As the aeroplane turns on to downwind my wife sits bravely beside me, more worried because I have had to brief her on the emergency exit procedures.

Short final. I come in as slowly as I dare. At twenty feet the engine is shut down and the propeller slows to a halt. Holding the nose high, I thump the mains on to the runway, harking back to taildragger days.

It is enough of a jar to knock the offending leg into a locked position. The third green light appears. We run true. I can hardly believe it. Thanking the tower for their help, my wife and I wave to the police and emergency vehicles as we taxi normally to the apron.

All at once, with normality restored, that cappuccino returns to our thoughts. That night we see ourselves on the national news and the real upset of the day occurs as they start the segment, "A sixty-year-old pilot ..." it begins. Hang on, I cry, I'm only fifty-nine!

Not content with having the beautiful Trinidad, in Dec 1995 Santa brought David a cute little Cessna 150 NWP as a Christmas present. Now what would David want with a simple little two-seater like that? Apart from being a fun little aircraft to fly as a leisure activity on weekends or after work, NWP became the aircraft that Michael and Anthony would use for their training. Since infancy the boys had been keen aviators. Propped on cushions in the co-pilot's seat, they would spend hours accompanying their father and while not being actively taught, absorbed aviation skills by observation and doing. Now it was time to start the real thing.

A family friend, Lyn Butler, started their ab initio training. Lyn came to the task with an impressive aviation pedigree. Her father was Jack Clancy, an early aviator in the 1930s. He and his brother Allan designed and built a tiny aircraft called the Clancy Skybaby in 1933. It is considered a prototype of modern aviation and showcased how quickly advancements were made in aircraft design. It was, after all, not long since the Wright Brothers began it all in 1903. Jack kept a Skybaby on his property outside Gunnedah. David had the thrill of flying it one beautiful afternoon. It was even older than the Tiger Moth and Chipmunk he had trained on! An important part of Australia's aviation history, the original Skybaby has now been retired to the Powerhouse Museum in Sydney.

Both boys of course loved their flying and were keen students if a little tardy some mornings if there had been a night out before the lesson! A great day was Michael's first solo cross-country which was Gunnedah-Mullaley-Gunnedah, an enormous distance of 38 kms from Gunnedah. As he climbed out of the Cessna after returning safely, he remarked in usual offhand teenage tones, "That was a bit daunting!" This man now pilots luxury corporate jets and thinks nothing of jetting off to anywhere in the world at a moment's notice. A far cry from nervously heading to Mullaley!

The Cessna 150 proved a reliable little workhorse. Apart from providing a safe trainer for the boys, it was a fun machine for pure recreation. After the boys had no further need for it the Cessna was sold to the Gunnedah Aero Club where it worked for years as a trainer and also a cheap aircraft for local pilots to hire. Sadly, it is no longer with us. Some years ago it was flown to Inverell for some major maintenance. Prior to the work being done, NWP waited quietly outside the hangar. That afternoon a huge summer storm blew up. The little Cessna suffered catastrophic damage and was written off. On the positive side, the Aero Club came out of this situation rather well. Just imagine if the storm had destroyed it after the maintenance had been done! You can be lucky sometimes.

While David was busy with all his extra-curricular activities, his main duty was to his many patients that loyally and patiently waited to see him in the surgery each day. The life of a rural GP is not an easy one. Gunnedah in the nineties was slowly going the way of so many country towns and becoming under-doctored. David's practice was now reduced to two. The workload, of course, did not diminish in any way. David worked five days a week with a brief afternoon off on Wednesday. They were busy days in the surgery. Outside the surgery, there was work to do as well. Hospital in-patients required visiting in the morning before heading to the surgery and the doctor may well have to deal with a new admission overnight as well as the existing in-patients. No wonder the doctor would sometimes be late to the surgery and hence behind with appointments all day. This was a strain on both patients and doctor and also on the surgery staff who were caught in the middle trying to keep everyone happy.

One afternoon a week, after work David would visit the local nursing home and do a routine check on his patients. This was generally fairly straightforward medicine managing the elderly, balancing their medication and tending to any change in their condition.

Leaving the surgery at the end of a long day of consultations did not necessarily mean being off duty. Gunnedah was a town that had no resident doctors on staff at the hospital. All doctoring was done by the doctors in general practice. At 6.00pm a doctor was rostered on call for the night. This might mean being called either by a patient directly or by the hospital at any hour to attend a patient who had presented at Accident and Emergency. Sometimes the situation could be dealt with over the phone via the RN on duty at the hospital. Nevertheless, this meant being woken up from a deep sleep, roused to full doctor cognitive ability while advice or treatment was relayed over the phone before attempting, often unsuccessfully, to fall asleep again. As the shortage of doctors became more problematic, the A and E department would become almost a default doctor's surgery and an A and E visit would often be part of the drive home after surgery had finished for the day. Rather than attempt to get an appointment it was easier to simply turn up at Emergency knowing that a doctor would come, it was simply a matter of waiting.

After hours calls were often a nightmare, particularly the annoying, trivial ones. It was common to get a call at 10.00pm concerning a crying baby who would not settle.

> Might it have an ear infection?
>
> Has any pain relief been administered?
>
> No.
>
> Do you have any in the house?
>
> No.

It was an exhausting treadmill and after a night on call, surgery was still waiting for the doctor next morning.

Babies, of course, had their own special sense of timing. A mother would present to the hospital in labour, the doctor would be advised of her admission and given details as to the progress of the labour. If this happened at night, it was difficult to sleep soundly knowing that a further call would come to summon the doctor to the delivery. A Caesarean of course was an additional ordeal to face. David loved his obstetrics and although most deliveries go smoothly and have a joyful outcome this is not always the case. Intervention is sometimes required to enable a baby to be delivered safely. An emergency Caesarean could not wait for the next morning when the sun had risen. Imagine operating in a critical situation at 2.00 am, saving mother and baby, then returning home full of adrenalin only to head back to work a few hours later!

A person working at this high level obviously needs regular time off work. Herein lay another problem. It was well-nigh impossible to obtain a locum willing to come to Gunnedah. Doctors who worked as locums were far more likely to accept a position for a few weeks or longer at a more congenial location, say a coastal town. Hot, dusty Gunnedah was not a preferred location. A doctor's absence for an extended break of a few weeks meant that the other doctors in the town had to take over this extra load. Each doctor in town was busy enough without the added burden of a few extra patients because their regular doctor was in Europe on a holiday. It was a difficult situation and made taking time off for a well-earned break a problem for all concerned.

In the 1990s David's practice consisted of himself and Dr Arthur Lundie. Because of his age, Arthur worked only a few hours each morning. He was, however, deeply loved by his faithful patients. Arthur was the epitome of the old-school family doctor that, in this day and age of medicine seems increasingly difficult to find. Arthur's ability to still practice medicine depended on David's presence in the practice. David became his overseer and allowed Arthur to keep doing what he loved.

By this time David was getting itchy feet. The long hours, hospital in-patients, after hours on-call and the inability to obtain locum relief made moving elsewhere look extremely attractive. Arriving in Gunnedah in 1974 he had had no intention of still being in residence twenty-five years later. Life intervenes and it is not easy to uproot children and cart them off to another town. Now it was dear old Arthur who was holding him back. While Arthur was well and working his mornings, David would stay in Gunnedah.

An escape plan was nevertheless being hatched. The Port Macquarie bolt hole at Flynns Beach was now looking like a more permanent proposition when the time was right. David even went so far as to look at practices in this growing seaside town and found two to his liking that were looking for an experienced family GP.

In late 1998 Arthur fell ill and after a brief illness he died peacefully in Gunnedah Hospital. After a life of service and devotion to others he was now at peace. David delivered one of the eulogies to this great man at his funeral. Later that same night the decision was made. After a phone call to the doctor in charge of the Lighthouse Beach Medical Centre, the plans were put in place. A move to Port Macquarie was happening!

Port Macquarie

1999 to present

David was no stranger to Port Macquarie having holidayed there in the past. For the last four years he had enjoyed weekend escapes from the searing heat and dryness of Gunnedah for Port Macquarie's milder coastal climate. He was however a stranger to the new practice at Lighthouse Beach. He had spent twenty-five years, the bulk of his adult working life, in Gunnedah. Every patient was now new, with no family history or shared experiences to make consultations and diagnoses easier and more amenable. It would be a challenge.

But, to make the task easier, there would be no hospital patients, no weekend surgery, no nursing home patients and minimal after hours on call. Working conditions would be a lot less stressful.

David began working at the Lighthouse Beach Medical Centre on 25th January 1999, turning up on day one with only a few patients to see and all of them completely unknown. He survived this strange day and recovered by enjoying a Public Holiday on the 26th. The first week was almost over!

It did not take much time until David's patient load grew. Return visits helped with filling in the background story of each patient. It was slow work. Each new patient meant taking a full medical history and this takes time. He did however have quite a few familiar faces as many Gunnedah people continued to see David professionally. They were more than happy to travel the long, winding road over the hill to Port Macquarie. Although the numbers of Gunnedah patients have dropped off there is a core of regulars who still visit after twenty years. That's loyalty, or an indication of the medical situation in our inland country towns.

David's doctoring in Port Macquarie was quite different to what he was used to in Gunnedah. Port Macquarie was a much bigger city with a staffed Base Hospital. David now had no need to visit and be responsible for any patients admitted to hospital. Similarly, he no longer did surgery. He missed the challenge and stimulation this provided. He does continue to do skin work and enjoys this surgical side to his work. The other interesting work that he enjoys is looking after pilots as a DAME (Designated Aircrew Medical Examiner). The regular medicals that pilots require is the cause of much despair and headshaking among the receptionist staff. The raucous laughter and overlong consultations suggest that flying and not medical issues seems to be the topic of conversation! How lovely to combine the two.

Combining the two – medicine and flying - also happened during the working week. In Gunnedah, David had established the clinic at Premer once a week to assist people living in a small rural community. He was keen to continue this on the Mid-North Coast and settled on the small town of South West Rocks about one hour north of Port Macquarie. This growing little town was serviced by two medical practices but was short on doctors. David decided to visit the town for two mornings a week. Luckily there is an airstrip on the edge of town on a property that raises Santa Gertrudis cattle. Rex, the owner, is a retired pharmacist, although this is hard to believe. A wiry nuggetty man, Rex is in his element on his property. His favourite dress code is shorts, shirt and generally bare feet. As a pilot of long standing, Rex is invaluable in maintaining the strip in good condition and attempting (mostly successfully) to keep the cattle off it. In rainy times his test of the strip's ability to take the weight of the Bonanza was to stand on the runway in his bare feet. If the water oozed up between his toes it was not a flying day and driving to South West Rocks was the unhappy result. In flood times the strip has been inundated not just from the amount of rain but also with the river overflowing on to the strip, particularly at high tide.

Flying to the Rocks certainly has its challenges. The cattle occasionally break through the fence and wander into the path of the aircraft. This also has the spinoff result of manure left behind ready to connect with the aircraft wheels on landing or take-off. This is a messy, smelly and difficult to remove splatter especially if David is racing back to attend afternoon surgery at Lighthouse. Transport to the surgery does not end with landing on Rex's airstrip. There is the slight issue of travelling from there into the town, a distance of about five kilometres. What better solution to the problem than a small 110cc Honda motor scooter. On a good day, there is nothing better than heading off to work in your beloved aeroplane, landing on a grass airstrip and then tootling into town on a scooter.

The interesting thing to note is that door-to-door, from home to surgery, it is only five minutes longer by car! Now why would you bother?

Why do you think?

South West Rocks Doctor

2007

"What's that smell, Doctor?"

It is one of my South West Rocks fly-in clinic days. These are days I look forward to, flying to work despite the occasional hassle. All night there has been gentle rain pattering on the tiles and the day seems gloomy as I look out at the grey sea and low cloud hanging above it.

Although I can return to Port Macquarie on instruments if necessary, I must fly "contact" outbound as the airstrip at the Rocks is a modified cow pasture with a one thousand foot hill abutting the circuit area.

Ten minutes before I leave the house, I ring Rex, the octogenarian owner of the property, a long time pilot and aircraft owner. By this time he has walked along his strip with his bare feet, deciding by the amount his toes sink into the turf that the ground can take my Bonanza aircraft today, albeit with care.

He tells me to keep in the centre, but stay out of the cow track if I can, or I will get mud on the aeroplane. Apparently there is a lot of cloud around, he cannot see the mountain nearby and there is some fog over the strip. The cows are off the grass but he admits there may be some dung. Rex finally advises me to use the "river approach".

As this is marginal, I throw my approach plates and maps in the Bonanza and regret having washed it the day before. It stands outside the hangar gleaming in the damp morning as I pre-flight for the short leg to work. The airport weather states broken cloud at 700 feet and visibility of eight kilometres, so once airborne I turn to the coast to follow the shoreline northbound. It is days like this that I recall why I went to live in Mount Isa many years ago where a cloud was a novelty.

At 500 feet I cruise along keeping the coastline on the left and knowing that there is only the sea with its grey breakers and breaching whales to my right.

Crescent Head passes in the gloom and the southeast wind creates constant turbulence as I hand fly the aircraft. Looking inland it seems the cloud base is lower and I can see why Rex has suggested the "river approach" where one circles the town and arrives from the north. I make a radio call inbound but the only traffic is the cows in the adjoining paddock and I hope that none of them decides to hop the fence and need chasing off.

I turn in from the bay along the river putting down the wheels and first flap and reducing the power. Planning ahead for an upgrade to instrument flying I have my plan ready on my kneeboard and the Brisbane Centre frequency selected on my second radio. I know exactly what heading to take up so that I will climb away from the hill to the east. The river bends and I see the wet strip. Wisps of fog hang nearby. Full flap. Power back. I am confident of Rex's appraisal of the ground. Being a pilot, he knows exactly what my heavy-footed aircraft needs to set down upon. What he does not know as I flare is that there is a large soft cowpat before me. There is a silent splat as the nose wheel throws the green substance on the underside of my beautiful clean aircraft and over the wings and tail.

An appropriate expletive is muttered into the silent intercom.

Rex is there with his bare feet to welcome me and help me pull my motor scooter out of his hangar, and I putt into town to heal the sick and stamp out disease, glad that I have plastic pants and leather jacket to keep me dry. This is the dangerous part of the operation!

Three hours later I am back at the Bonanza preflighting in the drizzle. Port Macquarie is in low cloud and requires Tamworth as an alternate. What will the afternoon patients say if the doctor is over the ranges! I try not to think about that.

I file my flight plan on my mobile and climb into the gloom to intercept the approach on to runway 21 back home. It amazes me as I gaze out at the wings in the grey cocoon that the cow dung remains stuck to the aeroplane. What fantastic adhesive properties this substance has that neither 170 knots nor heavy rain dislodges it!

Bouncing around in the turbulence and close to minima I break out and land at my home airport. Lunchtime is spent under the aeroplane with a hose and an umbrella washing off this revolting green excrement. As I walk into the surgery at Port Macquarie for my afternoon's work, I am somewhat tired by the morning's activities and I think I can detect the faint aroma of cow dung on my shoes.

Shortly after arriving in Port Macquarie, David decided to broaden his flying experience. He had admired the beautiful Cessna 172 seaplane taking off on the Hastings River and climbing up in the blue sky to complete a scenic for fortunate tourists. Twenty minutes later it would reappear, touch down like a giant pelican and taxi slowly back to the jetty to await its next passengers.

This looks like a bit of fun, thought David. Not being one to let the seaweed grow under his feet, David quickly made the acquaintance of the owner and arranged to do his seaplane endorsement.

This involved firstly attaining a boat licence. The seaplane operates as a boat on the water, then an aircraft once it has taken off. Red and green lights, power and sail craft, dodging dolphins, it was a whole new world of navigation and rules.

Once legally able to begin instruction David was amazed at just how different it was to bounce along a water runway until enough speed allows the aircraft to lift from its floats and finally into the air. The thrill of the water splashing over and the different noises produced by the floats and the water made the whole experience a totally new, exciting type of flying.

Watch out for the Pelicans

1999

When a pilot imagines he has no more to learn and nothing to occupy his mind, he has reached only the limit of his own ability to learn and be interested.

P G Taylor

I lined up the white Cessna into the biting turbulence, its little wings rocking. As it came to the take-off position, I opened the throttle.

But today was to be a different experience. For 41 years and 9500 flying hours I have always had the ground beneath me on take-off. Admittedly it has not always been the perfect surface, what with grassy and wet country airstrips, not to mention cow dung and wheat stubble!

The power came on and I held the stick right back. As the nose rose up to block my view, the aircraft shuddered and spray streamed from the floats. I eased the back pressure and the aeroplane rose on to the step, planing across the wind risen wavelets. In a few seconds the wings took the weight and the speedboat sensation ceased. We were airborne and climbing and the feel of the aircraft was more familiar. In fact, I was quite surprised at how similar the float plane handled in the air. Stalls and steep turns felt just like all the other Cessna singles I had known, the only feature of note was the need to use rudder so much – almost more than the Austers and Tiger Moths I had flown many years ago.

The excitement of the take-off was still in my mind as we circled around a small saltwater lake ten miles south of my home base in Port Macquarie, looking for wind lanes and sand bars, logs and wind surfers.

My instructor, Bill Lane, who runs Saint Air, looked like a typical flight instructor but the four gold bars on his shirt contrasted with the shorts and bare feet below. With 29000 flying hours and 12000 in sea planes alone, he must be one of the most experienced in Australia for this type of flying.

Happy that the lake was suitable for alighting, I lined up the smoothest patch of water and descended with power. The nose lifted, much like a taildragger, and as I eased off the power the floats bit into the water. There was some slight shuddering and then we were floating at rest on the lake. I could not hide my enthusiasm and grinned from ear to ear. After taxiing up and down wind for a while, it was time for "circuits". Around and around we went, taking off, curving around the rugged landscape, and touching or sometimes plonking on to the lake. I was thrilled with this totally new experience. My mind leapt forward to the anticipation of flying to rivers and other lakes, of nosing up to sandy shores away from the usual hassles and traffic of the busy Port Macquarie airport.

It was time to return to the Hastings River and home base, and as I levelled off at 1000 feet, I became aware of my muscles. The exertion of using large inputs into the rudder and control column for two hours of training had given me a much greater workout than a land craft, and I felt very virtuous.

On final for our last landing, I had to watch for marker buoys, boats and ferries. Once down we taxied to the ramp, manoeuvring very slowly past wharves, pleasure craft and pelicans.

As I wrote up my logbook that night, I was very pleased to write, "C172 floatplane," a seemingly incongruous entry under the previous day's, "IFR renewal" flight.

Aviation has so many different aspects to enrich the experience. It started for me with open cockpits in the fifties and progressed through the Vampire jet, twins and ultralights, to IFR and night flying. I have glided and parachuted and flown the Pacific, and I guess I felt that there were few surprises in aviation. Eight engine failures and accidental penetration of thunderstorm and icing conditions have added to tales I could tell, but the surprise of flying from the water caught me unawares. What a thrill it is. I can recommend this type of flying for opening up a whole new world of aviation.

In 2000 David was invited to become a founding member of the Aviation Safety Forum. This group, meeting every three months for a day, was to work in an advisory capacity to CASA, the main aviation regulatory body. David was appointed by The Right Honourable John Anderson, Gunnedah's local Federal member and at the time the Minister for Aviation. David would be representing the pilots in the general aviation sector. There were fifteen members representing both the commercial and general side of aviation. Fired with enthusiasm and anxious to promote general aviation, he became tired of the slowness of the bureaucratic process. After appearing to make progress on an issue it became frustrating to discover some months later that nothing had been done. Other pressing issues had ousted the problem that David was attempting to solve. This mentality did not sit well with David's ability to carry through a task to completion as soon as possible. Procrastination and dilly-dallying are not in his vocabulary. In 2005 he resigned. It was an eye-opening experience and certainly shed light on the issues that he still faces today through his work as a DAME (Designated Aircrew Medical Examiner).

In 2000, one beautiful Anzac Day holiday, David and an old friend from Gunnedah, Mike Barnier, were sitting enjoying a coffee overlooking the green valleys inland from Port Macquarie. One of them (neither will admit which one) suggested it would be a great idea to start a small air charter business. Out came a piece of paper and before you could blink a plan was in place. A hangar was available, an aircraft or two could be sourced, a pilot was available and plenty more could be hired. There are always young pilots eager for a job. At this time young Michael Cooke was living in Port Macquarie. Michael had started his flying training in 1996 in Gunnedah obtaining his Commercial Licence and Instrument rating in 1998. He decided to move from Brisbane in 2000 to undertake his Instructor rating in Port Macquarie. From there he quickly became employed as an instructor with a local flying school. Michael was set on an aviation career. What a delight to be part of this new venture!

Coastwings was established in 2001, up and running and ready for business. Setting up a charter company is no mean feat. The regulations set by CASA are formidable but finally an AOC (Air Operator's Certificate) was obtained allowing the company to undertake commercial work. Now what are the essentials a charter company needs? The two obvious requirements are aircraft and pilots qualified to fly them! A ready-made and very keen pilot, Michael Cooke, was already in residence but acquiring aircraft is a different proposition. Aircraft are hugely expensive and would be an enormous capital outlay for a startup business. The common practice is to cross hire an aircraft from an owner and pay an hourly rate for when the aircraft is being used. The running costs, apart from the fuel, are met by the owner.

November 2001 saw David, Michael and Mike Barnier heading in the Trinidad to Moorabbin Airport in Melbourne. Waiting to meet them was the owner of a Cessna 340. This aircraft is a pressurised light two engine passenger aircraft with seating for five passengers. As it is pressurised it is generally able to fly above the weather making for a more comfortable passenger experience. It was an excellent aircraft for charter work and not too expensive to operate. Michael needed to be checked out in it and after a couple of circuits he was ready to head back to Port Macquarie while David and Mike Barnier returned in the Trinidad.

Of course they flew in tandem and communicated on the radio on the "chatter" frequency that does not interfere with the airways communications. After some time, Michael had reached a higher altitude than the unpressurised Trinidad. David realised Michael's communications were a little slow and drawly. He suspected (correctly) that there was either a problem with the pressurisation or Michael had inadvertently forgotten to switch it on. This was a new luxury for him. Lack of oxygen induces a sense of euphoria, nothing worries you, everything is just wonderful.

"Descend Michael," says David now in doctor mode, "you're hypoxic."

"Juust fine, Dad, all's goood," slurs Michael's reply.

"It's not, descend now, right now before you black out."

Whether it was Dad being Dad or Michael still retaining a modicum of sense, he did descend, saving himself from a sticky situation before it became worse.

Coastwings was based in one of the local hangars at Port Macquarie Airport. Business slowly started to build up. They obtained some regular contracts with local companies including collecting and delivering spare parts for the then Impulse Airlines. This usually meant a night flight to collect an aircraft part from Williamtown to deliver to another airport where the unserviceable aircraft was grounded. Airlines don't make money with an aircraft stuck on the ground, hence the company is willing to pay to ensure it's back in the air as soon as possible.

Now if this situation occurred on a Friday or Saturday night a slight but not insurmountable problem arose. Most young men are keen to socialise at the weekend. Michael and the other young pilot Simon were no different. It was not unusual for the phone to ring at perhaps 10.00pm or even later and a slightly slurred voice would ask Dad if he was able to do a flight to Brisbane or Mackay or even Hobart to collect or drop off a part for Impulse.

Of course he would! After a busy day at the surgery David would drag himself out of bed, do a flight plan and without even thinking about the hideous weather that may confront him, he would head out in the dark to begin his second job. Good old Dad to the rescue again!

A regular passenger was a local politician whose home town was not serviced by a regular passenger air service. It was often the task of Coastwings to fly him to and from Canberra. A Coastwings VIP!

On one flight from Sydney he was not feeling well and was extremely happy that the pilot/co-pilot was not only able to fly the aircraft but also to dispense medical advice and some medication to fix the problem. With Qantas and other airlines you take a chance that there might be a doctor on board should you require medical assistance. One up to Coastwings!

Other regular contracts were obtained involving transfers of ambulant patients. who did not require the services provided by the Air Ambulance. Coastwings provided a cost-effective way to get them to or from a medical appointment. Another regular run was flying doctors and nurses to Lismore to service the Breastscreen program.

In 2002 David decided that a Tiger Moth would significantly boost the company's profile. Apart from his own passion for these legendary aircraft, they are much loved by the general population who like nothing better than seeing these old biplanes bring back a taste of yesteryear. David relished spending Saturdays or odd afternoons doing joy flights around the local area. A voucher for a thirty-minute flight was a popular gift, particularly for a significant birthday. The word joy flight was true to its name judging by the delighted grins and beaming smiles from the happy passengers. It was a special part of the business and did not have the time constraints and weather issues that other charter flights could encounter. If the weather, especially the wind was too strong (remember the leaf!) a scenic flight could be simply rescheduled to a more equable weather pattern.

Things were going well, so it was decided to branch into maintenance with the formation of Avcair, and flying training under the title Aviation Academy. Students began to arrive and Michael, a qualified Instructor, took on this task as well as charter flying as needed. Another instructor was sourced to provide a backup. An aircraft was required of course and having parted with the little Cessna 150 on leaving Gunnedah, that one was not available. Fortunately, Lyn Butler, the boys' first instructor, and her husband Athol, were selling their much-loved Cessna 150. It was the ideal aircraft for the task. Its history was known and trusted and it proved to be an ideal and reliable aircraft for trainee pilots. Students were of all ages and it is surprising how many older people wish to fulfill a life-long dream to learn to fly. It is not always important for them to obtain a private licence. Sometimes it is enough to just be at the controls with the security of an instructor in the other seat. The sensation and thrill of flight is sufficient for them. Others may aspire to going solo, to be totally in control and responsible for all decisions and actions. Others may take their training further doing the theory and flight tests to gain a private pilot's licence. Everyone is different with different needs and desires. Coastwings helped a variety of people enjoy the dream of piloting an aircraft to whatever level they wished.

Coastwings was an interesting, challenging undertaking. Any aircraft business is tricky to run and extremely difficult to run profitably. Staffing issues, workloads and maintenance are all problematic areas. David, especially, did not enjoy the organisational and business side of it. His busy medical practice also meant he did not have the time needed to attend to the business. It finally all got too much. Michael was ready to move on to advance his career. He wanted to gain hours in multi-engine and turboprop aircraft. Coastwings could supply neither of those. In 2005 the business was wound up after an interesting, certainly challenging few years. It was all invaluable experience and certainly there were no regrets. The Tiger Moth was moved to Queensland where it was ultimately sold.

Michael certainly went ahead with his flying after his return to Brisbane. He gained valuable multi-engine experience flying out of Toowoomba to the oil and gas fields along the southern part of Queensland and out as far as Moomba in South Australia. Another way to quickly build up flying hours was to undertake ferry flying, bringing single engine aircraft across the Pacific from the USA to their new home in Australia. Imagine a tiny four or six seater aircraft forging its way across the Pacific Ocean at a maximum of 10,000 feet altitude. Limited fuelling spots along the way mean that the aircraft is packed to the gunnels with fuel tanks placed inside the fuselage. The pilot transfers fuel from these tanks to the aircraft's own tanks. This enables the aircraft to fly the long distance from the Californian coast to the first fuel stop in Hawaii. All in all, it was a heartstopping way to earn money and gain flying hours.

Michael remained keen to start and manage his own business. In 2010 he resurrected the name Avcair, the maintenance side of the Coastwings business, and formed a company which has developed, with the help of his brother, Anthony, into one of the best charter management businesses in Australia. Today it does mainly executive charter and medical evacuation flights. Michael's company, Avcair, now operates ten aircraft including Lear jets and Citation jets and has twenty-five pilots on its staff. What a difference to his great grandfather, Lionel Cooke's flying experience of a Bristol Boxkite in 1915! He would be very proud of his great grandsons – their father certainly is!

In 2023, David's daughter, Amelia, joined the company and is working to keep Avcair in a healthy financial position.

Since leaving Gunnedah, David had not done any more overseas flying. That was about to change. With two sons undertaking ferry flying, the temptation to accompany them was too great to resist.

The first was relatively simple, involving a mere hop across the Tasman from New Zealand to Port Macquarie. Fortunately this aircraft was a substantial Piper Chieftain, an aircraft used extensively for commuter flying and charter work. This flight worked well so of course he was eager to do a few more!

Back in Port Macquarie and with a willing ferry pilot on hand, David decided it was time to replace the Trinidad with something a bit newer. A beautiful Bonanza A36 Jaguar was located in the USA. After the inevitable reports, flight and engineering checks, plus haggling of course, the aircraft was purchased. Michael was given the task of ferrying out his father's precious new baby. Both arrived in one piece and the Bonanza since then has been a reliable and comfortable aircraft to fly in.

Just to make sure they knew how clever Michael had been, David and Anthony ferried another Bonanza across the Pacific about two years later. This flight was to have been a tandem flight with Michael ferrying another aircraft at the same time. This plan fell to pieces when Michael's aeroplane was experiencing problems hence not ready to undertake the flight. It was suggested that Anthony and his father go ahead anyway, despite Anthony's relative inexperience in ferry flying. Michael was the expert. Was Anthony up for the challenge? With reservations, yes, and of course Dad would be there with his years of experience to hold his hand.

Ferry flying presents many problems. Despite having extra fuel tanks on board, it is crucial to calculate if there is enough fuel to reach the next airport where fuel is available. There are headwinds which hopefully will turn into tailwinds by the vital point-of-no-return. If there is not sufficient fuel by this time then the pilot has no option but to turn around and head back to the starting point. It's a carefully calculated mathematical procedure.

This trip was relatively straightforward apart from Anthony suffering from a severe stomach upset during the stopover in Hawaii. Just as well the co-pilot was a doctor!

You would think that flying in a small aircraft for thirteen hours straight over the ocean would be tedious. Far from it! There are instruments to watch with hawk eyes lest one of them should indicate a flicker of an impending problem. There are radio calls to make to ensure contact with the outside world. Sometimes a broadcast would be made over the radio by a wide-bodied jet carrying hundreds of happy tourists to or from Hawaii or the West Coast of America. This little diversion could result in a brief exchange between the two crews on the "chatter frequency" where pilots can talk without being on the official radio channels. The flight crew of the Boeing 747 were amazed that down below them at 6000 feet altitude two brave men were squashed in a narrow cockpit enjoying their lunch of muesli bars and dried fruit. Up in the lofty realm of flight levels the Qantas crew were enjoying a fish or chicken meal with the freedom to walk around and stretch their legs at regular intervals.

It comes as no surprise that on landing back in Australia after this marathon flight, both pairs of legs are reluctant to work after such a long period of inactivity. It takes a little while for land legs to get back in working mode.

Pacific Ferry Flight

2007

"Most people tiptoe their way through life, hoping to make it safely to death."

Earl Nightingale

I am standing at the counter in an FBO in the small town of Hollister, California, having just completed tanking up a new single engine aeroplane to be delivered to Australia. Next to me is a retired eighty-five-year-old test pilot who flew such exciting aircraft as the Northrup Flying Wing and the X-4 transonic fighter. He is passing the time of day with me as my son Anthony pays the operator for services and fuel we have received.

"So, your son is the ferry pilot for this aircraft? Does it require two pilots?"

"No," I reply.

There is a pause.

"Then why are you going with him?"

Why indeed?

What could possibly induce a sixty-five-year-old doctor, albeit one with 11000 flying hours to leave his normal environment and fly the Pacific Ocean in a light aircraft?

"It is there to be done and I am looking forward to the challenge," I reply, hopefully disguising the apprehension and unease I am feeling. He looks sideways at me with a puzzled frown.

The following morning, we taxi from the parking area with our huge load of ferry fuel, muesli bars, wide neck bottles and Mae Wests.

It is fortunately VFR conditions, and the briefing officers have given us a forecast of five knots average tailwinds over the 2100 nautical mile flight to Hilo, Hawaii. We type in the route and the Garmin 1000 glass cockpit colourfully displays the first few waypoints. Our dinghy pushes my seat forward into an uncomfortable upright position as we ready ourselves for takeoff. This flight will be a far cry from the previous flight to the US in the Boeing 747 with the unbelievable facilities of economy class food, drink, entertainment, rest rooms, helpful flight attendants and most important of all, a deep sense of security. Luxury! I'll never complain again.

Prior to rolling, we are given an eighty mile dogleg up the coast due to military operations. No amount of arguing that we need to avoid this, will change their minds and we are off and climbing. Soon we are cruising at 6000 feet, an unbroken cloud layer hiding the empty ocean. The winds are on the nose, but we live in hope.

Anthony is flying the first leg, and he busies himself with the fuel flow and pumping from the ferry tank every half hour. With not a lot to do I muse over the previous day when, during a test flight, a transducer failed, and all the engine instruments went black on the glass cockpit display.

When we took to the sky to test the HF and ferry tank, we discovered that the fuel flow indication was not registering on the screen. This was of great concern and we hunted for any reason which may have been caused by the installations.

On the next trial flight, we discover that the engine indications all disappeared on take-off, only to return on the landing roll.

We could not transfer the readings to the second screen and the only backup was for flight instruments.

A desperate call to the manufacturer resulted in a hurried flight to North California where the engineers examined the systems. After hours of head scratching, they change the fuel flow transducer and all was well – we hoped!

When one is to fly for extreme range it certainly induces a modicum of insecurity. What if it failed again leaving us with no way to set power and lean for maximum range? Give me real instruments any day, even though it has only taken a couple of flying hours to master this new technology.

We try a higher level, but the headwinds are stronger.

"Where are the tailwinds?" I text on the satellite phone to my other son Mike, a veteran of ferry flying and still in the USA.

After six hours there is a rise in the ground speed and almost within minutes we are getting a healthy ten knots from behind. Anthony and I smile and celebrate with some bawdy songs written at university, a muesli bar or two and we reach for the wide neck bottles.

With thirty minutes to go we see the 10000 foot volcano behind Hilo appearing above the cloud deck.

Landing after thirteen hours in the air, we repair to a nearby hotel for some real food and some blissful rest.

Mike rings. "You two are not doing any more ferry flights without me. I can't stand the worry!"

"Well, now you know how I felt when you started this work," I reply.

At midnight I awake to the unmistakeable sound of vomiting. Anthony has suffered food poisoning and is running at both ends. He looks and feels ghastly and I doubt we will be able to proceed next day. Fortunately, I have brought the appropriate medications and by morning he is well enough to continue.

It is my leg and I lift the heavy aircraft from the Hilo strip and climb slowly around the south eastern end of the island past the smoking volcano.

We charge through the intertropic convergence zone, weaving easily between the 40000 foot storms.

Anthony is recovering slowly and after eight hours we land at Christmas Island, site of the early atomic tests. It is a rustic island, where it takes three hotel rooms before we find one with air conditioning that works. The people however are friendly and helpful and by the following morning Anthony is well enough to fly his leg to Pago Pago, another seven hours away.

This part of the ocean is devoid of shipping and for hours we gaze at the empty sea and wonder if anyone would find us here if disaster struck.

I continue to eyeball the instruments and fuel flow. We pump the ferry tank and call San Francisco on HF every half hour. There is always something to do and one is never bored. It is a practice to monitor the guard or emergency frequency 121.5 over the ocean and we call blindly to any aircraft in the area.

A great Aussie voice booms back.

"G'day, this is Qantas 4, can I help?"

"No mate, thanks, but it is good to hear a friendly voice."

American Samoa looms up ahead and we curve around the dramatic green hills and sparkling shoreline to land on a runway placarded for us to take care with the sea spray drifting across the strip.

The last day is to be our longest. We load extra fuel although we do track over Fiji and New Caledonia en route to Brisbane in case of adverse winds.

On the way to the airport half an hour before dawn, Anthony is obviously recovered as he devours a bacon and egg McMuffin for breakfast. The first light of the new day is etching the clouds as we take off and climb between early morning storms. We calculate our fuel reserves and decide we can make it through to Brisbane without a stop. Despite the fourteen hour trip it seems quicker because of the islands that dot the way.

Eventually we are past Tontouta and heading for Brisbane with ninety minutes fuel in reserve.

The last of the ferry tank fuel is pumped and Anthony climbs into the back to tidy up. In the clear afternoon light we see the welcome coast of Australia, the Glasshouse Mountains and Moreton Bay. It is a moment of great excitement. He has done a magnificent job in command of the flight. Despite only having 600 flying hours Anthony has shown great professionalism and skill and his confidence has helped me to overcome my own fears.

It is strange to park near two huge Boeings at the International Terminal. We are sprayed, clear customs and finally relax. A tremendous tiredness suddenly comes over us. We no longer have to consider power settings, leaning, weather, fuel and serviceability of the equipment. We do not even have to get up early the next day.

People do not really understand what it is like in a small aircraft on such a long flight. Forty-three hours over four days sitting half a metre from another person ready to deal with any emergency is an intensely binding experience, hard to explain to those who have not been there.

Two days later I was talking to a medical colleague who asked me what I had been doing lately.

"I flew the Pacific in a small aircraft last week," I replied. He looked a bit vague and changed the subject!

I am reminded of the American test pilot's comment five days ago.

"Why are you going along when you don't have to?"

I don't really know why. Sharing the flying with my son as we cross the Pacific Ocean is a most memorable event. There is apprehension and stress and insecurity and I am so glad I did.

And, yes, I would probably do it again!

David's two other long flights were with Michael. He had been contracted to fly a Piper Aerostar from South Africa to Australia, and after a quick phone call to David, "Want to come with me, Dad?" a co-pilot was organised. This was new territory for both of them and involved departing from Lanseria in South Africa and tracking up over Mozambique for the first refuelling spot in Dar-es-Salaam in Tanzania.

It was here that they had a wonderful experience with the Tanzanian refueller. This happy young man gladly took their money for the fuel and disappeared on his bicycle to "get change!" After a period of time the pilots decided they had seen the last of their change and began their departure procedure. They were about to close the aircraft door when a frantically pedaling young man appeared, his face shining with sweat. "You forgot your change," he shouted with beaming face. They departed Tanzania with happy memories.

The flight continued smoothly with stopovers in the Seychelles, then on to Sri Lanka. At the time Sri Lanka was undergoing civil disturbance. It was not an easy place to transit. The pilots were escorted under armed guard as they refuelled, exited the airport and also on their return. It was a slightly daunting experience. The final port of call before reaching Australia was Cocos Island. When the two intrepid aviators saw the coast of Australia in the distance, they both relaxed and enjoyed the banter of the Aussie voice on the radio as they approached Port Hedland, their entry point.

Rolla Cooke's grave, Yorkshire.

Site of Rolla's crash, Killerby Hall, Yorkshire.

David and uncle, Digby Cooke

With Michael on Cocos Island, Indian Ocean

Solo in Robinson 44 helicopter, 2018.

Looking brave departing California with Anthony in a Bonanza.

South West Rocks paddock on clinic day

Leaving Prestwick, Scotland with Michael.

Flying the Spitfire, New Zealand, 2012

Flying the Spitfire.

Chipmunk arrives in Port Macquarie.

Bobcat emblem.

Cartoon by Canadian RCMP friend, Norm Muffitt.

Last Post Ceremony at Australian War Memorial Canberra for Rolla Cooke, 2019

With Liz at Last Post Ceremony.

The original Bobcats: Alan Bradtke, David, Rod Hall, Steve Woodham, John Hayler. Absent Greg Kemp

Awarding of Order of Australia, Government House, Sydney, 2020.

Rolla and Betty, 1941.

Rolla enroute to UK, 1941.

Bobcats.

David's 80th birthday, December, 2021.

With Vietnamese nurse, An, at work in Vietnam.

David with Liz and sister Debbie Higginson at Government House, OAM ceremony.

David with a Spitfire in Oshkosh, USA.

Aerostar Adventure

2005

"... flying is pure passion and desire which fill a lifetime."

Adolf Galland

It is pitch dark over the Indian Ocean at 10.00pm local time as my twenty-six year old son Michael, in command of the Piper Aerostar 600, calls Seychelles approach. The reply is welcome as our HF radio has failed and we have had no communication for five hours. Although conditions are visual, we are told to do an ILS approach in order to bring us safely between the mountains.

What the hell am I doing here in the dark over a foreign ocean?

***

I have been partially responsible for training Michael over the years, but with twenty-five major ocean ferries to his credit, tonight he is the captain and I am the co-pilot. I have every faith in his abilities but after fourteen hours in the air we are tired and were not expecting an instrument approach. Intercepting the localiser, I call visual. Michael fights exhaustion as he slides down the ILS and we touch down.

Is this the same son who, aged sixteen, said it was "quite daunting" on completing his first area solo around Gunnedah?

A smiling islander marshals us to a halt and suddenly the engines are silent.

Although he has a "real" job flying a King Air in Queensland, ferry flying is no stranger to Mike. He accepted this ferry of the PA 600 from Johannesburg to Kempsey on behalf of a Sydney man but when Michael tried to depart five months ago, the weather had been shocking, the winds unfavourable and the aircraft not performing as advertised.

After frightening himself in Mozambique taking off in 40 degree temperatures with the necessary ferry overload, he aborted the flight and left the aeroplane to be fixed back in Johannesburg. Now we are assured it is AOK and of course the weather is more favourable.

***

Four-thirty am, and we are driving through the dark roads to Lanseria Airport in South Africa on the outskirts of Johannesburg, anxious that the 4000 foot elevation and short runway will not be covered by the forecast fog.

The Aerostar is often "bagged" by pilots as being dangerous, but as long as one can achieve 120 knots shortly after rotation, it will fly with the overload. The cabin is already filled with nine hours fuel for Dar-Es-Salaam in Tanzania. It looks like a black waterbed on which our maps and bags are loaded.

We taxi to the run-up bay as the first traces of dawn appear and the Aerostar vibrates as the power comes up.

Ninety knots. Rotate.

Gear up, almost 120 knots and we start a 100 foot per minute climb and ease up the flaps in tiny stages. Mike smiles. It feels better than all the detractors had told us. We climb into the cloudy African air, heading for Dar-Es-Salaam, 7½ hours away. The country looks very like Australia with flat scrub which soon turns into the beautiful volcanic plugs of Zimbabwe. It is fascinating to be flying over such strange terrain. We speak to heavily accented controllers as we pass over Mozambique, Malawi and finally Tanzania.

The beaming airport staff in Dar are very welcoming as we try to refuel quickly in the steamy afternoon. We are starting to improve the take-off technique as, overloaded again, I handle the gear and the milking of the flaps. Mike locks on to the speeds, so critical in this configuration. The tiny laminar wing of the aircraft, good for cruising at 190 knots, is not conducive to lifting overloads of fuel. We head due east for the Seychelles weaving to avoid thunderheads while racing away from the low set sun.

We decide to spend a day in this tropical paradise and so we potter around the aeroplane adjusting transfer pumps and fuelling eleven hours of Avgas into the "waterbed" behind us.

We ring our engineer in NSW about the failed HF radio but despite many suggestions it will not transmit, and we have no choice but to proceed all the way to Australia without this communication.

With first light we race down the 9000 foot runway, crossing the far threshold at 100 feet. With our third leg a routine develops. We are quiet for the first two or three hours and I find myself listening to the engine note with great interest. A tiny flicker in a fuel pressure gauge widens my eyes for a few seconds and I hit the booster pump.

> "The engineers say that's OK," says Mike seemingly disinterested, but I am not entirely convinced and watch it like a hawk.

Five hours, halfway to Colombo and we play some music on a CD player and start to converse on philosophical topics. I sing Mike some of the songs I wrote when in Medical School.

Two and a half hours to go and we find ourselves over the turquoise Maldives – a pattern of scores of flat islands beset by tourist cabins. Mike finds we now have mobile phone coverage over this country, and we text everyone we can think of with our progress.

Land looms up. Sri Lanka is on the verge of civil war after a Tamil Tiger blew herself up near an army general five days prior, but we do not really feel insecure taxiing into the apron. There are plenty of guns visible, but our agent smooths our way through the bureaucratic procedures. It is amusing to see eight people turn up to take turns pumping the 1000 litres with a wobble pump.

Another dawn take-off and we head for Cocos Island. The morning is hazy with moisture and as we cross the southern end of Sri Lanka, we see mist between the hills.

> "Bad weather for 400 miles before Cocos," the weather briefer tells us, "with embedded thunderstorms to 45000 feet."
>
> "Great!"
>
> "What is your alternate for Cocos, captain?"
>
> "No alternate, mate," says Mike, "we're landing at Cocos, there's nowhere else."

At three hours I start the transfer pump and look in horror at the sight gauge in the system. No fuel transferring. Mike takes off his shoes and climbs on to the black bladder which wobbles under his weight. I am left up the front watching the shop.

"Hold your nose, I'm going to burp the tank," yells Mike and we become unwilling petrol sniffers as he opens the filler cap and lets the air out. Immediately the fuel flows and I relax a little with the thought that I may indeed not die today. I strain ahead looking for the dreaded intertropical front and after twenty minutes look round puzzled. Mike has not come back to the flight deck. I twist around to see him asleep on the bladder, a pillow under his head. Eventually he comes forward. "You can sleep now Dad."

"No thanks, I'll just stay up here and worry."

Halfway to Cocos we make contact with an Emirates jet pilot who passes on our position. As he flies over us, no doubt enjoying a three course meal, we eat yet another muesli bar. By the time he is out of range we have exchanged names and addresses. The convergence zone fizzles, and we are able to weave easily between the build ups before landing at Cocos. The island is barely bigger than the airstrip itself. The Australian staff are helpful and after fuelling we walk the 50 metres to our accommodation, dodging birds and land crabs as we go.

Our impression that we are almost in Australia dissolves the next day as it is still seven and a half hours to Port Hedland and the sea and airwaves seem devoid of life.

I muse over the fact that we are so heavy that if we lost an engine, we would go down anyway. I plan how to get across the cockpit to the door underwater and then take a philosophical attitude and start to enjoy the flight.

An hour out and we start to see the oil and gas platforms off the WA coast

"Civilisation as we know it!"

A faint blue line appears on the horizon, gradually materialising into Australia. I sing Peter Allen's song and we let down on to the flat lands of the coast now made green by the recent cyclone.

"The eagle has landed," says Mike over the Unicom frequency and we shut down while awaiting customs.

"Which one is the eagle?" the lady official asks. "Anything else to declare?" she asks eyeing one of us emptying the wide-necked bottles, "I have to get back to the footy."

Yes, this is definitely Australia.

By comparison, the flight to Cunnamulla is so relaxed. With a stop for a pie at Alice Springs, we only see one other town, Birdsville in the whole nine hours. We are over hostile desert most of the day and yet there is something comforting about being over land and being in Australian airspace. Hitting Cunnamulla at dusk we find that the PAL (pilot activated lights) are not working. We are tired and already talking about what we want for dinner and it takes all my concentration to land in the oncoming gloom.

"Lucky you didn't hit a kangaroo," says the groundsman.

Two hours flying the next day and we are home in Port Macquarie. After fifty-two flying hours in seven days, it seems very quick.

We help pull out the ferry tank, the "waterbed" and ask the engineer if he will please fix the HF radio, if only for next time.

Suddenly it's all over. We have come 9000 nautical miles and now we will go back to reality. I, back to my surgery in Port Macquarie as an ordinary doctor, and Mike to his real job flying his Super King Air taking crews back and forth to the oil and gas fields of Queensland and South Australia.

I have flown for forty-eight years and spent 11000 hours in the air, and I don't often get big surprises and yet this week has been a great learning experience for me. I have flown the Pacific and the Tasman several times, but this was a real thrill and how much more so to fly co-pilot to one of my sons, the fourth generation of Cooke pilots.

The last ferry flight that David did with Michael was by far the most challenging. This flight involved bringing a Cessna 404 Titan from Prestwick in Scotland to Darwin. This type of aircraft is used as a small commuter airliner which can fly at altitude to avoid all but the very worst of weather. David was more than happy to undertake this task. Flying from the UK to Australia is no mean feat and offers invaluable experience in radio calls and navigation. David did not have to be asked twice.

Michael went on ahead and was there at Glasgow airport to collect his father and head down to Prestwick. Scotland is not known for its benign weather, far from it, and the Cessna awaiting them was living proof. It had spent the best part of the last two years sitting out in the weather, facing all the icy rain, winds, snow and occasional sun that Scotland had to offer. It looked terrible.

A cousin who lived close to Prestwick had expressed interest in going for a test flight when it was ready to go. He took one look at it and changed his mind! No way was he boarding it, let alone flying in it. Michael and David felt much the same way, but a contract is a contract and you can't judge a book by its cover! It had been deemed fit to fly and who can argue with the aircraft engineers?

The flight in the Cessna 404 Titan has gone down in the annals of Cooke flying as The Scottish Tragedy or Macbeth. It's not hard to see why.

From take-off in Prestwick on April 21, 2007, things started to go wrong. As well as coping with flying in a different country where radio frequency changes happen more regularly than in Australia, a magneto decided to pack it in en route to Southampton. This was easily fixed by the simple aeronautical technique known as wobbling wires. With greatly renewed confidence they took off again, heading to Genoa on the Mediterranean where an overnight stop was planned. The wire wobbling ensured no further problem with the magneto but unfortunately the aircraft heaters failed. Now this is not a problem that would cause grief to the pilots or threaten their safety, but it certainly, at 11,000 feet altitude at the end of April, caused the cabin to be icy cold. There was father and son sitting side by side in control of a sophisticated aircraft while huddled like an old couple under a couple of rugs that were fortunately provided on board. Who said that flying was glamorous?

After a restful night spent in a cosy hotel room in Genoa they set off again heading for Luxor in Egypt via Brindisi on the heel of Italy's boot. What was going through their minds? No doubt some thoughts about what misfortune would befall them on today's leg. They found out soon enough when the left fuel pump failed. This meant that the left engine would have to be started by using the right fuel pump and crossfeeding to the left. Not an ideal way to start an engine.

By this stage both David and Michael were just a little tired of coping with these problems, especially as the more difficult countries and longer legs were still ahead of them. After an overnight in Luxor, Egypt, it was off to Bahrein which meant flying along a 20 mile corridor over Saudi. If one strayed outside that zone there was a likelihood of being shot down! This flight was getting more terrifying by the moment. The last straw occurred after take-off from Luxor. The hydraulic line fractured. The hydraulics are responsible for powering the undercarriage and flaps on board the aircraft and their absence can cause great problems. Michael went down the back of the aircraft and unscrewed a floor panel, discovering the dreaded reddish hydraulic fluid sloshing around beneath him. Facing a landing in Bahrain with no undercarriage was a real possibility. Adding to the stress was the hour spent circling over the airport waiting for it to open. Amazingly the undercarriage came down but not the flaps causing the aircraft to land at a faster speed than desirable. Safely down, its shameful defect was clearly visible as the reddish fluid dripped steadily on the tarmac.

As they climbed out of the Cessna, David said to his son, "I'm not going any further in that machine."

"Neither am I," said Michael.

They both returned to Australia by airliner leaving the 404 to its fate. It was repaired and after two more attempts by Michael sometime later, with more problems and dramas, Michael gave up and left it for the owners to solve how it would get back to Australia. Amazingly it did. Some time later it was shipped to Darwin and is happily working for its living in the tropical north.

The curtain fell on the Scottish Tragedy.

Interrupted Journey

2007

There are old pilots and bold pilots, but no old bold pilots.

"Bahrain radio, we have a hydraulic problem. We may not be able to lower the undercarriage."

Thirty miles from this Gulf island my son Michael is flying inbound from Luxor. I am handling communications. The ten seat Cessna 404 is bouncing in the heat turbulence of Saudi Arabia.

"Are you declaring an emergency sir?"

"Negative, we have had a hydraulic failure and would like priority to land please."

"You cannot land for one hour; the airport is having repairs. Please hold at thirty miles."

Suddenly the quiet, relatively unstressed life of a GP in Port Macquarie seems very attractive to me as we circle in the holding pattern. There is little to do but anticipate the outcome.

***

Michael, who ferries for a living, rang me a week prior to this moment. He was to pick up the aeroplane in Scotland and fly it to Australia.

"It hasn't flown for two years but has been thoroughly checked out," says Mike, "but it would be great to have another pilot."

It takes me half a minute to agree and he leaves four days ahead to test fly the small airliner and prepare it for the long trip.

Over three days of flying in Scotland he finds a few problems – one fuel pump has seized, a hydraulic line has fractured, the heater keeps blowing its circuit breaker, the autopilot turns itself off in turbulence and the second transponder, second ADF and DME do not work.

There is, also, persistent muddy water in one fuel tank which no doubt caused the pump to seize. Despite repeated draining, every morning there are brown bubbles in the fuel drain. The delightful Scottish engineers drain this tank, repair the hydraulic line and replace the pump.

On the morning I am to arrive, Mike takes delivery of the aeroplane.

"All OK?" he asks.

"Aye."

"Is it OK?"

"Aye."

Pause. He opens his mouth to repeat himself and then twigs to the vernacular.

"Are you saying 'yes'?"

"Aye, laddie."

I tumble out of the airliner at Glasgow and, kept awake by adrenalin, help Mike preflight for our first leg to Southampton.

The engines are sweet, and we take off, tracking by the Isle of Man to Wales, then south to our destination. I am fascinated by the continual frequency changes and minor adjustments to our flight plan as we proceed the length of England.

Coming back over the coast of Wales we become aware that the right engine is rough. The EGT rises and the CHT slumps. We diagnose a magneto failure on this right engine, but all is otherwise well and we continue to Southampton landing on a beautiful spring afternoon.

The magneto is checked out and fixed (a loose wire), and we are ready for our leg to Italy next morning. It is comforting to me to ring a friend in Tamworth NSW, a magneto expert, who tells me it should be fine to continue the flight.

We climb out over the Channel and cross the French coast at Le Havre. All is going well as I ponder on the American B17s cruising over to France in the forties to be mauled by waiting Messerschmitts. The sea sparkles in the sunlight and I wonder how many fallen aircraft lie on the seabed beneath us. We sail on over France and turn to cruise along the Riviera towards Genoa.

We have descended to 7000 feet when the Italian controller says,

"Climb to flight level 110."

"Negative," says Mike.

There is a pause.

Did you say 'negative'?"

Yea, mate. We want to come down, not up."

We stand by until a resigned Italian gives us permission to descend to the beautiful little city and we land after four and a half hours.

The locals are charming and helpful. Early next day we climb over the snow-capped central mountains via Florence to Brindisi on Italy's heel.

A quick fuel stop and we depart for the seven hour flight to Egypt. As we track beside the many Greek isles the heater fails again and we try to rug up with extra clothes, looking like two old people in a nursing home. Mike leaves me to do his exercises in the aisle – part of a get fit campaign - but comes back shortly, puffing.

"Boy, I must be unfit. I could barely do them," he gasps.

"Mikey we are at 11000 feet, of course you will be puffed!"

We dine on our salami and cheese sandwiches and marvel how big the Mediterranean Sea is, until the coast of Egypt slips by and we plunge into sand and dust haze reaching well above us.

Cairo control routes us to Luxor via a place in the Libyan desert, adding a hundred miles to our flight.

"G'day mate." The Oz accent is laid on. "Can we track direct to Luxor please?"

"Stay on the route," comes the terse reply.

Five miles from the River Nile the desert abruptly becomes green as we descend over the Valley of the Kings to this exciting city, a great tourist destination.

Another early start and we drain all the muddy water out of the left tank and climb into the sunrise, crossing the Red Sea and the dramatic mountains of western Saudi Arabia.

The hydraulic flow lights flicker and come on indicating a failure. Mike and I stare at them and realise that gear and flaps on landing will be a problem. He talks to our engineer in Australia via a satellite phone and we discuss the causes. We can land without flaps on the long runway at Bahrain and we can always blow the gear down with the nitrogen bottle. We continue in relative calm.

"I notice the left fuel pump circuit breaker has popped," says the captain. He resets it. The pumps are placarded to be used in take-off, landing, climb and descent and to keep the engines smooth.

"OK, Dad, if we get surging in the left engine as we land, be ready to switch the left fuel selector to cross feed. We'll use the right fuel pump for both engines." He goes aft to study the operating handbook and takes some photographs of the scenery whilst I handle the brewing thunderstorms surprising us over this desolate moonscape.

The turbulence fails the autopilot and I attempt to keep us as level as possible, singing to myself as a form of relaxation.

Mike appears again.

"I am starting to feel a little insecure about this aeroplane," I state, remembering the many articles in our safety digest where accidents seem to be caused by multiple problems developing.

The satellite phone rings.

"I have called a couple of times and you didn't answer. I was worried," says the engineer back in Australia.

"Sorry mate," says Mike, "Dad and I had the storm window open taking photos of the countryside."

He recommends a certain engineer in Bahrain and it is soon time to descend over the Gulf.

Mike puts his hand on the gear lever and hesitates.

"Get it over with, Mikey," I say.

There is a slow grinding and after an interminable time three greens appear.

"Try the flaps."

There is more grinding and we achieve a small amount of flap and then no more. We shut down on the baking tarmac and inspect the Cessna. The bilge is awash with red fluid which drips on to the tarmac. The partially lowered flaps are immobile but nevertheless we are down.

Engineers crawl over the machine and show us the hydraulic lines which had hidden corrosion causing the blowout. We agree it is time to leave the aeroplane in Bahrain and come home until repairs can be undertaken.

Three days later I am again sitting in my quiet surgery in Port Macquarie discussing coughs and blood pressure – a different hat on – and yet I am missing the excitement. But it is my real job. My flying will only consist of medical clinics on the Mid North Coast of NSW in my Bonanza and giving scenic rides in our company Tiger Moth.

Do I have any regrets about this last week? Certainly not!

Would I do it again?

I can't wait.

David's last international flying excitement was a stark contrast to The Scottish Tragedy. In 2014 he put his hand up to bring a King Air back from the USA with Anthony. Michael's company was managing this aircraft and using it for charter work. At the same time Michael was arranging to bring back a Gulfstream jet for its owner. This aircraft was also to be used for corporate work.

On arriving in the USA David discovered that the King Air had some issues that needed to be addressed. Time was at a premium – David still had a job waiting back in Australia. He could not afford to hang around indefinitely while the repairs were carried out. It was decided that they would all return to Australia in the Gulfstream. This was a slight disappointment but only slight. Instead of having the thrill of doing a Pacific crossing in the large, powerful and comfortable King Air with his son Anthony, David was now reduced to passenger status. But what a passenger! Flying across the Pacific in a sleek, modern corporate jet such as the rich and famous own is not something that everyone experiences. Most people cross the Pacific crammed in an economy seat with limited legroom and indifferent food. This aircraft was a different experience altogether, in fact it had once been the personal jet of Oprah Winfrey. It had noble heritage indeed.

This flight was very special. Father and his two sons plus a cousin, Andrew and his girlfriend. They could not believe their luck in hitching a ride back to Australia in such luxury. Would David be allowed to do any of the flying? He was not endorsed nor had any experience in jet flying. He was however permitted to sit in the jump seat and observe his two sons skilfully operating this sophisticated aircraft. He was also allowed to do the occasional radio call when one of the boys temporarily vacated the cockpit.

"Keep an eye on the instruments, Dad, but please, don't touch anything!" And so the Gulfstream forged its way across the Pacific at 45000 feet on autopilot under the watchful eye of second officer David Cooke.

David laughed to himself. As a young, and not so young child, Michael was an inveterate fiddler and toucher of everything he could get his hands on in the aeroplane. It was a source of some stress for his father, drawn between not wanting to dampen the young aviator's enthusiasm and keeping the aircraft safe! How the tables had turned with Michael now issuing orders from the cockpit.

With a couple of days in Hawaii thrown in for good measure this was declared one of the best flights ever!

It may seem that David spent every waking moment up in the air. Nothing could be further from the truth. Most of his time involved being a conscientious and devoted doctor to his many loyal patients at both Lighthouse Beach and South West Rocks.

Medicine in Port Macquarie, although blessedly quieter than in Gunnedah, lacked the stimulation that surgery and emergency work provided. In 2009 an opportunity arose to change all that for a few weeks. The Hoi An Foundation is a charity run from the USA which provides medical and surgical care for isolated villages around the historic, heritage town of Hoi An in central

Vietnam. David decided to donate his time for three weeks and with what seemed like minimal preparation, David, Elizabeth and an RN, Judy were winging their way to a very different part of the world. They were met at Da Nang airport by Carol, an Australian nurse who had worked at the foundation for a number of years. She was comfortable with the locals and had a smattering of Vietnamese, a notoriously difficult language to master even at a basic level. Carol co-incidentally had a Gunnedah connection having been born and raised there. A small world.

Hoi An was a culture shock. Hot, crowded, teeming with motor cycles and pushbikes, it was an ordeal just moving around. Thank goodness for Carol who strode with confidence into the traffic with her hand outstretched and her head down. "Whatever you do, don't pause or baulk. The bikes will weave around you, they can judge your pace," she said. Miraculously they did. Carol also knew where to buy cheap bottled water and how to get "small nose" prices. Tourists are apparently known for their big noses and always pay more!

On the first morning, David was picked up early and whisked away by his interpreter, An. Off he went, swallowed up by the traffic and holding on for dear life on the back of An's small motor bike.

David was soon to discover that doctoring in these outlying clinics was a far cry from sitting in his air-conditioned surgery at Lighthouse Beach. Two of the most prevalent conditions that he faced were hypertension and diabetes. Both these common and highly treatable conditions provided very real risks for the Vietnamese people. Why were these conditions so common among these slight and certainly far from obese people? Obesity tends to be a risk factor for type 2 diabetes but the Viets are on the whole slender. The risk factor lies in their diet. Delicious Vietnamese food is generally high in sugar and salt, both poisons to the human body when consumed at high levels.

Unfortunately, treating both these conditions is not simply a matter of prescribing a few pills and regular monitoring. Medication is freely available over the counter but the cost to the average person prohibits regular consumption. Another issue is the understanding that the medication is an ongoing treatment. After a few days of hypertension medication the patient, feeling a bit better, will simply cease taking the tablets or be unable to afford to continue. More worrying still was the medication available in the pharmacies.

Medications that had been removed from prescribing elsewhere because of dangerous side effects were available in Vietnam, having been dumped on the market by the pharmaceutical companies.

Evidence of what is called The American War was frequently seen. One elderly woman had a nasty scar on her abdomen. On being asked about it she replied matter-of-factly, "That's where the Americans shot me." She was unperturbed. That was then, this is now, is the philosophical viewpoint and after all, they say with a smile, "We won!"

David saw many children with simple heart defects that could be fixed with an operation in childhood. Costs prohibited this happening. Any person lucky enough to have surgery would be treated at the nearby Da Nang hospital. It was common for patients to share a bed and it was the job of the family to ensure the patient was adequately fed. The Hoi An Foundation would fund surgery for serious cases and provide a future for those lucky enough to undergo the treatment.

Three weeks in Hoi An were an eye opener for David. Although used to the poverty and sickness among the Indigenous community during his time in the outback, this was a whole different situation. It was a very thankful doctor who came back to Lighthouse Beach to treat and care for his very fortunate and basically "worried well" patients.

Vietnam Doctor

2009

…far from the worried well

Five am. The loudspeakers on telegraph poles blare out scratchy music to wake the populace and induce them to start their day's work. I wonder why they couldn't wait another hour or so to let me sleep till a reasonable time. Later in the day the tourists will be entertained with Vivaldi broadcast from these same speakers.

Already the day is heating to its 35° and 98% humidity, and the hazy sun beats down on the ever busy roads. Motorbikes and pushbikes stream in a procession past the hotel in a seemingly chaotic traffic system that strangely appears to work. It is not unusual for bikes to accommodate four people, weaving like fighter pilots with incessant tooting of horns.

After twenty minutes we are still alive, and Judy has managed to open her eyes for the last two kilometres.

We enter the clinic building which is proudly shown to us by the local "EC", a man trained somewhere between a nurse and a doctor. A fan is fetched, and Judy begins to screen the patients for diabetes and blood pressure before handing them on to myself and Mai, an Australian nurse who manages the Hoi An Foundation and has been here for many years. American doctor, Joshua Solomon started the organisation some years ago and spends many months of each year in Vietnam.

The people are gentle and appreciative but suffer from these two diseases due to the high salt and sugar content of their diet.

"Are you taking the tablets?" the interpreter asks on my behalf.

"No, I felt better," is a common reply and indicative of the amount of education these patients need about their treatment.

I sigh and the interpreter explains that the blood pressure is 200/100 and that this fifty year old is at risk of a stroke. We give advice and prescribe the available medications some of which we stopped using in Australia twenty years ago. One such is Cozaar, I note, stopped in a hurry in the western world because of serious side effects, and so I take people off this treatment. I wonder why we are doing this work when there are locally trained doctors until I learn that they have no continuing medical education, never meet for discussion and are reluctant to share any medical information.

With vast amounts of bottled water to counteract the enervating heat, we wade through the day seeing more heart murmurs in my three weeks in Hoi An than I have seen in forty years of Australian practice. It is largely rheumatic disease with a smattering of Fallot's tetralogy and septal defects. These go unrepaired in the majority of cases due to the cost ($US5000) of surgery for people whose annual income may be around US$6000. These people would be lucky to reach twenty years of age.

I see wounds from the "American War" and there seems no resentment by these ex Viet Cong men and women. "That was then," they say, "this is now."

The pathology is gross and plentiful – hydrocephalus, Marfan's syndrome, cerebral palsy, marked clubbing and of course the horrific effects of Agent Orange.

The people seem happy and accepting of their situation, and, as doctor is spelt "GOD", I seem to have more success in getting patients to stop smoking than in Australia.

Today we see about seventy patients although each day is totally different. Some days we travel far out into the countryside while others involve loading the bike on a ferry and working across the river on one of the many islands.

What a momentous experience. What a learning curve! My wife and I live in a comfortable hotel for US$25 a day including breakfast and it is possible to eat for US$20 a day for the two of us.

Would I go again? Ask me in a year's time when I've got over the exhaustion, but probably yes! The two Vietnamese girls, Nguyet and An are stimulating, energetic and full of knowledge as well as being clever on a bike and Mai and Carol, two Aussie nurses who run the Hoi An Foundation, are truly inspirational, dedicated and selfless.

Three weeks of this experience and I return to my Lighthouse Beach surgery. The rooms are air conditioned, there are no frogs jumping across the floor and the computer generated scripts for modern medicines are paid for by the government. A man needing heart surgery is taken by air ambulance to Sydney where a surgeon will perform the operation at no cost to the patient.

I muse on the difference and I shall never be the same again.

Over the last two decades the town of Port Macquarie has experienced something of a boom in growth. The demographics of "God's waiting room" have undergone a dramatic change. Many retirees sell the family home in Sydney, move to Port Macquarie, buy a smaller home and still have plenty left over to finance a relaxed coastal lifestyle. Likewise, many younger families have found the town to be an ideal place to settle and bring up young children. The increased population has meant increased infrastructure and job opportunities for these young families. Education too has flourished and for many years now the UNSW has had medical students finishing the last three years in regional areas including Port Macquarie. More recently the UNSW has commenced full medical degree training here bringing more and more young people to the area and keeping local school leavers in their hometown. Charles Sturt University has developed a large campus here too offering a variety of undergraduate courses and is undergoing constant expansion.

For five years David took part in a lecturing program with the final year medical students. Each Tuesday he would take one student with him to South West Rocks in the aeroplane and if it was appropriate, they would sit in with patients' consultations, observing and learning about rural medicine. For some students the flight was the highlight. One young woman declared on being asked what she had learned that day announced, "You can have fun being a doctor!"

In 2003 David's mother, Betty, died. After enduring the loss of David's father Rolla and her second husband, Ken, in World War II, she had finally settled to a happy life and fifty-four years of marriage to Bruce. Two children, Ian and Debbie completed the family. Five years later, in 2008, Bruce died. This man had an outstanding military career as a Catalina pilot and was hugely influential in David's formative years. David's love of flying was nurtured and supported by Bruce. His mother, however, with her history of loss, was not quite so sure. But she had always been enormously proud of her son's achievements.

Three weeks before Bruce died, David was able to visit him in his own home prior to being transferred to a nursing home. Bruce was weak and knew that the end was near. David took him by the hand and thanked him for being such a loving and caring stepfather. Never one to show emotion, Bruce replied by thanking David for being a loving and loyal stepson. It was a moving end for a relationship that had started with a young man taking on the care of a little boy who had lost two fathers and who had then been protected and indulged by a female household. It would have been no easy task!

With the loss of his mother and stepfather David now moved up the ladder to assume the role of family patriarch. But something was missing. Where was the next generation after his children? There was obviously a family conference held on the topic of who would be the one to make David a grandparent. Now as we know this is not a decision that can be made with a definite outcome! However the decision must have been, "Well, let's just see what happens!"

And happen it did! In the space of three years, five little girls entered the world and joined the growing Cooke family. In 2010, Michael and Anthony each had daughters, Charlotte in September and Nellie in November. Nellie was named after her maternal great-great grandmother Nellie Harrison, nee Mosman.

The following June 2011, David's firstborn Sarah gave birth to Phoenix followed in 2012 by sister Pippa for Nellie in May, and sister Gabriella for Charlotte in November.

These five little cousins have formed strong bonds with each other; let's hope their friendship survives those turbulent teenage years! Of course the as yet unanswered question is, "Will there be a first female pilot in the family?" That remains to be seen but with the encouragement from parents and one grandparent in particular, it is a distinct possibility. Time will tell, and a fifth generation Cooke pilot may yet emerge.

With the disposal of the Tiger Moth in 2006 when Coastwings was wound up, David had settled down to a flying life based around the Bonanza. However just before Christmas 2008 he received an offer too good to refuse. An old friend, Jack Jones, rang one night asking David if he was interested in going down to Cessnock in the Hunter Valley to view and test fly a De Havilland Chipmunk with a view to a shared purchase.

A Chipmunk! Remember the crashing disappointment when at the age of seventeen David was allotted a Tiger Moth in his initial training. How he used to envy the other cadets as they strode out to their smart little Chipmunks while he walked to the old fashioned biplane. How exciting it was when he moved on in his training and finally climbed into the sleek, modern Chippie. And now, here was a chance of having his very own Chipmunk!

The opportunity was badly timed, being just a few days from Christmas with its present and food buying panic stations. This escapade to Cessnock received a slightly frosty reception on the home front, but when the test flight was done, with the Chipmunk inspected and gazed upon, there was no question. This Chipmunk would be moving to Port Macquarie, arriving to great delight on January 1, 2009.

The Chipmunk was fun, pure and simple. The solid Bonanza was the workhorse, transporting David to South West Rocks in comfort each week. It also gave easy access for family visits to Sydney or Brisbane and of course was invaluable in providing the opportunity to cover Australia's vast distances on holidays. The Chipmunk was another story altogether. This little aircraft was perfect for a quick fly after work and was a popular thrill for visiting friends and relatives. It was a special treat for birthdays or other celebrations. Being slow, it was an ideal aircraft for viewing the stunning Port Macquarie scenery, especially during whale watching season.

Co-owner Jack, too, enjoyed the pleasure of reacquainting himself with the Chippie. Many an afternoon or Saturday morning was spent with the two of them enjoying this shared activity. Considerably older than David, Jack gradually found it more difficult to fly himself but was a willing and happy co-pilot. After some years, with increasing ill health, he stopped flying altogether and David took over as sole owner.

Waiting for a Chipmunk

2010

If God had meant us to fly, he would have given us more money.

I stand to attention and salute the Chief Flying Instructor.

He informs me that I will have three weeks intensive training in which time I must go solo. I will then fly most weekends while doing my university studies during the week.

My strict Air Force officer training prevents an overt smile but my heart beats quickly. As I turn to go, however, he informs me that I will be training on the Tiger Moth. A sinking feeling overcomes me. I understood all ten of us were to train on the beautiful little Chipmunks standing proudly in line outside the flight hut. But no, two of us have been singled out to fly the antiquated Tigers to compare our progress.

Why me?

We used to say that if you drop a leaf and it lands outside your spread legs it is too windy to fly the biplane and so it is for three long days.

Insult to injury!

For three days my fellow hot shots strut out to their shiny craft bragging about how light the Canadian designed Chipmunk is on the controls. Meanwhile I sit in the Tiger Moth's silent cockpit or drop leaves between my feet. They talk about the funny Chipmunk brake system and flap speeds, but when I look in the Tiger cockpit there are no brakes and no flaps. How primitive.

On the fourth day the wind drops and I climb aboard for my first lesson.

I find it hard to fly smoothly. The heavy dragging ailerons and constant need for rudder inputs is hard work and I cannot seem to balance the turns. Being in the rear cockpit too, I cannot see forward with my instructor's head in the way.

I see the sleek Chipmunks in the circuit looking like little fighters whilst I stagger around the aerodrome in what amounts to a pre-war biplane held together with wires.

The kids on the aerodrome fence gaze with envy at the Chippy pilots whilst I slink out to the stringbag that wobbles and sways on its way to the grass field. My instructor cheerily tells me the Moth flies better when I am not touching it! The hotshots are greasing their landings whilst I bounce across the grass unable to keep straight. I am not helped by the lack of forward visibility, being forced to look sideways to land.

At last I am sent solo at about eleven hours and pull it off more by accident than skill. My second solo is almost a disaster as I have to go around three times before I manage to set my bouncing steed on the ground. The engineers have to examine the results of my heavy landings.

I plough on with my training realising, by comparing notes, that although the Tiger is a safe training aeroplane, it is much harder to fly well than the Chipmunk. I am so disappointed at my bad luck, as no matter how hard I try I cannot fly as smoothly as my fellow pilots tell me they can.

***

Fifty years of flying pass and the maturity of thousands of hours has taught me how lucky I was to have learnt on the iconic Tiger. I no longer decry the Air Force decision all those years ago.

Of the aeroplanes I have owned over the years, two have been Tiger Moths, but one December day two years ago a friend asked me if I was interested in sharing the purchase of a DHC-1 Chipmunk and could we fly down to Cessnock to see it? Shining in the sun it stood, its proud little nose pointing purposefully to the sky. Complete with Air Force roundels its small cockpit smelt of fuel, oil and military paint. I read the very basic handling notes, written in the fifties and brief myself on the controls as I sit in the pilot seat.

It is so easy to fly and so forgiving. What a joy. I am seventeen years old again. I loop and roll and even pull off some relatively good three pointers. It sits now in the *hangar at Port Macquarie and I smile standing beside this sixty year old aeroplane that has been so much worth the wait.*

"Aviation therapy" is a term used by pilots and aviators to describe a form of recreation peculiar to them. It may or may not involve actual flying. It definitely involves a trip to the airport and the hangar. It can be a solitary form of therapy but is generally more effective if practised with others. It can involve nothing more taxing than standing around talking. The topic of conversation is not hard to imagine. Aviation therapy can be as simple as needing to fuel, or wipe off some oil (the Chipmunk is particularly useful in this regard). A tyre may need inflating, a wash is occasionally required and of course, on special occasions, a complete polish. This is an excellent task as a polish takes some time and can be broken down into smaller components thus providing a few trips to the hangar for therapy polishing!

Another keen aviation therapist is David's mate Alan. Alan, like David is the proud owner of two aircraft, one an RV 12 and the other a KR 2. Aviation therapy sessions would often include flying in one aircraft or another or occasionally in two. Alan is an experienced ex-naval fighter pilot with finely honed skills. They gradually developed the habit of doing some formation flying together, a challenging and skilful exercise that requires supreme concentration. This is high-level aviation therapy.

Some time later, David was doing an aircrew medical on a local flying instructor, Greg. David noticed on Greg's licence that he had a formation endorsement. Formation flying is a skill requiring an official endorsement. He mentioned it to Greg.

> "Yes, I enjoy formation but there's nobody here to do it with," he replied.

"Oh yes there is," said David and the very next Saturday for the first time, three pilots took off and flew in formation over the town and coast. When Greg arrived at the airport for his first formation session, he moved into instructor mode.

> "We'll just go into the office for a quick briefing," he said to the other two.

Alan and David exchanged surreptitious looks. A briefing? They just took off and took turns to lead and follow. Greg was right of course. With three aloft it was a whole different exercise. It was important to have a plan and of course much more visually interesting for those on the ground.

That was the beginning of the Bobcats Formation Team. Shortly after, John, a retired Cathay captain, joined the team and the four became a tight group. The formation team is a regular sight over Port Macquarie each Saturday providing much enjoyment to the public, who are quick to criticise if they get the chance. "You were a bit far out today," is a popular comment. Another comment from those on the ground is often, "Did you see me wave as you went over the Golf Course?" But of course! With another aircraft off your wing tip, no formation pilot is looking at the scenery or those on the ground.

In 2016 Greg left Port Macquarie to pursue his career in Queensland. His place in the team was filled by Rod in his Yak 52, a Czech trainer. Rod was followed by Steve in his Sonic which he built himself. Two flying instructors, Pete and Anthony also increased the numbers although Anthony has since left to continue his career in Western Australia. The latest keen recruits are Charles and John who both fly Slings. Barring people on holidays, bad weather or unserviceable aircraft, the Bobcats Formation Team continue to fly much to the delight of the general public. For safety reasons the flight lasts only about thirty minutes as it requires intense concentration which can only be maintained for that amount of time. It is followed by a Debrief Session, an important and therapeutic part of the whole experience. It involves visiting a local café, discussing the flight in detail and generally talking at the tops of their voices, so relieved are they that they survived another flight. As well as the pilots there are others who may have been passengers or are simply enjoying the aviation company. A seat on the formation team is a popular place for the airport people. Join the queue and you too can fly! Occasionally they will be joined by a helicopter with pilot Eric, who although not strictly in formation, accompanies the team down the coast. And of course, to the coffee session!

Buying aircraft is never an easy business. Over his sixty years of flying David has certainly bought his fair share, being now up to aircraft number 14.

Some purchases are more successful than others and on occasions the heart can unfortunately rule the head. One such purchase was a BE33 Bonanza TYL. David took delivery of this aircraft in May 2001 from its previous owner

Jack Jones. Jack was also the co-owner of the Chipmunk. David always loved Bonanzas for their strength and durability. In Gunnedah he happily flew the Bonanza VH-KEY that he held a third share in. VH-TYL was a smaller four seat Bonanza and was purchased to provide another Coastwings aircraft for short VFR charters or scenics.

TYL was a lovely little aircraft and was kept busy with scenic flights. It was also useful for training and was popular for checking out pilots who wished to upgrade to constant speed propellers or to do a BFR check. Although it had some issues with various mechanical problems it wasn't until 2005 that things started to go expensively wrong. When it had its 100 hourly maintenance check it was discovered that it had corrosion in the wing spar which needed urgent attention. Now this is the piece of metal that attaches the wing to the fuselage of the aeroplane. It is fairly important! It is also very expensive to fix and means that the aircraft is grounded and therefore not earning its keep.

A wing spar is not something that is easily found in the Bonanza spare parts department. This particular item has to be sourced from the USA and is not generally available, often having to be specifically made. After much time, expense and frustration, the repair was made and TYL was fit to fly again. It was decided however to sell the aircraft. It moved away to a new home and a new owner.

Another aircraft horror involved a twin engine Piper Seminole. This aircraft was to form part of the Coastwings fleet. When sourced it was in a sorry state of repair, needing a considerable amount of work done to bring it up to scratch. However, on good authority by the engineers, they were reassured that the outgoings would not be too horrific and the outcome would be a very versatile, comfortable little twin. It seemed like an excellent opportunity to obtain a twin at a reasonable cost.

Sadly it was not to be. Repairs were slow, parts were difficult to obtain and the Seminole always seemed to be at the end of the line when work was allocated. Other maintenance jobs took precedence. The Seminole languished unhappily in the hangar awaiting its turn. Costs spiralled. What should have been basically a refurbishment and some general repairs morphed into an extensive repair work and a huge expense. Eventually it was ready to take to the sky. Although it provided comfortable transport for a trip to Brampton

Island, its working life with Coastwings was short and it too was sold and is still flying happily elsewhere in Australia.

Even David's beloved Bonanza has not been without its problems. Some minor corrosion was noticed on the wing and further investigation revealed a far more serious problem. This aircraft too had a wingspar problem and it would need replacing. Like the other smaller Bonanza, it was no easy feat to source and freight this item from the USA. A replacement is not readily available but is generally custom made and takes an inordinate amount of time. Meanwhile David had no appropriate aircraft to do his clinics in South West Rocks let alone any other recreational flying. It was a stressful, frustrating time trying to source replacement aircraft. The Chipmunk was a possibility and occasionally a private Cessna 182 was available. Fortunately, David had decided to obtain his Recreational Pilot Licence for the sheer fun of it. This is a licence that is becoming increasingly popular in flying clubs as it allows people to fly a lightweight aircraft without the need for a medical. It is purely a leisure licence and has opened up the world of aviation to more people. Now it could provide David with much needed transport until the Bonanza was airworthy again.

Aviation can be a cruel mistress. Unexpected expenses on top of the fixed costs and the vagaries of weather can keep a pilot on the ground. And no pilot wants to be on the ground.

It's commonly said in aviation land that the second happiest day of your life is when you buy an aircraft. The happiest? When you sell it! No aviator would argue with that and yet no true aviator would have it any other way.

Over the years in Port Macquarie, each new aviation adventure afforded David the opportunity to continue his writing. Once he puts his mind to it an article about his latest adventure can be written longhand in an afternoon. Many of these articles have found the light of day in various aviation magazines including the Bonanza society and the local Hastings District Flying Club's *Propwash*.

In 2011 he launched into another artistic pursuit. About ten years ago David's brother Ian and his partner Sally made a sea change, relocating to Kendall where they built a studio and residence in a stunning location. Sally is an artist and her light flooded studio would make anyone keen to take up a brush and start painting. She commenced lessons and soon convinced David to give it a go. Friday mornings would see him head out the door with canvas, paints, brushes and boundless enthusiasm.

His early attempts were directed at copying great works of art. The first was a Rembrandt, *Joris de Caulerif*, a fearsome looking man. It was interesting to watch the progress of this exercise as photos were taken regularly to assess the development of this first masterpiece. Acrylics is a forgiving medium as layer upon layer can be applied until something fairly pleasing is created. And, by the time the brush was finally put down this was a very thick painting!

Many copies were made over those first few months. One copy, done very reluctantly by Sally's latest student, was the well-known *Whistler's Mother*. No one could say it was an attractive painting but for teaching purposes it apparently had something to offer. The painting was dutifully done, and teacher seemed reasonably satisfied. What she didn't notice until it was pointed out was the tiny little aeroplane that had been painted into the art work on the wall behind mother! A lovely little anachronism which personalised the work very much as David's. Sally loved it!

Once David had graduated from copies he moved on to his own creations. Over the next five years he produced around seventy paintings. Many were of the outback that he loves, sometimes from personal memories or from photos. Some became abstracts, especially if they "weren't working" they could be, well, whatever you liked!

David painted energetically and consistently for about five years. Apart from giving some to various family members and hanging a few on the surgery walls, most of them are spread around the house, crammed into cupboards or piled up behind doors. One day he decided he'd done enough and laid down his brush.

This artistic pursuit provided a creative outlet for David that was a different stimulation to his writing, acting and singing over the years. Perhaps it is only a matter of time before he decides to learn a musical instrument. Now what could it be? Something difficult, no doubt, and probably cumbersome. Maybe a tuba or a double bass would be a good challenge. Nothing is impossible.

David is never one to shirk from a challenge and at the ripe old age of seventy-seven he decided to extend his flying career in a new direction. In 2018 David's last surviving aunt died. Dot was the wife of David's Uncle Bruce, the brother of his mother Betty. Dot and Bruce were childless and the estate was mainly divided between their nieces and nephews. What to do with this unexpected windfall? David decided that instead of stashing the money into consolidated revenue it should be used for something different, something fun, something exciting. But what?

Enter Eric, an aviation friend. Eric has owned many aircraft over the years and at this time had a Citation Mustang and his pride and joy, a smart red Robinson 44 helicopter. Eric often joins in the Saturday Morning Aviation Therapy Group and has been kind enough to take David up in the Robbie a couple of times. A great experience and a certain someone's appetite was whetted! Eric decided to challenge himself by becoming an instructor. His wife Dagmara wanted to have a bit of basic instruction and Eric's pilot, Nico, wanted to do an instructor's rating as well. An instructor could be procured from Goulburn to come to Port Macquarie and do the training in weekly blocks every month or so. A few students would help with the expenses and four students would be a whole lot better than three. Thus it was that David, aged seventy-seven, became a student pilot again and began training in flying a rotary-wing aircraft.

This experienced pilot with over 13000 flying hours was now back to being a raw beginner. Rotary-wing aircrafts are a completely different form of flying and many processes are the exact opposite of what they are in a fixed wing. David said over and over, "This is the hardest thing I've ever done." Progress seemed slow and hovering was a supreme challenge that must be conquered. Take-off and landing too were quite unlike anything experienced in an aeroplane. And how do you cope with an itchy nose or a nose that needs blowing? An aeroplane flying at altitude can be left hands free for a little while without any drastic movement happening. It will just keep flying. Take your hands off the helicopter control for just a second or two and you're in big trouble.

It was worth it. On 7th July 2019 David went solo! Another achievement in his flying adventure, another feather in his cap.

Helicopter Surprise

2019

Helicopters just beat gravity into submission

After sixty years of flying fixed wing aircraft, I started a helicopter rating.

For 13000 hours I have simply thought, flying is flying. From Tiger Moths to King Airs, I have flown a wide variety of aircraft or crewed with my sons. Formation flying, aerobatics and the thrill of the seaplane have added stimulation while landing on paddocks dodging cows has provided a contrast to the precise environment of the IFR scene,

Twenty years ago, when I obtained the seaplane rating, I was surprised then at just how different this was to what I had known in aviation. Now I was in for another surprise.

My total experience of helicopters had consisted of many movies and of being taken once in a Bell 47 to a patient in flooded North Queensland whilst a flying doctor.

One day last year a friend, Eric Saacks of Port Macquarie Helicopters took me up for a fly in his Robinson 44.

That started my interest. I had heard that to fly one was akin to balancing on a basketball. It would be a hard task to master.

When I announced my intention to all and sundry, I received comments ranging from, "Good on you!" to "Do you have to do this at your age?"

An instructor was arranged from Hughes Helicopters Goulburn to come to Port Macquarie, I took a week off work, my friend's Robinson was available for hire, it was all organised.

On the first day the instructor, Neil Hughes (what a brave man!), showed me a preflight then we climbed up in the lovely red Robinson to cruise along the coastline. I was then asked to take the controls one at a time.

My nervous hand trembled a little and the Robinson trembled also.

"Just rest your hand on your knee," Neil instructed, and the trembling stopped. We progressed along the beach, surprisingly not falling to the ground. I started a turn so gently that unless Neil had encouraged me to tighten it, would not have had us going in the opposite direction under a radius of several miles. Round we came.

"You can breathe now, Dave," said Neil and apart from going up and down a hundred feet or so we were still upright and alive.

After forty-five minutes of staying aloft I was looking forward to landing and a coffee only to be told we were to hover for a bit.

The "bit" turned out to be twenty minutes of up, down, sideways, forward and backwards seemingly with very little control by myself.

I hadn't found straight and level too hard, not even turns and climbing and descending but hovering is the challenge.

The next two days we sat for long periods of time over the Helipad staring at the fence (not the ground in front) and coinciding over the big H only very occasionally. Even these brief moments were more by fluke than ability. Whenever my fearless companion took over, we stayed immobile about two metres above the required position. Whilst I was relaxed at altitude, near the ground I over controlled. Neil then started asking me irrelevant questions such as, "What is your wife's birthdate?" or "add 124 and 124." When he did this I gradually relaxed and became a better hoverer. I was apparently overthinking it. Occasionally he would lay a finger on the cyclic control without any input and I settled down.

"I'm a slow learner," I moaned.

"You've only done three hours, you're doing well. You're confusing the helicopter with the jerky over controlling. Use small movements and wait!"

I had been programed over the years being told how unstable a helicopter was and so felt quite stressed.

"Breathe Dave!"

Unhunching my shoulders I tried to relax as I do flying formation in the Chipmunk. Occasionally the wobble stopped.

"Use the pedal to turn 180 degrees," said Neil.

I touched the left pedal and we started to turn.

"A little more Dave or we will run out of fuel before we get around."

I danced on these controls and we turned better albeit moving forwards, backwards, sideways, not to mention up and down.

I longed to stop and land.

"Getting tired, Neil."

"No you're not, keep going, you're doing well."

I didn't feel I was.

Having shown me an autorotation we proceeded to do circuits. Around the airport we went climbing from the hover to 1000 feet and down to the hover again. I have sixty years of pulling the stick back to go up and now I am putting it forward, filling the window with a view of the ground. Up we leapt and I relaxed a bit.

"Now put it on the ground." Lowering the collective control, we are about to touch but so ingrained in me is the desire to flare that at the last second I can't help pulling the cyclic control back and we slide backwards. Neil takes over and I try again and again to think don't flare, put the stick forward!

We touch down.

I want to stay there but no, we rise again.

The same thing happens on the next circuit. I try to out think my "muscle memory". Every now and then we touch down in the "foreign feeling" level attitude. It feels like a fluke.

"I told you I was a slow learner."

"No, you're not," said my mentor.

I wondered how much of my problem was the preconceived expectations I had and how much was the ingrained effect of fixed wing flying.

The next day I was thinking so much about touching down that the hovering seemed to be a bit easier and apart from when concentration lapsed, we stayed within a moderate distance of the helipad. Maybe not always pointing in the right direction.

I spent the nights lying awake trying to overcome my fixed wing reflexes but the next day I would muck it up again. It felt like December 1958 when I first learnt to fly in the RAAF Reserve. I could rise from the ground without too much wobbling but putting it down was another matter. How trusting is this instructor to let me muck it up but then let me sort it out. How lucky I was to have Neil grinning at me in my peripheral vision.

Bad weather sets in. The next day is too gusty, the following day is windy and not a solo day. On the third day we start doing normal circuits until a rain storm blows in and we call it off.

This is starting to spook me. I am prepared for solo only to be delayed. I just can't imagine going solo. Every now and then Neil tells me I am doing well.

"Your radio calls are very good," he says.

"I have 13000 hours, Neil, radio is something I can do."

We come out to the helipad on the fourth day and do a few circuits.

Suddenly Neil is unbuckling his seatbelt. How clearly I remember that December day in 1958 when I went solo in the Airforce.

> "I'm getting out this time Dave. You'll notice a difference without me. When you lift off, the nose will want to rise. Put the cyclic forward and a bit to the left. You will climb quite quickly too."

I feel strangely relaxed. The inevitable has come. Finally my hands respond to the plea to relax and enjoy. I unhunch my shoulders as the Hughes Helicopters orange T-shirt moves away. What faith he has!

Up into the hover I correct for the lack of weight and suddenly I am accelerating through translational lift and then I hear another helicopter moving to the big H.

I press the transmit button.

> *"Helicopter taxiing at Port Macquarie will you be long at the helipad. I am downwind on my first solo?"*
>
> *"No worries, mate, I'll get out of your way", he replies*

I thank him. Then from another aircraft in the circuit, "Hey Dave, have you left someone behind?" Yes, I think, as I look down at the airport and see Neil pretending not to look in my direction.

The other helicopter disappears from view as I turn on to final over the busy terminal building where an airliner is loading its passengers.

The landing is surprisingly reasonable despite overshooting the helipad by ten metres and Neil wanders back and climbs aboard.

"How did you go?" Hey, wasn't he watching? I smile. I have done it. A little bit of confidence comes over me and I feel a milestone has been passed. I think of the naysayers who said why are you doing this at seventy-seven years of age.

Why not?

I ring my friend, an ex-Navy helicopter pilot but all he says is, "Helicopters don't fly. They're just so ugly the earth repels them!"

I beg to differ. The Robinson is beautiful.

Where to now? What other flying adventures lie ahead? Perhaps he can take up flying kites and watch them soar in the sky from the safety of the ground. Maybe not. Gliding might appeal but an engine would be sadly missed by a powered pilot and Port Macquarie is not suited to gliding at all. Paragliding? No engine there either. Balloon flying? Again, Port Macquarie is not an appropriate environment. Enrol in Richard Branson's space flight crews? That would be a challenge. Perhaps a drone might be an exciting alternative hobby.

Rest assured, something will turn up to appeal and challenge this passionate aviator. In his sixty plus years of flying David has been the epitome of the famous motto of the RAAF, "Per ardua ad astra" – By Labour to the Stars.

David can look back with pride on his flying career. He has achieved 13900 flying hours, a huge accomplishment for someone in general aviation. He has flown over 110 types of aircraft, from an ultralight to a King Air. He has held an instrument rating since 1978. He has dabbled in aerobatics. He has flown formation particularly latterly in the famous Bobcats team. He has flown across the ocean in a single engine aircraft to Bali, Fiji, Samoa and New Caledonia. He has flown from the east coast of Africa to Australia via the Seychelles and Colombo. He has even crossed the Pacific, also in a single engine aircraft. At the age of 77 he went solo in a helicopter, a completely different flying experience. He has even leapt out of an aircraft wearing a parachute. He has faced storms, engine failures and landing gear problems with a cool head and a brave heart. It is an amazing record from someone who has also worked with devotion and loyalty as a gifted and caring general practitioner for over fifty years. If only there were more hours in each day to fly more, to heal more, to accomplish more.

His accomplishments, however satisfying to him, are not limited to his own flying. More fulfilling to David over the years has been the interest and enthusiasm he has had in encouraging others to fly and share what he loves to do. From his earliest days as a pilot, David has loved flying with, and inspiring other pilots. There are many private pilots flying today who would have given up the struggle were it not for David's support. In particular he has encouraged young people into aviation. One particular young lad liked nothing better than to fly to South West Rocks during the school holidays. The phone would ring on Monday or Wednesday evening and a piping voice would ask to speak to "Doctor Dave" in order to request a ride to the Rocks. Latterly the voice changed to a rumbly bass and eventually school morphed into university where a Bachelor of Aviation was studied. This young man is now based in Hong Kong with Cathay Pacific Airlines, following his dream.

Another young friend with a passion for aviation was determined to join the RAAF. This is no mean feat and depends on physical, psychological, academic ability and a definite aptitude for flying. David was his rock and support, tirelessly dealing with the issues that blocked his path. This persistent young man was based in Amberley air base in Queensland as a captain of the C 17 transport aircraft. He now flies the F35 fighters, a far cry from the PC 9 trainer!

On the other end of the age spectrum are many people who have longed to fly but work, family and life in general have prevented it from happening. Now retired, these people can fulfil their dream. David loves nothing better than to encourage and fly with them in between their regular flying lessons.

As a DAME, David fights like a terrier to allow pilots to continue flying when facing medical issues. He refuses to face defeat. It is a personal challenge to ensure that a pilot can keep his licence by simply persisting with the paperwork required to deal with the medical system.

Just when you think he has nothing new to learn in the world of aviation, David has recently taken up a different challenge. He is now undertaking instruction learning to fly a gyrocopter, a strange beast something between a fixed wing aircraft and a helicopter. Like helicopter flying this is a completely weird and wonderful way to fly. It's early days with only a few hours completed. Stay tuned, who knows where this new adventure will lead? With David, anything is possible!

Finding Rolla

David's father, Rolla Maxwell Cooke, died on November 4, 1941. He had travelled to the UK as a Pilot Officer of the RAAF to serve with the RAF. After arriving in England and undergoing training in the Spitfire he was stationed in Catterick in North Yorkshire. From here the squadron undertook fighter duties out over the North Sea and over Europe.

On the 2nd of November his usual aircraft became unserviceable with an undercarriage problem. Rolla was allocated another Spitfire to continue his flying. It was a week of foul wintry weather with low cloud and icy precipitation. On the morning of the 4th of November, Rolla was instructed to take the repaired aircraft up for a test fly and check the faulty undercarriage. Keen to be back in his old familiar cockpit, he was only too happy to oblige.

Rolla was a young man with all the bravado of the young. He was only twenty-three years old. The Spitfire took off in the November gloom and its keen pilot tested the undercarriage. All seemed well. On his return to the circuit area he decided, with the foolhardiness of youth, to do a low-level roll over the airfield. As the aircraft rolled the undercarriage partially extended, destabilising the aircraft. At such a low altitude there was no time to recover. The aircraft plunged to the ground in a ploughed field five miles from the airfield. It exploded on impact and was destroyed by fire.

One month later, on 2nd of December 1941, David Rolla Cooke was born at the Mater Hospital in North Sydney. His mother, Betty, turned to Nellie, her own mother for solace, gritted her teeth and got on with the business of raising this precious baby. At this time, and for reasons that can only be speculated on, there was a fierce disagreement between the families. As a result, David had very little contact with his father's family. The Cooke grandparents rarely saw their little grandson and elected not to involve themselves in his upbringing. It is hard to understand how or why this continued for so long, but the end result was the lack of paternal grandparents in his life. As David grew up however, Lionel his grandfather, established a clandestine relationship with his grandson, meeting him some afternoons at work when David travelled in from school to join him. He encouraged him to box, a favoured pastime of

Rolla's. As a university student David would meet Lionel at Long Reef Golf Course for an occasional round of golf followed by some fish and chips. All this was done in secret, David's grandmother never knew of these meetings. These outings were treasured moments for David but in no way the memories that most children have of loving and doting grandparents.

At David's twenty-first birthday, to everyone's astonishment, both Cooke grandparents turned up to the party. They stayed only thirty minutes, and on departing, grandmother remarked, "He's nothing like Rolla," as she walked out the door.

Sadly, neither grandparent attended his first marriage in 1965 despite receiving an invitation to attend

Here was a sad and troubled woman who never got over the loss of her firstborn. It is well to remember that in the 1940s people either got over a tragedy in time and carried on with their lives or they fell into depression and suffered the consequences. Mental illness was a source of shame in those days. Maybe this was the real cause of the rift between the families. We shall never know.

As a little boy, David grew up surrounded by loving family. His maternal grandmother Nellie, Nanny to David, spent much time with him as his mother attempted to rebuild her life. Of course, as a tiny boy he never missed the lack of a father, you don't miss what you've never had. He knew his father was killed in a Spitfire. This, for David, was an exciting fact and something to brag about as he grew up and attended school. It was not until maturity that David slowly became aware of the true extent of his loss. By this stage Betty had remarried twice. Her second husband, Ken, had been tragically killed when shot down over Borneo one week before the cessation of hostilities. After the war she married yet another pilot, Bruce, and went on to live a happy fulfilled family life that included the birth of two children, Ian and Debbie.

Despite being in a happy, secure and loving family, David had a growing awareness as he reached adulthood of "being different". He had a different name, having kept his father's name of Cooke and he looked different to stepfather Bruce and the other two children. Bruce and Ian were tall, so different from David. And he felt different. Because of the family rift, he had no one to say, "You look just like your uncle" or "You have your father's nose". As well as the lack of Cooke grandparents, David also had no contact with Rolla's younger brother, Digby. He was twelve years younger than his big brother, the pilot... How proud he must have been of this young pilot who went away one day, resplendent in his Air Force uniform and never returned. What a devastating loss for this twelve year old and how sad that he was kept from a little nephew who was coincidentally twelve years younger than he was.

The love of speed was really in these Cooke genes. Digby grew up to be a racing car driver of note, participating in the Redex trials among other car races. What a hero he would have been for young David if only they had known each other.

David's adult life has been a constant search to learn and fill in the blanks of Rolla's life. It was many years after that first visit in 1970 to Rolla's lonely grave in Catterick Parish Cemetery before he visited there again. In 1995, seeing the grave after more than twenty years, a decision was made. Contact would be made with Digby, David's closest blood relative to his father. Surely after all these years the rift, when Digby was just a small boy, would by now be irrelevant.

On return from the UK a letter was duly written expressing a desire to reconnect. Off it went to the last known address in Wollstonecraft, and the waiting began. A few weeks elapsed with hope fading. David put it to the back of his mind, accepting that nothing was going to be forthcoming.

Two months later David was busily working in the surgery one morning when a call came through. "A Digby Cooke would like to speak to you," said David's secretary, "are you free to talk?" What a question! Of course he was. The months of anxiously waiting now faded away. Digby had been away from home cruising in the Whitsundays and had only just collected his mail. A warm and lengthy catchup concluded with plans to meet up very soon.

Digby and his wife Gwen visited Gunnedah one weekend and that visit cemented the bond between the two men. Despite their age difference and the different paths they had taken in their lives, these men bore quite a startling resemblance to each other. Here was a man who shared Rolla's genes most closely. Here was a man who looked like David. It was a moving experience to see them talking and recognise similar mannerisms and gestures in them both.

The weekend passed with endless talk and sharing of letters and photos that they had brought with them. David saw and read letters written by his father to his parents and little brother all those years ago. They were happy letters written by a young man so far from home facing the danger and excitement of flying for his country. He wrote of his excitement about becoming a father, a daunting prospect for a pilot so far from home.

Of course Digby's visit had to include a flight in David's Trinidad. On the beautiful clear Saturday afternoon, the two couples went out to the airport, the men climbed aboard and took off. Their smiling faces on their return said it all. Shortly after climbing out of the Trinidad Digby moved away from the aeroplane and stood by himself with his back to the others.

"He's crying," whispered Gwen to David. And so he was. Composing himself he returned to the group. He put his arm round David.

"I always wanted to fly with my brother and today I have."

David's Uncle Digby is now ninety and contact with him, although infrequent, remains happy and loving. As a result, David now has treasured mementoes of his father in the form of letters, photos, school documents, far more than the watch and logbook that were his only items. Time has certainly healed this wound at least.

Filling in the details of Rolla's life in Catterick required a little more detective work. One visit to Yorkshire involved a visit to the Elvington Air Museum outside the city of York. This little museum has been modelled on an actual airfield in wartime Britain. Vera Lynn songs carry in the air to add to the atmosphere. In one of the Nissan huts there was a huge map of Yorkshire showing the location of every air accident in the county during the hostilities. Pressing the name of the casualty caused a small red light to light up indicating the exact location of the accident. There for the first time David could locate the precise site of Rolla's accident. This little red light told him that Rolla's Spitfire crashed in the grounds of Killerby Hall, a large farm southeast of Catterick.

Killerby Hall is located just off the A1, one of the main north-south roads running down the centre of England. With the speed of traffic on this highway it was difficult to slow down sufficiently to read the small signs that indicated a farm location. A glimpse of the word "Killerby" made it possible to make a quick left turn down a rutted farm road in the little hire car. A mile or so down the track there was a farmhouse with a sign outside, Killerby Farm. A knock on the front door produced a young woman carrying a small child on her hip. She smiled a friendly Yorkshire smile and kindly pointed further down the road to the "big house" Killerby Hall, a much grander place altogether.

She was right. Arriving at Killerby Hall was like stepping on to the set of a BBC drama. This was an imposing place, a huge stone residence surrounded by extensive stables with inquisitive horses peeking out of the half doors. A whip thin woman, immaculately dressed in jodhpurs, long shiny riding boots, tweed hacking jacket and hat was astride a chestnut mare. After a courteous greeting she summoned her husband to attend to these strangers from the Antipodes then clattered over the cobbles to continue her ride.

The charming lord of the manor was surprisingly helpful. In true English fashion he had inherited The Hall from his father who was in residence during the war. "Yes," said the owner, "a Spitfire crashed here in 1941, my father often spoke of it." He went on to say that for years after it was not unusual to turn up bits of metal when the fields were ploughed. Directions were given to the field which was not far away.

Early October 2006 was cold and drizzly. The ground had been newly ploughed and was heavy and wet. The field was generally flat but rose on one side with a gentle slope towards a copse of trees. It was heavy going. In totally inappropriate footwear, (who packs wellies in their suitcase) the trek was made across the field and up the rise to the trees. Even after all those years there was still a faint depression in the earth where the Spitfire ended up. That was enough. After some photo taking and a plod back across the sodden ground, Killerby Hall was left to its rural pursuits and another little piece of the story had been discovered.

Despite being killed and buried so far from home, Rolla is remembered and honoured as are all war victims. The Parish Cemetery in Catterick is a typical little village graveyard but the war graves, forty-five of them, are beautifully maintained by The Commonwealth War Graves Commission. Close by the cemetery is the Anglican Church of St Anne. There is a memorial here to remember those who served locally during the war. Stained glass windows and embroidered panels are permanent reminders of those who gave their lives for others. It has always been a sadness for David to think of Rolla's lonely grave that never has a loved one stop and visit, leave a flower or simply think of the young man who lies in the ground. In July 2018, David left a laminated business card at the grave with his contact details in the faint hope that someone may get in touch.

In early September 2018 he received an email from a local Catterick resident who regularly visits the cemetery and had found David's card. He is an ex-Air Force Warrant Officer. Part of his retirement activities is to check on the war graves to ensure that all is well, and none needs attention or maintenance. He had been based in Catterick during his service time and had decided to retire in the town. An email correspondence developed between the two men as David shared Rolla's story and his own with him. It was decided that on David's next visit to Catterick they would meet up. In August 2019 David and I had arranged to meet Patrick and his wife Ros at their home at 2.00pm. Prior to that, the usual visit to Rolla's graveside was made and a small plant placed in front of the headstone. A man was seen approaching from the entrance, making his way to the graveside. It was none other than Patrick himself. Soon an email friendship became more personal. After much imagining what this man who checked on war graves would look like, Patrick turned out to be a jovial Irishman, instantly welcoming and personable.

After a happy afternoon together, it was good to depart knowing that someone cared, someone visited, and someone checked Rolla's grave on a regular basis. The cemetery was no longer such a lonely place for Rolla to rest in.

Another impressive Air Force Memorial is in York Minster itself. Part of the RAF Memorial consists of an enormous book, an honour roll with the name of every deceased serviceman written in beautiful calligraphy. For some reason, perhaps because he was Australian, Rolla's name had been omitted. It took some five years of visits, emails and endless effort to rectify this oversight. In August 2016 a verger escorted David to the book, unlocked the case and turned the heavy pages to the appropriate one to show the name of Rolla

Maxwell Cooke now recorded in perpetuity in York Minster. Maybe a small thing to fight so hard for, but surely the right thing to do for this young pilot.

Not long after visiting York Minster a stop was made in the Cotswold town of Moreton on Marsh. Here was located a museum dedicated to Wellington bombers and therefore worthy of a quick visit. Most of these smaller museums are staffed by elderly gentlemen keen to chat and share their knowledge. One pointed David to a few shelves of secondhand books and being the voracious reader of aviation literature he happily obliged. He picked out a book at random. *Airfields of Yorkshire in the Second World War* and flicked through the pages. He opened at a page showing a squadron photo of four rows of smiling young men. There in the front row was Rolla looking back at David. What a coincidence and what a dearly treasured book for David to have in his possession.

David has been an avid aviator for over sixty years and has had the privilege of flying over a hundred different aircraft from the tiny lightweight Foxbat to the somewhat larger Beechcraft King Air. The jewel in the crown, the aircraft that had fascinated and troubled him all his life, had eluded him. The Spitfire had been constructed and flown as a single seat aircraft and hence unavailable to mere civilian pilots.

But not all were single seaters. An Englishman, Nick Grace acquired a two seat Spitfire from a museum and proceeded to bring it back to airworthy standard. In 1985 it flew again with Nick at the controls and his wife Caroline in the rear seat. Tragically Nick was killed in a car accident three years later. Caroline had no intention of letting her husband's dream collapse. She underwent the huge task of learning to fly the Spitfire, even obtaining aerobatic and formation endorsements.

This beautiful aircraft, now known as the Grace Spitfire in Nick's honour is used in airshows and to give people the thrill of their life in a joy flight.

On discovering the story of the Grace Spitfire David was keen to sign up for a flight. The first stumbling block was its location; it is based in Northamptonshire in the UK. Second stumbling block was the price: a thirty minute flight is almost £3000. Now these two problems are definitely surmountable. David visits the UK regularly and is financially able to splurge on a life-changing event such as flying the Spitfire. The third stumbling block proved a bigger problem. There was an eight year waiting list for flights.

Would David even be alive in eight years?

Would he be fit and able to travel?

Only time would tell. David signed up to the Grace Trust, joining the long list of hopefuls. An unkind thought made one hope some of the old men further up the queue might quietly peg out before their time.

David put it to the back of his mind and got on with other things.

A few years later David was talking to a mate, Russell Delforce, about his recent trip to New Zealand. Russell had visited the small town of Ardmore outside Auckland, particularly the NZ Warbirds Museum. He discovered an interesting fact. Tucked away in this far flung spot so far from its birthplace was a two-seater Spitfire ready and willing to show its stuff to eager passengers.

David rang the contact number that night expecting to hear a similar story of wait lists and prohibitive cost.

"How long would I have to wait?" asked David.

"Well, when can you get here?" was the cheerful reply.

It didn't take long to organise. Surgery was cancelled for a week and two weeks later, destination Auckland!

June 2012, Ardmore Airfield. NZ weather is changeable at the best of times but more so in winter. The wind had to be right, as a Spitfire cannot tolerate high winds. A tentative time was set for the following day. An anxious wait began with much looking at weather reports and gazing skywards. The day was rainy, with scudding showers and a strong wind blowing across the runway. There would be no flying today.

The next day the weather was better, with billowing clouds racing across the sky and short sharp scuds of rain but a window of opportunity prevailed. On June 24, 2012 David flew a Spitfire. He finally took to the sky in this beautiful machine that his father Rolla had lived and died for.

At the age of seventy-one David felt for the first time in his life that he had truly shared an experience with his father.

On 4 November 2019 twenty-six family members and friends gathered at the Australian War Memorial in Canberra to attend the Last Post Ceremony which is held every evening before the Memorial closes. Each day a different serviceman from the Army, Navy or Air Force who served and died in any conflict from the Boer War to Iraq or Afghanistan is honoured. On 4 November 2019 it was time to honour Rolla. It was seventy-eight years to the day since he had given his life for his country.

The service was simple, brief, lasting only fifteen minutes and profoundly moving. It commenced with the National Anthem which was followed by a piper playing a lament as wreaths were laid. A biography outlining Rolla's personal and service life was read. The ceremony concluded with a reading of *The Ode of Remembrance* from Lawrence Binyon's *For the Fallen* and the sounding of the Last Post.

Rolla's descendants laid the wreaths: his son David, his four grandchildren Sarah, Amelia, Anthony and Michael and his five great-granddaughters Charlotte, Nellie, Phoenix, Pippa and Gabriella.

Sadly, Rolla's brother Digby was unable to attend. However, it was a great thrill to have Russell Cooke attend with his daughter and grandson. Russell is Rolla's cousin and the only person at the ceremony to have personally known him.

The ceremony and the gathering of family and friends afterwards was a fitting testimonial to just one man who died for his country. For David it was a moving public tribute for the father he never knew and has mourned all his life.

Postscript 6 June 2023

Michael and Fallon Cooke welcomed a baby boy into the family. He has been named Rolla Royce Cooke, a cherished brother to Charlotte, Ella and Fenella. On 9 June 2023, David met this new and very precious grandson, Rolla.

Waiting for a Spitfire

2012

"Oh! I have slipped the surly bonds of Earth..."

John Gillespie Magee

---

2 November 1941.
Entry in Logbook of Pilot Officer Rolla Cooke RAAF, 23 years old, attached to 145 Squadron RAF Catterick, Yorkshire.
Aircraft: Spitfire II N7657.
Remarks: Attacks
Time: 50 minutes.

I imagine the scene.

The Merlin engine starts and the pilot feels at once the hot blast of the exhaust past the cockpit. The noise. The vibration. Immediately the revs and boost register and the oil pressure climbs towards the green.

Take off. Bouncing on the grassy airfield. Slamming the perspex hood closed and selecting the undercarriage lever, curiously labeled "chassis", to the up position.

Wisps of cloud whip past the rain streaked canopy as he climbs at 150 knots. He cranes his neck left and right at the other aircraft rocking in formation on either side.

Ten thousand feet already, the oxygen is on and breathing is rapid as the coast slips by.

Fear, pulse racing.

The dull, white-capped North Sea blends with the grey sky. There is the convoy ploughing along below to protect.

The controller's metallic voice in the helmet, "Pimpernel aircraft, the 'trade' should be bearing 080 and slightly below you."

Breathing heavier, rotate the gun button to unsafe.

Eyes squinting. Goggles down. This is what all that training was for - Tiger Moths, Wirraways and now the Spitfire.

"OK, OK, I have them," the squadron leader's voice.

Little dots.

Messerschmitts! Dorniers!

Three thousand revs. Push forward on the stick. Black crosses flash past.

Turn. Turn. Where are they?

Something with black crosses in front. Fire. Missed. Try to see behind. Neck hurting. Turn. Turn tighter. Is that a Spitfire or a Messerschmitt behind? Holes appearing in the wing. Turn. Turn. Sweat. Into the cloud and straight out. He's gone. More rain. Turbulence, vibration. Neck straining left and right. Aircraft. Sea. Cloud.

"OK Pimpernel aircraft, home time."

Is it all over? What happened? The oxygen mask is chafing. Which way? Follow the others. Dive for the coast. Two missing – who are they?

Rocket across the gentle dales of Yorkshire. Shaking, arms aching. Undercarriage down and bump on to the green aerodrome. Exhaustion.

Was that really fifty minutes? The propeller slows to a stop and the engine tinkles as it cools. Legs still shake as the ground crew come up to count the holes in the wing.

Rolla Cooke – fighter pilot.

24 June 2012.
Entry in my logbook
Aircraft: Spitfire IX MH367.
Remarks: Handling.
Time: 45 minutes.

I am taxiing out on the green New Zealand airfield in a sixty-eight year old two seat Spitfire. All my flying life I have longed for this moment. The hot exhaust is blowing past my cockpit. I slide the canopy shut. We line up and I am pushed into the back of the seat. Gear up. 150 knots. Back to 2500 revs and plus four boost.

I gaze past the familiar elliptical wing with its camouflage paint and red and blue roundel. We are climbing over the beautiful hilly countryside. The clouds flash past. Shuddering. Turbulent.

"Handing over," says the instructor.

"Taking over," and my hands grasp the control column for the first time. Turning, turning left and right I look over my shoulder. For a big aeroplane it is remarkably light to handle. Slightly heavy on the ailerons but the elevator is very sensitive.

250 knots. I follow the instructor through a loop. The altimeter spins like I have never seen it do before. Into a roll, then a barrel roll.

Now, my turn.

Another roll and not enough forward stick. We plunge towards the sea and my mentor takes over.

A couple more and I am at home. It is more like a fast Chipmunk to roll than the Vampire I flew in the Airforce. Pulse racing with excitement we roar along the green rainswept New Zealand coast and turn towards the airport. It is so easy to handle. I hand over to the instructor for the landing.

Was that really forty-five minutes since we took off? The elliptical wing dips on to final approach. All those years of wondering what a Spitfire felt like and now I know. As we touch down I have tears in my eyes as I remember the last entry in my father's logbook in an unfamiliar handwriting.

4 November 1941.
Aircraft: Spitfire II N7657
Remarks: Killed on this flight.

Afterword

2020

Port Macquarie at the start of 2020 was a town facing severe water restrictions and the aftermath of catastrophic fires that had blanketed the town in smoke. One fire in particular, a peat fire, had been burning on the outskirts of the airport for six months. Despite the actions of fire bombers, the fire continued to flare up and refused to die. It had been an unpleasant and worrying few months. Destruction of property, wildlife and bushland had been extensive. It was an unhappy time for the district and its inhabitants.

The rains finally fell and the peat fire surrendered and was extinguished. Life in Port Macquarie was looking distinctly brighter. Not for long.

March brought the reality of Covid-19 to us all with its isolation, masks, social distancing and the cancellation of activities. Panic buying, loss of jobs, closed shops, travel restrictions introduced us to a new type of existence. Thankfully Port Macquarie has been lucky with little direct exposure to the virus. Compared to other areas, the town has been enormously fortunate.

Despite the ordeal of Covid-19, the year was not a total disaster. David has been blessed with some special events that have made 2020 a year to remember in a good way.

On April 4, David's firstborn, Sarah Alexandra Cooke and Tim Murphy were married in Beechmont, Queensland. They had already decided to have a small ceremony with just witnesses present. A gathering for family and friends was planned for later in the year. Covid-19 and border closures have put this celebration on hold but it is expected to take place in 2021. The wedding was viewed on Zoom by family and friends and was held early in the morning, the dawn of a new day and a new life together. Phoenix made a beautiful little attendant to her mother. It was a simple, happy ceremony and so appropriate to their life. David's only sadness was not being there in person to walk his daughter down the aisle – or in this case, the bush track!

In March an email dropped into the Inbox informing David that he was being awarded an OAM in the Queen's Birthday Honours List in June 2020. This was to be kept a secret until the announcements were made public. Provided David did not commit a crime in the intervening months all would be well. The secret was kept. On Monday 8th June it was announced that David was awarded an OAM for, "services to aviation and to medicine." What a well-deserved accolade for someone who has spent his adult life serving others.

The days, weeks and even months following the announcement produced an outpouring of congratulations and good wishes from an outstanding number of people. Particularly heartwarming was the contact with people from times past who wished to reconnect and congratulate him. It was all somewhat overwhelming for David.

Covid-19, of course, delayed the official investiture. Finally, on December 2, (David's birthday!) he was invested with the Order of Australia Medal at Government House on Sydney Harbour. There were only twelve people being presented on this occasion. The ceremony was intimate, warm and moving. Her Excellency the Honourable Margaret Beazley AC QC, Governor of NSW, said to the recipients who had all expressed their surprise and humility at receiving the honour, "Be proud today, you can be humble tomorrow!"

Everyone in the room agreed. We were so proud.

Appendix

Additional Writings by David Cooke 1979 - 2020

Flight into Night

1979

> *Most glorious night! Thou wert not sent for slumber!*
>
> Lord Byron

There is a slight lifting and falling felt through my seat. A droning that I don't hear except if it were to falter. I look down at the ground becoming monochromatic in its last moments before darkness. What tiger country! Nothing but trees and deep ravines. I will feel better in a little while when I cannot see it anymore. I know where I am so I can relax a little – at least I know how many DME miles and upon what radial. It means I do not need to use the ground to tell me where I am so I can really enjoy the flight without that desperation that comes of making sure I am not getting lost.

I lean forward to dim the panel, reticent to do anything to snap me out of my thoughts hoping that the electronic sounding voice will not invade my headset and require a reply. I do not want to talk to anyone just now, for just to do that reminds me that I will eventually have to trade where I sit for reality. I will have to come down to the world. It is so peaceful; the stars are appearing and a slender moon is becoming prominent. I breathe the clean air and find it hard to realise that more than a mile beneath me is pollution and conflict. Tonight it does not matter what the navigation fees or landing charges are. They remain on the ground with the pollution held down by some financial inversion layer that protects me up here.

The blackness has surrounded me now. Below, above and around I see very little, just the winking of my beacon on the wing's shiny surface. It brings my gaze back inside to the winking digits and circles which tell my hardly conscious thoughts that I am where I am supposed to be. I don't have to care too much because a little computer attached to my control cables is pulling and pushing me along a pathway. And I reach forward and turn off all my cabin lights.

Within a few moments the blackness pales outside and I can see dusky forms passing underneath. My tiger country again, and a little river's reply to the moon – no lights except for those above.

A little eddy lifts me then lowers me again, a tiny change occurs in the unconscious noise, the stars tilt and recover. I know where I am. I am just up, and that's all that matters. As far as I am concerned I am no longer going anywhere.

Something appears ahead – a light. That is the city's first herald. That is people. That is reality. That is landing charges and air route fees. It is not mine. I am not part of that. It is on the ground and I am not part of the ground. I shall stay up here even if that light passes under me and no matter how bright and large and prominent and coloured and ...

"...descend to 7000 feet, turn left heading 110, call approach on ..."

I lean forward and turn the lights back on again and press my talk button.

Aviators

1982

*The average pilot, despite the sometimes
swaggering exterior, is very much capable of such
feelings as love, affection, intimacy and caring.
These feelings just don't involve anyone else.*

Someone once said to me, "I have to have a reason to go flying." It was then I realised that people who fly are not homogeneous. There are two groups and they have little in common except the means by which they do it and the medium into which they enter.

The man I mentioned was a pilot; a person who steers, a technician who goes from A to B, a manipulator of machinery who "has to have a reason." The other group is the aviator; the Jonathan Livingstone Seagull, the flyer who needs in fact a reason to come down!

When I was about to buy my first aeroplane someone said to me, "It is not logical to buy an aeroplane and it is not financially sound to do so. If it is bent, you will not be able to rebuild it despite insurance." I agreed with all he said, but I stopped any further argument by saying that I never claimed to be thinking of it along logical lines. It was not because it was faster transport, nor more efficient, nor more comfortable. It was certainly not cheaper than surface travel and it was debatable regarding its efficiency in getting from place to place. I just wanted a vehicle to fly in, that's all. There was no other "reason". I did not really care where I was going. I just wanted to be aloft. I felt only the pinch and finiteness of my fuel endurance. This was my reason to come down.

You can discover the aviator amongst flying people. He can tell you how many hours he has within 100 or so, because each hour means so much to him. Each hour has been a golden experience away from the reality of the world. You will see him, for an hour or so before a flight commences, switch off in his communicating with you and a faraway look comes in his eyes. From that point it is useless to try to get *him to give you his attention for he is already drifting up into the air. You will see him try to concentrate on flight planning and he can barely read the forecast because of his trance-like state.*

As he approaches the aeroplane the excitement increases so that he has to really try hard to do any checking of airframe and engine. There is a sort of urgency to get in and get away and he will become impatient with anyone and anything that delays him.

There is just one moment that you can sometimes catch, when he is just about to start up. He pauses, and it is worth waiting for. There is a little look around and the faintest hint of a smile upon his lips that is for no one but himself. You will catch out aviators too at the end of a flight. They seem reluctant to leave the cockpit and the aerodrome and it seems to take an hour or so to "come down". It should never be thought that aviators are found only amongst non-professional pilots. Indeed, there are as many aviators flying professionally as not and I have in fact found the aviator syndrome amongst people who have not been lucky enough to learn to fly. You can tell the airline pilot who is an aviator, for behind all that braid and professional air, there lies a man who loves others to experience what he feels. He will be a man who appears more interested in your experience than you are in his. He will not try to scare you. He will not try to impress you. He may have 20000 hours, but to you he will be a fellow flyer.

It probably does not matter to the aeroplane, the air or in fact to aviation whether a flyer is one or the other. It only matters to the individual himself. He changes when he is flying, he is a different personality and it is a personality he likes better in himself than his earthly one. There is no snob value in being an aviator and certainly pilots who are technicians are often better at the job than he, being essentially more practical.

There have always been people of both types in the world, but some days, when one is lying in a grass field under the wing of an aeroplane "swapping lies" with another aviator, I wonder what aviators did before 1903.

Whatever Happened to the Kids on the Aerodrome Fence?

1982

> ...*none, not one who truly loves the sky would trade a hundred earthbound hours for one that he could fly.*
>
> G R Wilson

One of my earlier memories is of catching the tram out to Mascot Airport in the early post war period to while away the hours on my own just watching the aeroplanes coming and going.

I remember the thrill as I neared my destination and started to catch sight of aircraft climbing away or coming in to land. I remember being fascinated by a pilot who hopped out of his Tiger Moth and, picking up its tail, walked it backwards to park. I remember hump backed Ansons, people hand swinging props, Lockheeds with their nose lockers open and DC4s pouring out voluminous white smoke as they started.

I can remember too, that I was frequently so engrossed that I would forget to eat lunch.

Those memories recall excitement no zoo, nor Manly ferry, nor visit to the cinema could match.

The scene has changed over the years – or not so much changed as moved. The other day I spent a most enjoyable afternoon at a local country property. The owner, also a pilot, had bought a microlight "flying parachute" type minimum aircraft. He had invited a few friends to come and see it and perhaps to fly his pride and joy.

It was a very different experience to the sophisticated IFR machines I fly now or even to the classic old Tiger Moth I all too infrequently totter around in. The little microlight bounced along the strip and then with a deep breath I opened the throttle fully, felt it into the air and curved away over the sunflower crop at a breakneck 25 knots and a dizzy fifty feet.

After ten vibrating and exhilarating minutes, I put it back on the ground and then taxied back to the watching public … and then it hit me.

There was indeed something very different there that afternoon and yet something vaguely familiar. It was not just the experience of handling another type of aircraft, nor the particular thrill of flight not so far removed from that of Orville and Wilbur, it was the atmosphere. All the people standing around on the grassy strip watching, thinking, telling lies; the excitement, anticipation and satisfaction. Those facial expressions, the smiles and that laughter I realised I had not seen for many years.

What had happened to aviation over those years since I used to taxi in in my biplane and see the kids standing at the aerodrome fence just watching the aircraft come and go and longingly admiring the heroes who flew them? The shy little, "can I have a look in the cockpit mister?", the look in the eyes as you sat them at the controls or even took the odd one for a circuit. The sentiment as you yourself relived your first flight through the eyes of a young boy.

The aeroplanes have changed, the pilots have changed and there are no more kids on the fence.

Look at the young pilot of today in general aviation, private or commercial. See him business like, walking away from his instrumented, autopiloted, closed in airconditioned steed, a huge black nav bag in one hand, keys in the other, perhaps girded in a suit and a serious look on his face.

I realised that was it! That was the difference. Not the happy, relaxed yet exhilarated gleeful look, but a slightly furrowed brow which means, "Did I cancel SAR? How were my procedures today? How much will that thirty minutes holding add to the cost?"

How could a shy youth be game enough to call out to someone like that – almost a mini airline captain.

The aircraft have perforce become more sophisticated and the pilots have followed and the kids have given up and gone away. But as I've discovered, not right away. Sure, they are no longer hanging around the verges of our 5000 foot sealed airstrips but they have not forsaken aviation. They have moved to the little grass paddocks where this new generation of aeroplanes is starting from scratch all over again. Here, with these new aeroplanes, costs, procedures and paperwork are at a minimum.

The children have not changed and what they are looking for is still to be found. This is a place where pilots smile and lie around under fabric wings on sunny days and are nor hurrying to get going before some operational approval becomes void.

I know all this situation is unavoidable, it is necessary progress and we must move with the times. But if you want to know what aviation used to be like, wander out to someone's paddock one day when the microlights are flying and see those kids on the fence.

A Portrait of Turbulence

1982

Take-offs are optional, landings are mandatory.

I am looking down at the shadow of my aeroplane on the ground three thousand feet below. It is fascinating to me that it barely moves. The shadow is almost directly below and even from here it can be recognised as a biplane. There is not a cloud in the sky and the summer heat is scorching the tip of my nose and my lips. I crook my little finger under the flange of the stick to stop the incessant bumping from dislodging my hand as I try in vain to anticipate or even follow the continual rocking of wings and tail. The airspeed oscillates twenty knots and the tachometer which at best gives only an average reading, is swinging in unison. I take a deep breath which feels like the first one I have dared take since take off fifteen minutes ago.

I look back and in disbelief can still see the aerodrome. What is my ground speed? They used to say that to fly a Tiger the day must be so calm that a leaf, dropped, will land between your legs. Today I dropped one and it disappeared from sight! Two people handled the wings until I lined up and then at all-up weight I ran perhaps twenty yards before the turbulence took me from the ground and flung me sideways and upwards. I had thought to allow my unspeaking co-pilot the controls but so far I am so engrossed in hanging on myself, that I dare not let go. A crumpled map is pulled out of my pocket and a dirty finger estimates the distance – 30 knots. No! Surely not. I wish I were going the other way.

I wriggle under the straps and remember to relax. I can see my face in the turn and bank indicator and so I smile. "Anyone can fly on a nice day," I say to the needles. The altitude is varying tremendously in this standing wave. One minute I am climbing and down to 1000 feet and five minutes later I am at three thousand with the nose down – so much for precision flying. The smoke from a power station is streaming downwind below me and the dust is rising as trucks move along the drought parched roads.

At least there are no clouds today and even if it takes four hours, I have the fuel.

We are strong enough to handle the standing waves caused by 45 knot winds coming over the range … the range! Four thousand feet hills … on track …to come!

What height must I get to, to ensure that if I sink I will still get over the hills? I might not even be able to get over the range. The turbulence might be too much. At this rate I will have to sit here for an hour and a half before I reach the range just worrying about it. Obviously, I must get up a bit higher. I open the throttle in jerks made by my hand continually coming off the lever. We climb and I look over the side at the shadow. It has all but stopped. Look at those cars overtaking me. At least I am a bit cooler than they are in this hot northwest wind. I wonder what they think of me up here almost stopped in my progress. "This is fun," I say to the turn and bank indicator which is in full time motion from side to side. "No, it's not fun, but it's nearly fun and it's worth more experience than the last ten hours I spent elsewhere on some autopilot drinking coffee."

If I can get up to 5000 feet before the hills and then if I attack them at the lowest point, I will have a large buffer of air. The sun slowly swings ahead of me and my face becomes quite tight as it burns. I try changing hands as fatigue is causing my arm to ache from the continual movement. The rises and falls are interspersed with sudden jabs at my aeroplane - a combination of eddies and thermals. The range is taking an interminable time to come up. Thirty-one miles in the last hour!

I start now to breathe a bit deeper as the enemy looms up ahead. Fancy having to land because I could not clear the hills on a fine day! It comes closer and suddenly we are going up. Power back nose down. Up we ride on this bucking horse, 6000, 6500. I must make some nominal effort to get down, as I am not on radio procedures.

The turbulence becomes greater and the straps are hurting me. My pulse quickens. The ridge of the hills is quite clear in front of me and now we start on our downward ride. Five thousand … power to climb, nose up … four thousand … three and a half … 1500 feet between me and the hills. We are suddenly over.

As if by some switch we stop our buffeting and start to rise again. At once the ground which for two hours has barely passed me, starts to leap backwards. The wind has lessened.

I dive downwards to the flat plains below and wriggle again under my straps. The lips reflected in the turn and bank grin back at me.

Seagulls Beware

1982

"If black boxes survive air crashes why don't they make the whole plane of that stuff?'"

George Carlin

There is a certain quiet security in life sitting in one's office or even at 10000 feet in a modern light aircraft, autopilot on, hands off, coffee out and feet up, so one day my old friend and I decided that we might appreciate this security even more after a trip to Van Diemen's Land by Tiger Moth. With a whole three days off we set out at dawn from Old Bowral in our flying machine. Actually it would have been dawn instead of two hours later if we had not had to pack a tent, sleeping bags, tools and parts, food, survival gear, navigation gear, tie-down gear and clothing into our machine. It would have been nigh on impossible until it was decided to throw out the seats and sit on sundry items.

And so we rise above the hills and head south for Merimbula two hours away. There being no auxiliary tank we intend working out the point of no return for each leg or in some cases an alternative landing point, if winds are unfavourable.

Naturally, over the vicious looking Shoalhaven River the engine runs rough for a while and we both have silent thoughts of cancelling the over water part of the trip. I am sure that if either one of us says something of this to the other, there will have been a unanimous decision, but as it is, we push on to Yarram near Wilson's Promontory where the tent is pitched. The only concession is to clean the sparkplugs.

The second day begins with the drumming of dew running down the top wing and dropping to the lower wing. There is neither strong wind nor much cloud to use as an excuse to stay here, and, without further discussion, the operation of packing the aeroplane is undertaken and we leave the mainland.

Unless you have tried to use a radio in an open cockpit, you may not realise what a procedure it is. The head must be placed before the instrument panel to avoid wind noise in the microphone and whilst you are "saying again" and "again," the machine winds itself into a spiral dive!

You sit there thinking of whether the Mae West should be blown up before or after ditching, whether the axe will be able to cut off a wing to float on or whether the li-lo under the seat will be a good enough float. You ponder on how long it will take to get a helicopter out to Bass Strait and whether the flying boots should be left on or off. Time passes. Flinders Island appears and after forty-five minutes slides under the left wing. There is no wind.

It is decided to refuel here and then land on the soil of Tasmania at Bridport and start straight back for the mainland before the northerly winds forecast tomorrow come about.

A point of no return is calculated during this leg and it is just past Cape Portland. Alas, we cannot make Bridport and back and so we turn for Flinders Island again. Honour has been satisfied, however, we are actually all the way to Tasmania and have only to survive the re-crossing. All the while one sits there thinking, "I know it is a well maintained aeroplane, but it is forty years old!"

Australia looms up in the distance and I calculate how far I could swim to make dry land. It is still too far away to survive. All too suddenly we are cancelling SAR on the mainland and we are alive. It is too early to stop for the day and so we replan for Benalla, a route which takes us over wild mountainous country. We sit there and realise between shivers that in fact, it would be far safer to ditch in the sea than try to land in these mountains. We therefore criticise ourselves that night for poor airmanship in planning over such inhospitable terrain but our spirits are not down for too long.

The third day is an easy four hundred miles over civilisation and we are home. Back to autopilots and heaters, radar vectoring and DME. And what do we feel?

We are already planning to fly the Tiger over the Simpson Desert.

A Grip of Metal

1989

Do not stop the engines until you have finished with the wings.

There are some days when you feel you could stay aloft and fly on forever. Such was a day in spring when the visibility was unobstructed ninety-three million miles to the sun and the only movement at nine thousand feet seemed to be the mouths of my two daughters as they chattered over the intercom about their proposed move to Queensland.

Heading north we were approaching the rise in terrain north-east of Stanthorpe with Mount Lindsay, a great plug stuck in the border ranges easily visible.

Sitting there in my relaxed mode I gazed regularly at the midpoint of the instrument panel, letting my peripheral vision tell me that all the clocks were in the green. The engine played its smooth music and even the radio groundlings were not pestering me with requests on this Sunday morning.

A slight roughness suddenly widened my eyes and then was gone. A tiny vibration that lasted perhaps two seconds had brought my awareness to alert and then as time passed became an assumed imagination.

And then it recurred.

This time the tachometer flicked and the even engine note changed for just a few seconds.

Now I was staring at the instruments as I enriched the mixture a little and checked the magnetos — a normal variation. I looked down at the inhospitable wooded hills below and was surprised that my daughters continued to chat, obviously unaware of my worries.

Now the tacho swung down a hundred rpm and there was a very definite roughness which stopped the talkers in mid-sentence. Flying since birth had made them relaxed travellers but there were now questioning looks at the captain.

Something is wrong. Is it a magneto or a valve? My mind raced through the possibilities as I strove to maintain my deadpan expression for the benefit of the now very restless passengers.

"Is it alright, Dad?"

"Sure."

We are over the ranges and still thirty miles from Archerfield when there is a quite violent shudder. The tacho moves down two hundred and back again to normal.

"What if it stops?"

"Don't worry, we would just land in a paddock," I lie, looking down at the increasingly built-up area. The aircraft is now in trouble as I am called by radar.

"Cleared to leave nine thousand on descent."

"Er, Control, I have a problem with rough running. Could I remain at nine thousand as long as possible?" The engine backfires. I try the useless manoeuvre of checking switches and mixture again.

"Are you declaring an emergency?"

"Not yet, but stand by! I would like to stay up here until I know I can get into Archerfield please."

The controller is silent for a few minutes and then returns.

"Archer Tower has cleared the circuit for you. Track and descend as required."

I tighten the belt a bit more and motion the girls to do the same. Casting my eyes around the cabin I throw a couple of loose articles behind the back seat.

As we approach ten miles the aeroplane is being shocked by the intermittent shuddering and sounds of a very sick engine.

> "Leaving nine thousand."

> "Roger. Tower reports no traffic. Call them passing three thousand." The lower power setting seems to reduce the roughness for only a short while and by the time I call Archerfield we are riding a very rough Bronco, my thought of flying forever on this day long forgotten.

The officer on the radio is nothing but help. He confirms we have the aerodrome to ourselves. Now down to one thousand feet the engine feels like it is soon to seize. I use a little power and the wheels touch the tarmac. The girls are relieved and as they pop the cabin door the chatter returns. I suddenly realise I have been hunching my shoulders for quite a while and they are sore.

> "Thank you for your help," I tell the man who no doubt is watching us with his binoculars.

Over the years I have had eight engine failures, most of them partial, but all of them requiring a landing as soon as possible. No matter how often one thinks to anticipate such an event, it is always a surprise. That moment of stark terror that comes to spoil your day is unimagined until it happens. Strangely, time passes slowly in such emergencies and I have never had to utter the advertised expletive before the reactions are carried out. One thing has always stood however and that is how reassuring it is to talk to someone on the ground and know they are trying to help you. It is obviously up to the pilot and crew for the definitive actions but there is a comfort if it is possible to share the load.

Two hours later I learn that the problem was a shattered valve guide. We are lucky.

> "I reckon you had a minute or so left before the engine would have stopped completely," I am told by the engineer.

Somewhere in the Pacific

1994

"Urgent. Please pass to pilot of VH-KEY currently somewhere in the Pacific. Regret to advise that Avgas fuel stocks depleted in Tonga and not available for several weeks."

With a week off, fellow doctors Trevor Stewart and Grahame Deane and I had decided to fly halfway across the Pacific and back in Trevor's new extended range Bonanza.

The clearances took a minimum of two faxes to obtain a reply from some of the island nations on our route, and we set sail from Brisbane Airport in late August having taxied almost halfway to the NSW border to find the International Terminal.

Already we had suffered a delay when one of my co-pilots had rung for fuel. After waiting for forty-five minutes for the Avgas tanker to turn up, we found that he had in fact rung the Archerfield phone number, no doubt causing some annoyance of that refueller as he looked for a non-existent aeroplane on his airfield.

I always find it exciting when one changes format to use one's full international call sign and, requesting clearance for the Tontouta track, we lined up for departure. The Mae Wests were on and a yellow dinghy and three wide necked bottles were within reach.

The small trough that often sits off Brisbane coated us briefly with a haze of ice as we climbed into a sparkling sky and soon we were monitoring the oceanic frequencies that are common all the way to California.

The distinctive musical Selcal tones rang in our ears as Nadi or Auckland roused some Boeing crew high above us, and totally spoilt by the GPS we watched the miles tick by uneventfully.

After nearly five hours of motionless flight above the fair weather maritime clouds and following coffee and dried fruit with chatter and lies, we sighted the hazy *mountains of Nouvelle Calédonie. We obeyed the relaxed female controller who told us to descend when we wished. Friendly as ever, the Tontouta Airport staff helped us through customs, and I used my schoolboy French to order the weather for the following day.*

There was a problem with a broken fuel tanker and so after a short return flight to Magenta, a small and "interesting" airstrip close to the city of Noumea, to fuel the tanks, it was time to don our four gold bars, wings and AOPA aircrew cards and claim our hotel discount.

The morning flight to Fiji passed smoothly, but on descent into Nadi, the message was passed to us advising us that we would not be able to go to Tonga due to fuel problems. We were amused by the wording of the message and disappointed, as we had been looking forward to visiting such a beautiful group of islands.

Nevertheless, the Fijians were so helpful on our arrival and in fact proved to be the friendliest people on our travels. Their happy "Bula" greeting is recognised by anyone who has visited this republic.

Our next stop was Pago Pago in American Samoa and we left early the next morning preparing to lose a day as we crossed the dateline en route.

Crossing into the western hemisphere we had our video camera focussed on the GPS as it counted up toward 180°E longitude.

A strange thing took us a little by surprise as, at the point of crossing the dateline, the GPS appeared to lose its track and distance measurement and the auto pilot took a hard right for a few seconds. The same thing happened on our return flight and I wondered what would occur near Greenwich, or in fact crossing the equator.

Despite a fairly clear satellite picture and a good TAF for Pago, we needed to do an ILS into this American controlled airstrip. The approach chart stated that there could be drifting sea spray from a blow hole beside the runway and we were not disappointed as we landed in a roaring crosswind. The eerie mountain tops of some extinct volcano could be seen beside us partially covered by the scudding low cloud.

With its natural harbour surrounded by old tuna boats rusting on their sides, the town proved to be an experience that was different to the other countries we visited. US dollars are used as the currency and the fish was excellent, although served in amounts far exceeding our appetites.

Halfway across the Pacific, it was now time to start our return to Australia and although Raratonga, Tahiti and Bora Bora were within reach it was time to depart for Fiji again.

"VH-KEY you do not have a diplomatic clearance to land at Nadi," the American tower controller informed us. We quoted the date and number in vain.

"Nadi advises you will have to wait until the Office of Tourism opens at 8.30am to confirm!" We could not believe it. We had a five hour flight ahead and we now had to hold at the end of Pago runway with the cabin and engine temperatures rising, the only mild diversion being a car chasing two dogs off the duty runway. After forty-five minutes I could bear it no longer. We shut down and Grahame and I walked over to the tower to enlist the help of the American lady in charge.

After much talking to Nadi we were starting to get desperate and I finally rang the Ministry of Tourism in Suva.

"Your clearance is for tomorrow, and from Tonga, not Pago."

"Is that a problem to change?" We had gathered that nobody flew around this part of the ocean in a single engine light aircraft for fun. Perhaps they thought we were carrying some illicit cargo!

A quick fax to us with a new clearance and, three hours later we ran to our aircraft to get underway and avoid having to finish this long overwater leg at night. Our arrival at Nadi was paradoxically friendly again and we found it hard to understand why they are so particular about clearance.

During the next day's six hour leg to Norfolk Island, the only scenery was a small reef halfway out in this lonely sea, and a patch marked on the map as "Discoloured water."

One gets into a routine on a long overwater flight that is detached from the rest of the world. Also, there is a continual monitoring of the green arcs on the panel and an acute ear for the sound of the engine. A change in the sound could lead to a dramatic change in one's future. The Selcals and chit chat of the airliners giving their Mach numbers and Spot Winds are somehow in a different world to us at 8000 feet and the occasional cup of tea or nibble becomes a welcome break for us. It is also strange how when "two hours to go" comes up it seems to us as though the flight is almost over!

At seventy miles out we start looking at the cloud shadows ahead and eventually one persists as solid rock. Norfolk Island, green and welcoming with little rain showers, and surmounted by a beautiful rainbow, eventually lies beneath us as we talk to an Australian Unicom operator.

A happy afternoon followed driving around this historical island in a two-cylinder NIKI barely able to reach the top of the only mountain with three crew packed inside.

After a "brief" three hour flight we arrived at Lord Howe Island where the wind considerately blew straight down the short strip. With a halo of cloud on the two 3000 foot mountains, this part of Australia was the most attractive of the past week. We were able to unwind here for two days and let the adrenaline of the past week run down almost in sight of the mainland.

The week was certainly not relaxing. The fatigue of the long stages, the uncertainty of the weather, the single engine and the time-consuming handling by the foreign authorities is more than offset, though, by the tremendous experience of seeing other countries and flying in an environment so different to our own skies.

Smoke

1997

The only way for a flying man to keep alive is to be apprehensive.

H de Havilland

It had been a distressing day. My daughter, Sarah's boyfriend had committed suicide the week before and we had flown from Gunnedah to Brisbane for the funeral.

The hot summer had commenced, and severe bush fires were raging in the Pilliga State Forest to the west of the town. Today the strong north west wind had encouraged the spread of the smoke and embers, driving a black pall to the east.

As we commenced our turbulent descent into Gunnedah in clear air, we could see the smoke stretching over the flat landscape barring our way home. We were tired and emotionally exhausted after the funeral – my wife in the back seat was silent in thought and my son Michael was beside me. He was seventeen years old and a private pilot about to start his commercial licence. He had little experience in decision making in the air.

At seven miles from our destination and 4000 feet above the Namoi Valley we entered the smoke stream with a few extra bumps. A slight heightened awareness cut into my concentration. The white shroud closed in and the ground, until now quite visible, disappeared. Flying by instruments we descended, sure that over the runway at lowest safe altitude, we would see enough to land. The white cloak thickened and then suddenly, as though a light had been switched off, the sky turned orange-black. Day had become night in a few seconds as the stream of smoke became so thick that I could see nothing outside except cinders flashing by. My pulse rose as I sat upright in my seat. The wing tips were invisible, the turbulence vicious and it was so dark that I could not see the instruments. I stopped our descent, knowing that there were hills *nearby and switched on the cockpit lights, aware that these toxic fumes could drown the engine. One of those "moments of stark terror" for Michael and me.*

We climbed, hopeful that we would top the inferno of smoke and sparks and I turned to the east knowing that there was an instrument approach at Tamworth thirty miles away. The engine never faltered, and we reached 3500 feet, enough to clear the hills en route. The strong westerlies drove us quickly towards that airport and I hurriedly dialled the frequencies to tune into the approach aids and tower. My mind raced as I quickly tried to calculate remaining fuel and determine how long we could remain aloft if Tamworth proved too hard to find.

At two miles, virtually in the circuit area, we saw the runway, a brownish, almost faded version of its true self, and I turned tightly to land. As we taxied in, the sun glowed like a red ball causing an eerie desert-like landscape. My pulse already slowing, I was aware of the fear on my co-pilot's face.

Broken Wings

2000

An aeroplane will probably fly a little bit over gross, but it sure won't fly without fuel.

The sunlight sparkles on the moving sea and the waves are breaking on the sand a hundred metres away. The breeze, laden with cooling water, wafts towards the inland hills, and light white clouds build in the distance.

But something is missing.

There are no aeroplanes.

On a beautiful Sunday such as this, there are usually many small flying machines buzzing their way up and down the beaches. They're so common, they're treated as part of the scenery. The little white Cessna with floats that gives thrills to countless tourists is silent, rocking at its mooring in the Hastings River. On a day such as this, every half hour or so I see her streaking down the beach with the sun glinting on her wings, tempting me to fly.

I am reminded of that famous line, "and no birds sing," surely one of the saddest lines in British poetry. We could well be back in the 1800s today, except that they had not known of flight to suffer its loss.

I drive out to the airport slowly and without song. No breathless excitement and pulse quickening anticipation fills me as I turn the corner of the airport road. No risky acceleration above the legal speed limit today – rather the heavy-hearted feeling of travelling to a difficult exam.

Opening the door, I see my aeroplane shining in the shadows, its silent nose pointing toward the tarmac that will not bear its wheels today.

Except for a brief time studying medicine, I have flown continuously for over forty-one years. But for me the thrill of aviating has never gone. It is a love affair that has never waned. I am into my fifth logbook and yet still open the original

RAAF one and read that most special of entries, "first solo" written by a trembling seventeen year old. That day is like yesterday, the fear, the joy and the exhilaration still remembered as I read my words, long before my writing degenerated into a doctor's scrawl. Today, although I fly to work several days a week, I would have loved to have cruised along the beaches at five hundred feet or so just to relax and put perspective into my thoughts.

An international corporation has taken away my ability to take to the air in my little French aeroplane.

We have been told how we have needed to pay so much for Avgas because of all the extra checks and refining that must go on – and we accepted it. We believed that because we wanted to be safe in the sky. We wanted to go aloft with the confidence that an engine failure is a rare thing.

And now we learn that they have been less than conscientious in their checking. Through human or mechanical error 5000 aeroplanes are grounded – many, we are led to believe may have so much damage to their fuel systems that they are uneconomical to repair. To replace fuel tanks, lines, filters and carburetors will exceed the value of the aircraft.

General Aviation is vital to our country. Without it we cannot train airline pilots and we cannot spray our crops. Our commuter airlines and our charter firms, the RFDS and other medical services are all part of General Aviation and the bulk of their aeroplanes runs on Avgas. In one month, General Aviation has been dealt a lethal blow from which it may never recover. Even if the aircraft are repaired or replaced, for many companies it may well be too late.

It seems that honour, services and responsibility are unrealistic qualities to expect from a multinational company.

The clock in the cockpit rolls over a digit as I peer inside my silent cabin, immobile in the hangar. I brush away a cobweb and bend down to wipe some grease off a wheel, quietly close the hangar door and drive away.

Cloud

2002

Aeroplanes don't make money sitting on the ground.

2.00am 2002 Williamtown. I slam the door on the Baron and stick the torch in my mouth. "Clear left," and the engine turns a few blades of the propeller and fires. My co-pilot nods and the right engine comes to life. We call "taxiing" to Brisbane Centre and stare ahead to pick up the blue taxiing lights through the rain spotted windshield.

Our company, Coastwings, has been chartered to pick up a part to be urgently taken to Brisbane for an unserviceable airliner. The aircraft is due to leave at 7.00am and we must rush this part to the waiting engineers. As the on-call pilot at the weekends, this task falls to me. I line up at the threshold and wait a moment to plan the take-off and emergency actions should an engine fail.

It is pitch dark except for the runway lights stretching into the night. A pathway to nowhere. Where they end, we must be in the air and climbing. I glance at my co-pilot.

"Let's leave the district!"

The power comes up and the rows of lights start to pass behind us. Faster now and we rotate. I am concentrating slowly on the "clocks" – there is nothing to see outside. Nothing exists outside the dim cockpit lights.

At once we are bouncing around in the wind and rain. At 500 feet we know we are in cloud because the strobe lights on the wings flash a reflection back to the cockpit. We climb and turn to intercept the track to Brisbane. I dare not look away from the instruments. The aeroplane is lightly loaded tonight, and the climb rate is high, but we can hear the rain on the black windscreen. Up we go, the heavy turbulence preventing me using the autopilot. 6000 feet and we have almost reached cruising altitude. I check temperatures – we must watch for icing but so far we are above zero degrees outside.

Suddenly after a few wisps of cloud go by we see a different darkness above us. We are on top of the cloud. The turbulence ceases, it is smooth and above us is a beautiful quiet starry night. I reach down to select autopilot and smile at my co-pilot.

A Shared Sky

2003

Jet noise: the sound of freedom

The whine of the compressor increases slowly as the revolutions build up. There is a light smell of kerosene and an exciting smooth throbbing beneath the seat as the combustion kicks in. A deeper roar takes over and the engine instruments indicate a successful start.

I am strapped into the right seat of a retired Royal New Zealand Air Force British Aerospace Strikemaster beside Rod Hall owner and pilot of a fleet of ex Service aircraft called The International Fighter Flight Centre at Port Macquarie.

Prior to start, I have been briefed on the aircraft, including instrumentation and systems operations. I have donned a parachute with instructions on emergency separation of myself from the aeroplane in time of catastrophe. The original ejector seats have been disarmed as a legal requirement but it is still possible to blow off the canopy in an emergency. With a wave from the safety officer standing on the tarmac, the external battery is disconnected and we move forward to the runway.

Having essentially only one moving part, the jet engine is ready for flight with a minimum of warm up and we are ready for take-off. Power up to high revs, check temps, brakes release and we roll.

There is no torque and we run true.

Lift the nose wheel at eighty knots, off the ground at one hundred, accelerate with gear coming up to 180 knots at 400 feet.

We are now at safety speed to return to the strip if necessary. Rod pulls up into a climbing turn on to downwind, the rate of climb indicator hitting the stops at 6000 feet per minute. By downwind we are through 4000 feet and the world is dropping away, the aeroplane rock solid and relatively quiet in the cockpit.

I am trying to catch up with what is going on, familiar feelings of this type of aircraft returning to me. It was December 1959 that I last stepped out of a two seat Vampire at Williamtown. My fingers touch the column and the wings rock as I get the feel for this eager steed. The controls are amazingly light and the aircraft is ready to respond.

At 8500 feet we dive into a barrel roll and Rod continues with a Derry turn and a Cuban eight. It is effortless, and then I try my hand pulling over three Gs in a couple of evasive turns. It is all I can do to avoid the rapid climb into controlled airspace at 12500 feet. I am surprised at how well I am tolerating the G forces.

As we leave 10,000 feet inbound the instruments give energetic indications of speed and rate of descent and it is necessary to reduce power and throw out the air brakes to avoid overspeeding in the circuit.

It is hard to separate ourselves from a training Cessna as we turn over the runway on to a left initial approach, such is the disparity of our two speeds, but we curve around on to final approach and gently touch the runway.

The Fighter Centre gives us a glimpse of flying an Air Force jet fighter. The performance is way beyond anything that we fly in General Aviation. It is an overwhelming experience to throw around a service aeroplane and learn what our fighter pilots feel. There is, however, one thing missing, and that is the fear and revulsion of war.

I see my own father's logbook entries in 1941. One states simply,

"2 Nov 41. Spitfire SO-M . 50 minutes . ATTACKS."

What an understated entry! The cold windswept aerodrome covered with scudding low cloud. The race to the fighters, exploding into life, smoke and noise filling the air. The bouncing across the green airfield and the maximum rate climb, clawing for altitude. Fear, discomfort… the sightings, the dive with guns blazing, heart in mouth, the brief dogfight and then the slow descent to the landing ground, still shaking from the adrenaline… a little smile as the wheels touch the turf.

That, we cannot experience, but in flying in this exciting jet fighter, I can at least know something of the fighter pilots' realm, and as I step down from the wing of the Strikemaster I am a little closer to my father.

The Second Best Day of Your Life

2011

"You promised that this was the last one."

I am told the second best day of your life is when you purchase an aircraft and the best day is when you sell it. No doubt it is a truism but having owned fourteen aeroplanes over forty-five years I don't seem to have learnt this lesson. Apart from the obvious topic of costs, (what wealth I would have today if I had never bought a flying machine), the problems I have encountered have been legion.

My first aircraft was an Auster. Already twenty years old when it became mine, it made me quite good at forced landings after five engine failures, including one total on take-off at 450 feet. There was a bang and the propeller stopped in front of me. It has always been my policy to work out from what height I can get back to the runway and the Auster had a fairly flat glide. Asking him for a downwind landing, the controller, a friend of mine, cleared me and said later, the first he knew that anything was wrong was when I got out and pushed the machine off the runway. The next day he admonished me for not advising him the reason for my quick return. Ah, the brash confidence of youth!

In the late seventies I bought a Tiger Moth in Perth and flew it back to NSW with a fellow owner. Four and a half days at sixty-five knots was a great experience with "little old ladies" doing their shopping overtaking us.

Reacquainting myself with aerobatics one day, I could not remove the front control column (normally required) and so I bound the harness extra tightly over the seat insert in the front cockpit. At 4000 feet over the aerodrome I proceeded to roll and loop, when, coming out of an inverted position, I found the stick jammed partially to the left. I could not see why and of course the Tiger wanted to bank in that direction. Certain I was going to be injured, in my desperation I found that by jamming the throttle fully open and closed quickly, and kicking the right rudder at the same time, the aircraft would temporarily return to a level position. We came down like a falling leaf, and with more luck than ability, managed to coincide the wings level just above the strip. Apparently the seat insert had come partially loose and was jamming the front control column. Evidently I remained pale for a month.

Some months later I was taking off from a bush strip when a willy willy, hitherto unseen, came at me. The tail was up, but I had time to turn the fuel and switches off before the dusty whirlwind hit. We danced on to one wingtip and then the other and came to rest on the nose. The fuel was hissing on the hot engine. It was time to leave. I jumped from the cockpit which from that position was four metres from the ground. This would have been fine except I forgot to bend my legs resulting in a jarred spine. It must have looked very funny to the onlookers to see the pilot jump and start running away only to fall to the ground clutching his back after a few metres.

A Piper Warrior I owned for several years was severely damaged when a mini tornado ripped through the hangar and it later experienced marked hail damage in a storm. The insurance company paid for the machine to be reskinned, but as golf balls go better with all those dints, and it could happen again anyway, I elected to just take the money and repaint.

Picking it up one day after routine maintenance at a large airport I reached 600 feet when the engine stopped making any noise. Once again, I knew I could return from that height and so requested a downwind landing remembering this time to say exactly why. The fire truck escorted me off the runway where I found the engine ran normally. A check by the engineer failed to find anything wrong and I rolled into another take-off. At 1000 feet the engine stopped again, and I was fast becoming friendly with the fire engine driver. Finally, the engineer found that the fuel strainer bowl was not seated properly and was sucking air. The problem was solved. By now it was dark and although reassured by the maintenance man that all would be well, I insisted that he come for a circuit to show his confidence. As we taxied out, the tower asked if they should get the firemen out now or wait for my 500 foot call! All was well except for my shakes all the way home.

Apart from a boiling battery over Bass Strait and a fractured valve guide requiring a hurried landing, the Warrior gave little further trouble.

In the nineties I bought a Trinidad which I loved dearly. However, it was during this time that we all suffered the fuel contamination disaster necessitating that the whole avgas system be flushed with water. This of course led to corrosion in fuel selectors and lines and required the replacing of many components.

The Trinidad seemed to like taunting me with undercarriage problems. On one occasion at night I could only get two green lights. After circling the major airport for one and a half hours so that the ambulances and fire engines could be summoned along with half the town and television cameras, we landed safely. Strangely we were no longer feeling like visiting the restaurant we had booked. On another occasion at a capital city secondary airport we found the main wheels were locked but the nose wheel was hanging loosely. No amount of coaxing could lock it and with two ambulances waiting, one each, and a couple of my best, best friends the firemen, I managed by good luck to "three point "the aircraft on the main wheels and the tail cone. I jammed it so hard on the runway that the nose leg clicked into its locked position and all it cost us was twenty dollars to have the fibreglass cone repaired.

Three of my aircraft have been Bonanzas, an A36 in 1990 and an E33 in 2001. In 2005 I bought a Jaguar edition A36 which one of my sons ferried across the Pacific for me. As my thirteenth aeroplane, my wife, Liz, made me promise that it would be my last. Of course I agreed, being sixty-four at the time.

The aeroplane remains my steed and we have had many adventures in it, but I must confess that I did add a share of a De Havilland Canada Chipmunk in 2009. I explained to Liz that thirteen was a bad number to finish on, but it took her a long time to speak to me again!

If you fly for long enough, I guess one will have a few interesting things happen, and I certainly adhere to the old saying, "flying is safe as long as you remember it is dangerous". Overall the aviating experience has been enriching and worthwhile and owning aeroplanes, while stressful, is rewarding. I would not give back a minute of it and I am still therefore delaying that, " best day of my life" indefinitely.

It's a Disease

2011

Not responsive to treatment

There is a painting in the Point Cook Flying Museum. It features a handful of assorted flying officers in 1915 leaning against an old car – Richard Williams, later to become the father of the RAAF, Frank McNamara, soon to win the first Australian flying Victoria Cross, Laurence Wackett who achieved fame as the designer of several aeroplanes, and my grandfather, Lionel Cooke, not famous but who nevertheless gained the eleventh flying licence in Australia and number 1422 in the world. He went on to instruct in the Bristol Boxkite, a collection of wires and sticks, innovative in its day as they had the latest system of control called the aileron. This aircraft was equipped with a rotary engine and charged through the air at forty knots until one earthed the magneto, stopping the thrust for long enough to land. On one occasion this earthing button failed on my grandfather and with no way of slowing enough to land his machine, Lionel had to circle Point Cook until his fuel ran out.

On another occasion he beat up one of the Melbourne Racecourses during a race. He was grounded for a while for this misdemeanour probably more because of the embarrassment to the Army that the horses were travelling faster than the Boxkite, than for low flying! Sepia photographs of the time show him in front of the forerunner of the Concorde wearing an enormous, padded helmet, an early example of the noise-cancelling headset bespeaking the potential trauma of primitive flight. I see him perched on the front of the wing, his nose freezing in the cold air, the vibrating craft just above stall speed, the castor oil smell and the thrill of gazing at Port Phillip Bay from a dizzy one thousand feet.

How new all this was to the world and the war and how doubtful that it would be of any lasting use.

Twenty-six years later an RAAF logbook declares that my father Rolla having come to England, was converting to Spitfires. There are a couple of black and white photographs of him at Catterick in Yorkshire, sitting in front of a 145 Squadron Spitfire Mark II. The logbook stops with the entry, " 4 Nov 41 Spitfire SO-M killed on this flight."

He had graduated a Pilot Officer at Amberley on the Tiger Moths and Wirraway. In his beloved Spitfire he had operated over the North Sea and the continent for a few months until he died. His total hours were just two hundred and twenty-eight.

The RAF report states that whilst testing a faulty undercarriage he attempted a low level roll and the aircraft crashed.

"A good pilot who tends to be reckless at times," was the official finding. Sedateness was not a required quality of fighter pilots! The fading letters from England to my mother tell of his love of the Spitfire and the smile on his face in front of his mount reinforces that sentiment.

I see him roaring over the coast, climbing hard, the rain sweeping back in rivulets on the perspex canopy. Wings rocking, head twisting left and right, breathing hard with anxiety, squinting into the gloomy sky hanging over the white caps. The logbook entry 2 Nov 41 Spitfire SO-M 50 mins. Attacks.

What this conjures up to me, the angular Messerschmitts with black crosses flashing in front of him, the turning, the roaring engine, the inside of the windscreen partially fogging up, the vibration of the guns, the itching of the oxygen mask and then it is over. Still alive. Dive for the coast, stop shaking.

Another seventeen years and it is my turn. From the age of five I had told anyone who would listen that I wished to be a flying doctor and now in my first year of medicine the RAAF Reserve is teaching me to fly the Tiger Moth. Then came the years in the outback conning my RFDS pilots to let me do some of the flying, owning an antique aeroplane which kept me poor, writing flying articles and trying to teach others what I had learned.

One doctor covering an area in Queensland the size of Texas, setting fractures without x-rays and operating by hurricane lamps. No GPS in those days, we made mud maps of the country to navigate by as the WAC charts had so little detail. The excitement of a night call, using helicopters in the floods and bogging on soft strips in the wet and parachuting into patients when no other way was possible. And they even paid me to do it!

Having flown now for fifty-three years the disease persists. Back in civilisation I still use my aeroplane to service a satellite practice.

Fifteen years ago, my sons, Anthony and Michael started to fly. There were years when I had things to teach them until the positions reversed. For a few years we had a family aviation company before both of the boys became involved in ferrying aircraft all around the world. I was able to share this life at times but very much as the co-pilot. The weather, the breakdowns, the difficult countries, the overloaded take-offs and the improvising on remote Pacific Islands - what excitement! Now they fly for large corporations in sophisticated prop jet aircraft and yet they love every minute.

Both boys, the fourth generation of our family to fly have baby daughters. I have to admit that these two girls have fluffy aeroplane toys and mobiles above their cots. What chance have they got to avoid this terrible disease? Last week these little girls started their aviation careers with a flight in the arms of their fathers.

I suppose it is possible to be treated for this illness, but then again, do we want to?

Affair with a gyrocopter

2020

… at your age?

Late last year we were having dinner in a local restaurant with a friend, David Massey, when he asked me what Liz would think of us doing a conversion to a gyrocopter.

She was just getting over my learning to fly a helicopter after sixty years of fixed wing and I looked searchingly at her. Her resigned tolerant smile encouraged me.

My knowledge of gyrocopters consisted of an ancient Cierva Autogyro which resided at the back of a hangar in Bankstown. I also knew some brave maniacs in the bush who chased cattle around in homemade bits of wood and a wicker seat making lots of noise and frightening the populace – and the cows!

The rotorcraft of today have come of age with high standards of tuition and manufacture and so it was that my friend and I arranged for an instructor to teach us in a machine owned by local flying instructor Brian Chow.

The open cockpit craft was a little daunting, looking like a motor bike with a rotor on top and a pusher Rotax engine to make it go.

After helicopters, where "auto rotation" is an emergency, it seems that a gyrocopter is always in auto rotation – a concept that at first puzzled me until I studied the theory behind it all. Like a child's toy fan held out the car window, the airflow turns the rotor and the outer part of the blades provides lift.

The machine cannot stall and has a flight envelope of zero to one hundred knots, being able to turn in its own length!

Our instructor Neil Farr came from Liberty Sky, a company in Manilla near Tamworth. A very experienced and long-suffering tutor, he started our lessons between rain showers in the typical coastal climate.

I was told a gyrocopter looked like a helicopter and flew like an aeroplane, but that is not strictly true.

Taxiing out to the runway was fairly straightforward. So far so good. We line up on the runway and connect the rotor to the engine. With a bit of vibration, the blades speed up as one holds the cyclic stick forward. The engine is disconnected from the rotor and I release the brake and pull the stick back.

Within seconds and quite behind the whole exercise, I find the nose rises. The idea is to proceed with the nose wheel just above the ground. We are airborne before I am ready for it and Neil coaches me to hold the machine just above the ground by pushing the stick forward.

At 55 knots we start to rise like a lift. There is a lag when one moves the stick so that overcontrolling causes exaggerated movement and although the afternoon is unstable, I am making it worse trying to chase it. It is the opposite of fixed wing flight where small control movements smooth the bumps. It takes me a while to work this out and meantime I am squeezing the life out of the stick. In cruise, like a helicopter, it feels like an aeroplane although climb and descent is dependent upon power rather than attitude. It is strange to be out in the open, like riding a motorbike in the sky.

We come back to circuits. The approach is at 45 degrees. We thunder down and flare at one metre. It is quite spooky to be this close to the runway, and then touchdown and stop almost immediately.

Off we go again doing 500 feet circuits. There is a slight imbalance in the rotor blades, and I find it hard to ignore the shuddering. If it were my Chipmunk doing that, I would be worried.

"It's fine," says Neil. I try to relax.

"Your knuckles are white Dave."

I'll improve, Neil tells me, I will improve. It's not difficult, just different.

It is actually simple but because it is not intuitive, one has to think it through and try to change old habits into new ones.

It's given me a new challenge and I look forward to overcoming it, and it is so much fun!

We won't be having further lessons and going solo until the corona virus has gone away. Hope I haven't forgotten everything I've learnt by then!

Medicine Way Back Then

When we graduated in 1966 it was said that the medical half life was eight years. Nowadays we belong to a strange profession where medical advice changes every year or so.

You only have to look at HRT – good, bad, good, bad.

Eggs – bad, good, bad, good.

Think of IBS – we told everyone to go on a low residue diet until we realised that this was what caused it!

In my first week as a JRMO in a non-teaching hospital I was shown a tonsillectomy and then told, "next week you have four on your list, let me know if you have any problems."

It never occurred to us not to do surgery. We were Bachelor of Surgery as well as Medicine. Appendices, breast lumps, gall bladders were just part of the work. As for obstetrics, remember a comment from Bruce Mayes book, "The majority of obstetrics in Australia is done by the general practitioner, and done well."

IV fluids equipment was put together by us with red rubber tubing and huge needles shoved into glass bottles.

Surgical gloves were washed and reused, and hypodermic syringes were glass with reusable needles. We were even shown how to sharpen the bevel by putting it through a cork and filing it.

Resident "bashing" was par for the course by those above you and there was no such thing as an hourly duty limit per week.

My shifts would often start at 8.00am and go through to noon the following day without a break, and sleep was sometimes a luxury. How dangerous was this!

One morning doing my rounds, the sister asked me to sign for a change in insulin dosage she had obtained from me on the phone at 3.00am. I had no recollection of the phone call whatsoever but fortunately my advice had been correct.

I had always wanted to be a doctor from four or five years of age. I would surgically remove kapok from my teddy bear. Despite watching Dr Kildare and

Ben Casey, when I was thrown in the deep end on graduating, it was nothing like what I imagined.

The medications were fairly primitive. Systolic blood pressure was 100+ your age and who had ever heard of cholesterol? For blood pressure we had things like Reserpine which made the patient intensely depressed or Aldomet which was better than a sedative. Children were given morphine derivatives for diarrhoea and the pharmacists made up potions such as:

"Ung hydrarg nit" and "mist gent alk".

I am sure we caused a lot of damage.

I remember a certain doctor telling us in biochemistry lectures that we should have a book with two sections. One was a list, "Those who would have died but for our help" and the other, "Those who would have lived but for our help." As long as the first list was longer than the second, he told us, you should keep practising. We did our best without fear of legal action and mostly were appreciated.

A couple of years after I graduated, I moved to the Northern Territory to be a flying doctor, covering an area more than the size of the British Isles. A typhoid epidemic broke out in the Indigenous population at two settlements. They would recover on chloramphenicol only to be reinfected the next week. I asked the Director of Health who then asked World Health. They replied, "Don't know but go and fix it! And write it up!"

I was ill-prepared for this task having had only half a lecture on the disease from the professor. Over a beer I determined to take enough antibiotics and four nurses with me and treat the entire population, sick or well, for two weeks with the medication. It worked and I entered the medical literature. Not only was there no more typhoid, but also no more impetigo, chest infections, venereal disease and gastroenteritis. There were also no blood dyscrasias from the chloramphenicol.

For years I worked in the Northern Territory and Queensland without x-rays, blood tests and ECGs and only the nurse and pilot with whom to discuss the cases. We pulled out teeth and spayed dogs and cats too! Wherever we went we were appreciated. The service enabled the folk to live and work there secure in the knowledge that someone would rescue them, albeit by aeroplane, helicopter or even by parachute!

Even though I live on the NSW coast now, the outback is my spiritual home and I love to hop in my aircraft and head back out there.

Nowadays the RFDS have four or five doctors, with GPS and radar equipped flying intensive care wards at each base, and no doubt do a better job than I did. I am immensely proud, however, to have had the privilege of serving the outback of Australia all those years ago. At seventy-eight I am still practising family medicine covering two towns with the use of my aeroplane. When my students ask me why I am a GP I tell them that I love the honour of talking to nice people all day even though we are conscious of lawyers hovering and perhaps too much bureaucratic input.

I am glad I have done medicine and can see no reason to stop.

However, it is not a bit like taking the kapok out of my teddy bear!

David's aviation background

Grandfather: Lieutenant Lionel Ernest Cooke 1889-1972 Australian Flying Corps

Lionel Cooke was born in the Perth Observatory, the son of Professor William Ernest Cooke, Government Astronomer. Together with the Governor of Western Australia, Sir John Forrest, the Professor standardised time for this enormous state.

In the early part of World War 1, Lionel was a second lieutenant in the Royal Australian Engineers having a degree in engineering. In 1915 he applied to transfer to the Australian Flying Corps and was accepted into the second course to be taught to fly at Point Cook outside Melbourne. He received instruction in the Bristol Boxkite, an aircraft not unlike the Wright Brothers Flyer. The pupil and instructor perched on the leading edge of the of the lower wing with some very rudimentary controls. The wing was fitted with the latest invention, the ailerons – flaps on the trailing edge of the wing enabling the pilot to turn the aircraft in conjunction with the rudders. Previously the wing was warped to achieve this. The engine was a rotary engine where the propeller and cylinders rotated together causing great problems with the gyroscopic effect on the stability of the aeroplane. Not only this, but these engines were either going or stopped and apart from a rudimentary mixture control the only control was for the pilot to earth the magneto and stop the thrust by a button . One landed by "blipping" this button to reduce the output of the engine.

He graduated in May 1915 with the eleventh licence issued in Australia. He was indeed in good company and an early photograph of Lionel and fellow pilots included Frank McNamara, the first Australian pilot to be awarded the Victoria Cross, Richard Williams, the "father of the RAAF", and Lawrence Wackett who was responsible for the formation of the Commonwealth Aircraft Corporation and the production of many aeroplanes including the Wirraway and Boomerang. When the pilots went overseas to service, Lionel was kept in Australia to instruct. He was very distressed by this and begged to be allowed to fight overseas. Lionel was a fun-loving character and on one Saturday when his fellow officers had gone to Flemington Races and he was "minding the fort", he took a Boxkite and "beat up" the race track. Of course he was severely reprimanded by the Commanding officer and grounded for a while.

One another occasion whilst flying above Point Cook, the "blipping" button stopped working and he could not reduce the power to land. Around he went until he ran out of fuel and the engine stopped allowing him to land. Lionel remained in the flying Corps until 1919 and there is an old movie at Point Cook showing him welcoming Ross and Keith Smith in their Vickers Vimy ending their flight from England. He retired from the military after this but in the Second World War was recommissioned as a (non-flying) Squadron Leader.

Father: Flying Officer Rolla Maxwell Cooke RAAF 1917-1941

David's father, Rolla Cooke enlisted in the RAAF in 1940 as a trainee pilot. He was posted to Tamworth in NSW for his initial training on Tiger Moths and then Amberley in Queensland for his advanced training on Wirraways. It was here that he graduated top of his course and was presented with his wings in early 1941.

Coming first in his course, Rolla was asked which aircraft he would like to fly and without hesitation he requested the Spitfire. The Japanese war had not yet started and so he was sent to the UK by ship. He was based in Hawarden in North Wales where he underwent the necessary conversion to the beloved Spitfire. In letters to his young wife, Betty, he raved about this beautiful fighter and on 1st October 1941 he was posted to 145 squadron RAF in Catterick as an operational fighter pilot covering the North Sea as well as forays into Europe.

David has a picture of him with his fellow pilots in front of a squadron aeroplane in October. His flights, grossly understated in his flying log book, were often no more than an hour and in the "remarks" column just mentions "Attacks".

On November 4, 1941, he was killed on a test flight over Catterick. He is buried above the town in a little graveyard dedicated to servicemen. On his headstone is written, "His Duty Nobly Done."

First stepfather: Flight Lieutenant Kenneth John Hanson RAAF 1918-1945

Ken enlisted in the RAAF in World War II and became a pilot. He was posted to the UK and then India flying the Lockheed Hudson Bomber.

After some years he came back to Australia and married Betty, David's mother early in 1945.

Shortly after he was posted to Morotai north of Australia to fly the huge Liberator bomber operating against the Japanese.

In July 1945 Ken was asked to fly low over the Celebes islands to photograph enemy positions. On this flight his aircraft was hit by anti-aircraft fire, and Ken and all his crew were killed.

Betty's marriage to Ken lasted a mere six months.

Second stepfather: Squadron Leader Bruce Cunynghame Daymond DSO, DFC, RAAF 1919-2008

Bruce had been a good friend of Rolla's at university and he joined the RAAF as a pilot just after Rolla. He trained at Narromine on Tiger Moths and then went by sea to Canada to fly Avro Ansons. From here he received his wings, was commissioned and sailed to England.

Converting to Catalina flying boats he was involved in submarine hunting in the western approaches. Following this he performed similar flying from Kenya in east Africa and the Seychelles. In late 1944 he volunteered for special duties flying from Madras in India, dropping and picking up secret agents on the western coast of Burma by night. In these operations he won the Distinguished Flying Cross for flying 100 hours in the air in the course of one week. On one occasion he was asked to rescue "at all costs" an American agent whom the Japanese were chasing. He flew across the Bay of Bengal for twelve hours dodging thunderstorms and arrived over the pick up point in the moonlight at midnight. He could see a Japanese submarine lying in wait for them. A crew member said years later that Bruce remarked to them, "we can't leave the poor bugger down there."

He landed over the top of the enemy submarine, stopped the engines long enough to grab the agent out of his dinghy, restarted the engines and took off before the Japanese were able to see him in the dark. For this he received an instant award of the Distinguished Service Order (second only to the Victoria Cross). He was actually recommended for the Victoria Cross but because of the secrecy of the operation it could not be gazetted as this award necessitated declaring publicly its purpose.

On returning to Australia, he stopped flying despite being offered the job of chief of operations of Qantas by Hudson Fysh. His only post-war flying was with David. He married Betty, David's mother in 1949 and was a loving and caring stepfather to David, providing him with a longed-for male role model.

Acknowledgements

This book has been written mainly for family and friends as well as aviation and medical contacts. However it has grown over the years, caused in no small part by David's habit of adding events that need to be included. Learning to fly a helicopter at the age of 78, honouring his father, Rolla at the Australian War Memorial Last Post ceremony and being awarded the OAM in 2020 have all extended the book. A line has now been drawn and it is complete.

I owe grateful thanks to those who have encouraged me along this journey. Family members, who have been waiting for so long and my many friends, especially those belonging to my Storyweavers writing group, have been supportive, encouraging and now a little impatient. In particular, my thanks go to Janine Noy for her thorough editing and intelligent suggestions. It was a huge job and she accomplished it with grace and efficiency. I am grateful too for the assistance of my cousin, Anne Ritchie, who kindly proofread the final draft. Thank you Anne.

Finally, my undying thanks go to David himself, for keeping a steady hand on the wheel, keeping me focused and giving me the opportunity to write this book by being his amazing self with such a tale to tell. What a life he has had and I hope the readers enjoy sharing it.

About the Author

Elizabeth Cooke started life on the west coast of Scotland and came to Australia with her parents and sister when she was eleven years old. She trained as an English and French teacher and following an initial blooding at Pendle Hill High and Rooty Hill High in Sydney, spent the majority of her teaching career in Gunnedah. Here she experienced both the public and private school systems.

Port Macquarie has been home for the past twenty-four years. She has one son and after marrying David in 1988, gained two stepsons and two stepdaughters.

Twenty years ago she joined a writing group, Storyweavers, and generally writes short fiction and memoir. Leaving her homeland as a child made her intensely aware of the importance of place in our lives and much of what she writes stems from either place or the people connected to place.

Notable events in her writing career include: gaining a Highly Commended in Gunnedah Short Story Competition in 1997 and first prize in the Adult Learners' Week Short Story Competition in 2002. An article was also published in the Aeroplane Owners and Pilots' Association magazine.

Articles and short stories have been included in the *Storyweavers* collection and *Beyond the Three Brothers*, a publication of the Port Writers.

Temps and Pressures is her first book.

www.ingramcontent.com/pod-product-compliance
Lightning Source LLC
Chambersburg PA
CBHW062032290426
44109CB00026B/2609